BY S. J. PERELMAN

Dawn Ginsbergh's Revenge
Strictly from Hunger
Look Who's Talking
The Dream Department
Crazy like a Fox
Keep It Crisp
Acres and Pains
Westward Ha!
Listen to the Mocking Bird
The Swiss Family Perelman
The Ill-Tempered Clavichord
Perelman's Home Companion
The Road to Miltown
The Most of S. J. Perelman
The Rising Gorge
The Beauty Part
Chicken Inspector No. 23
Baby, It's Cold Inside
Vinegar Puss
Eastward Ha!
The Last Laugh

THE LAST LAUGH

S. J. Perelman

INTRODUCTION BY
PAUL THEROUX

SIMON AND SCHUSTER
NEW YORK

Foreword copyright © 1981 by Cape Cod Scrivners Company
Copyright © 1981 by James H. Mathias, as Executor of the Estate of S. J.
Perelman
All rights reserved
including the right of reproduction
in whole or in part in any form
Published by Simon and Schuster
A Division of Gulf & Western Corporation
Simon & Schuster Building
Rockefeller Center
1230 Avenue of the Americas
New York, New York 10020
SIMON AND SCHUSTER and colophon are trademarks of Simon & Schuster
Designed by Irving Perkins
Manufactured in the United States of America
10 9 8 7 6 5 4 3 2 1
Library of Congress Cataloging in Publication Data
Perelman, S. J. (Sidney Joseph)
    The last laugh.
    I. Title.
PS3531.E6544L3   814'.52   81-4695
ISBN 0-671-42515-3   AACR2
Portions of this book were previously published as articles in
The New Yorker

Contents

6   Contents

PART TWO

INTRODUCTION

By Paul Theroux

Humorists are often unhappy men and satirists downright miserable, but S. J. Perelman was a cheery soul who, when he flew into one of his exalted rages, seemed to have the gift of tongues. He gave his mockery a bewitching style. In his stories, or feuilletons as he liked to call them, he represented himself as a victimized clown. He was "button-cute, wafer-thin" and reared turkeys ("which he occasionally exhibits on Broadway"); or Dr. Perelman, "small bore in Africa"; or a mixture of Sad Sack and Pierre Loti, haplessly sampling the pleasures of out-of-the-way places; or finally as a sort of boulevardier and roué who, at the moment of sexual conquest, is defeated by a wayward bedspring.

When I first began reading him in the 1950s—I was in junior high school—I was excited by his malicious humor, his huge vocabulary and what I took to be his lunatic fantasy. I sensed a spirit of rebellion in him that stirred the anarchy in my schoolboy soul. After I started to travel, it struck me that much of what he wrote was true: Perelman's Africa was the Africa no one else had noticed. His stories were bizarre because he sought out the bizarre. He cherished oddity and, being truly adventurous, was willing to put himself to a lot of trouble to find it (he strolled around Shanghai in 1947 looking for it). Then I met him. He *was* button-cute, and also a bit of a roué, and accident-prone. If he had been writing fantasies, we would think of him as a humorist, a writer of gags, whose object was merely to entertain. But he wrote about the world, and his intensity and his anger made him into a satirist.

A satirist seems a sour and forbidding figure—a mocker, a pessimist, a grudge-bearer, a smirker, something of a curmudgeon, perhaps with a streak of cruelty, who, in inviting the reader to jeer at his victim, never misses a trick or withholds a nudge. How does one suggest that such a man may also have a great deal of charm? Perelman's friends liked him very much. He was generous, he was funny, he was enormously social, he didn't boast. Travel has the effect of turning most people into monologuists; it made Perelman an accomplished watcher and an appreciative listener. When he talked in his croaky drawl he did so in the elaborate way he wrote, with unlikely locutions and slang and precise descriptions diverted into strings of subordinate clauses. He was small and neatly made; he wore very handsome clothes, usually of an English cut; and in his pockets he carried clippings he tore from the newspapers—one he showed me was about the movie *The Texas Chain-Saw Massacre*, which he eventually worked into a story. He read the London *Times* every day (he had an airmail subscription), more, I think, for the unusual names than for anything else. In today's *Times*, Sir Ranulph Twisleton-Wykeham-Fiennes has just reached the South Pole; Captain Sir Weldon Dalrymple-Champneys has just died; and both Miss C. Inch and Miss E. L. F. I. Lunkenheimer have just got married. Perelman welcomed news of this kind.

In his way, he was a man of the world. A man of the world, almost by definition, is never content anywhere. Perelman was a bit like that. He had a great capacity for pleasure, but he was restless, always active, game for anything; he fed himself on change. He began writing at Brown University, where a fellow classmate was Nathanael West (Perelman married West's sister Laura in 1929), and at the age of 25, with the success of his first book, *Dawn Ginsbergh's Revenge*, he was invited to Hollywood to write jokes for the Marx Brothers. He went, and he liked to say that Hollywood reminded him of a novel he had read in Providence as a boy, *In the Sargasso Sea*, by Thomas Janvier (anyone who has the luck to find this 1899 story of marooning and murder in the nightmare swamp will immediately see the connection). From time to time throughout his life, Perelman returned to Hollywood, struggled with scripts and then fought free. At the age of 74, fresh from the travels he recounted in *Eastward Ha!*, he tried to drive his vintage 1949 MG from Paris to Peking, commemorating the trip of Count Something-or-other. It was not such a crazy scheme. He had been around the world a dozen times. He was in good health, his car had recently had a tune-up, he had a generous sponsor and many well-wishers, and he liked to say (though joshing himself with his chain-smoker's chuckle) that he knew Malaysia and Hong Kong like the back of his hand.

In a Thai restaurant, in London, on Christmas Eve, he told me about his drive to Peking. He had just flown in from China. The trip, he said, was a total disaster. The glamour girl he had chosen for navigator had been fired at the outset for selling her story to a magazine. He had quarreled with his fellow drivers all the way through India. There had been kerfuffles with customs men in Turkey. The car was not allowed through Burma and, as there was no room on a ship to Malaysia, the car had been air-freighted to Hong Kong. There were more scenes in Hong Kong. "The others freaked out," Perelman said, but with the old car now parked in Kowloon, he flew to Peking and spent two weeks in a Chinese hospital with a severe case of bronchitis, aggravated by double pneumonia.

"Now I have to write about it," he said. "It'll be horrible."

Frankly, I thought the subject was made for him. Nothing is more Perelmanesque than a marathon drive across the world interlarded with setbacks, blown gaskets, howling Turks and long delays in flea-ridden Indian hotels. And pneumonia in Peking was the perfect ending for someone who always racked his brain for grand finales. (His editor at *The New Yorker*, William Shawn, told me recently, "He always had trouble with endings.") But this last collection of Perelman pieces contains nothing about that Paris to Peking trip. This is odd, because he had made his reputation by describing the complicated orchestration of fiascos.

A month before he died, he wrote me a letter in which he said, "I myself have spent altogether too much time this year breaking my nails on the account of the Paris–Peking trip I made . . . and after a lot of bleeding cuticle, I decided to abandon it. I guess there are certain subjects—or maybe one's subjective reactions to them—that in spite of the most manful attempts are totally unproductive. The one I picked certainly was, and it took a lot of Sturm und Drang to make me realize that my Sisyphean labors were getting me nowhere."

This was the only gloomy paragraph in an otherwise chirpy letter. His letters were long, frequent, and sensationally funny— indeed, so funny that, after receiving a few, Raymond Chandler (always a hoarder and procrastinator where writing was concerned) replied worriedly, warning Perelman against squandering his wit: "You shouldn't give the stuff away like that when you can sell it, unless of course your letters are just rough notes for articles."

But they weren't "just rough notes for articles." They were generous and intelligent expressions of friendship and most of them far too scandalous to be retailed. Here is the opening paragraph of a letter Perelman wrote me on Christmas Eve, 1976:

Between the constant repetition of "White Christmas" and "Jingle Bells" on station WPAT and the increasing frenzy of the Saks and Gimbels newspaper ads as these fucking holidays draw near, I have been in a zombie-like state for weeks, totally incapable of rational thought or action. I must have arrived at near-paralysis yesterday afternoon when I was in the 4th-floor lingerie section ("Intimate Apparel") in Saks 5th Avenue. I had just purchased two such intimate garments for gifties to a couple of ladies of my acquaintance, a tall blonde and a somewhat shorter brunette. For the former, I had chosen a black lace chemise in the style known as a teddy back in the twenties (familiar to you as the scanty garment worn by Rita Hayworth in the wartime pinup). For the shorter brunette, a similar peach-colored job. Both of these real silk, parenthetically, and as I signed the charge slip, I knew that when the bill came in after January 1st, I would kick myself for my prodigality. Anyway, while the hard-featured saleslady was wrapping them up with appropriate mash notes to each bimbo, I went upstairs to the men's dept. to buy myself a cheap tie-tack. When I returned for the feminine frillies, I found (a) that the saleslady had forgotten to identify which box was which, and (b) that she had switched the notes. In other words, the blonde Amazon would find herself with the brunette's undershirt and some steamy sentiment addressed to the latter, and vice versa. I broke out into a perspiration—it's tropically hot in those department stores anyway—and insisted on the saleslady clawing open the boxes, which meant destroying all the fake holly berries, silver cord, and mishmash they were entwined in. This of course put her in a foul temper, and meanwhile a waiting queue of customers became incensed. The upshot was a group shot of seven or eight people leering and cackling obscenely as I stood there holding the two chemises and the notes appropriate to the recipients. Given the savoir faire of Cary Grant I might have risen above it, but the only savoir faire I possess is Oliver Hardy's, and little enough of that. . . .

When Perelman's letters are collected, as they surely deserve to be, they will comprise the autobiography he promised and began, but never get around to finishing. The three chapters printed here are all we have of *The Hindsight Saga.* Anyway, with a title that good you hardly need a book; or did its promise of disclosures intimidate him? He was always more personal and ruminative and risqué in his letters than he was in his stories, and he heartily disliked people who boasted by reminiscing about the past. "I see Scott Fitzgerald's gossip-columnist mistress has been cleaning out the contents of a thimble," he wrote me when Sheilah Graham's *The Real Scott Fitzgerald* appeared.

Perelman knew Fitzgerald as a sober, hard-working scriptwriter, who had gone to Hollywood for the money, much as today's writers accept tenure at universities. Fitzgerald believed himself a failure, but Perelman was one man (Faulkner was another) who used Hollywood to fuel his other projects; his script-writing career coincided with his first appearance in the pages of *The New Yorker*. It seems extraordinary that he was able to keep his enthusiasms separate, but to California and New York he added the world. From the thirties onward he traveled widely, first in the Pacific and then in Africa, Europe and Asia. I cannot think of another writer who was so adept as Perelman in prevailing over such vast cultural incongruities and whose appreciations included B-movies, pulp magazines, Joyce's *Ulysses*, Hollywood dives, the societal norms in Bucks County, Manhattan and Nairobi, detective fiction, English country-house weekends, vintage cars, dogs (he once, on a whim, bought a bloodhound), cantankerous producers and pretty women. He talked with passionate energy about Fellini's *Satyricon* and Alfred Russel Wallace's *The Malay Archipelago*. He knew Dorothy Parker well and had a close friendship with Eric Ambler. He was the only person I have ever known who dropped in on J. D. Salinger, whom he called "Jerry."

His greatest passion was language. In "Listen to the Mockingbird" he wrote, "As recently as 1918, it was possible for a housewife in Providence, where I grew up, to march into a store with a five-cent piece, purchase a firkin of cocoa butter, a good second-hand copy of Bowditch, a hundredweight of quahogs, a shagreen spectacle case and sufficient nainsook for a corset cover and emerge with enough left over to buy a balcony admission to *The Masquerader* with Guy Bates Post, and a box of maxixe cherries." He was parodying inflation, but it is impossible to read "cocoa butter," "Bowditch," "quahogs," "shagreen," "nainsook," and the rest without a sense of mounting hilarity. He worked hard for a kind of insane exactitude in his prose and would not settle for "sad" if he could use "chopfallen." I think his travels were bound up with his quest to find odd words or possible puns. They were more than mere souvenirs of travel: they were the object of his arduous jaunts. The uniqueness of his writing depends for its effects on linguistic virtuosity, finding room for "oppidan" or the verb "swan" or the weirder lingo he abstracted in India and Africa. E. B. White once wrote about how Perelman, after crashing his car in Florida, savored the phrase "We totaled it!" and how his pleasure in being able to use it took the sting out of the accident.

His interests and his travels swelled his vocabulary and gave him his style. But none of this would have been accessible without his memory, which was faultless. That too is a distinguishing feature in his fiction. A good memory is one of the most valuable assets a writer has, and Perelman's memory amounted to genius. One day, years ago, he was passing through Shropshire, and a glimpse of that green countryside stayed with him. He plotted to return to Shropshire and rent a house and live there like a squire; but though he visited England often, he always became restive. Apart from the precincts of *Punch*, where he was feted, he found England tight and dry and a little dull. And the house rents in Shropshire were too high. He was too much of an Anglophile to like England greatly.

He died on October 17, 1979, in New York City, where he was born. The stories that are collected here previously appeared in *The New Yorker*, but the chapters from *The Hindsight Saga* are being published for the first time. His writing did not flag in fifty years, and this, his twentieth book, is as funny as anything he ever wrote.

PART ONE

"And Then the Whining
Schoolboy, with His Satchel"
and Other Pieces
1974–1979

And Then the Whining Schoolboy, with His Satchel

At four o'clock of a late-February afternoon in 1919, an icicle four feet long depending from the nose of Sultan Abdul-Hamid II, the potentate whose granite countenance graced the façade of the Turk's Head Building in Providence, cascaded four stories to the sidewalk below, narrowly missing Morris Schreiber, an insurance salesman who was hurrying at that moment to sell Azouf Harootunian, the manager of the Weybosset Market, an accident policy. In the barbershop of the Crown Hotel, simultaneously, Walt Zymchuck, in charge of the second chair, was lathering Edward Gipf, a retired jewelry executive, when, because of the intense cold, the Bakelite handle of his shaving brush broke off and lodged a soapy pellicle of badger hair in his client's throat, occasioning momentary strangulation. Less than twenty minutes later, the accumulation of frozen snow on the roof of Cherry & Webb's specialty shop on Westminster Street caused a skylight to buckle in such wise that icy drafts whipped down an interior wall. A family of mice domiciled there scampered into the corset department, and in the resultant stampede Mrs. Anna Rubashkin of Central Falls suffered a number of contusions from splintered whalebone.

While these and similar human-interest stories were breaking all over Providence in what was inevitably described as the worst freeze in weather annals, another event, far more epochal from my point of view, was about to occur in the city. On Exchange Place, the municipal mall dominated by an equestrian statue of General Ambrose Burnside, stood a popular tearoom and soda fountain—an Elysian temple of goodies which, to avoid any imputation that it was run by Greeks, bore the prosaic name of Gibson's. So seductive was the ambrosial smell of its cakes, pies, cookies, twists, and rings, its chocolates, caramels, mints, and nougats, and the syrups and garnishes employed in its parfaits, smashes, cabinets, and banana splits that travellers had been known to leap from trains passing through the Union Station, three blocks away, and squander their patrimony there with no thought for the morrow. Five or six years earlier, indeed, a stockroom clerk at the Pussy Willow Ruching Corporation, famed throughout New England for feminine neckwear, had embezzled a quantity of jabots, altered the labels on their boxes, and sold them to unsuspecting French Canadians as sabots. Since the offender had spent the entire proceeds on brownies, éclairs, and macaroons at Gibson's and lapsed into a state of coma, the judge, a compassionate man with a sweet tooth, tempered justice with mercy and remitted the sentence.

It was to the foregoing establishment, then, that I had been invited that afternoon for a rendezvous with a lady a dozen years my senior—a situation that, considering I was a raw youth, might suggest the sort of liaison popularized by Colette or Arthur Schnitzler. Actually, the inception of the meeting was quite innocent. Just as our sophomore English class at high school was dispersing that morning, the teacher, Miss Cronjager, summoned me to her desk. Over the weekend, it emerged, she had been grading some compositions of an autobiographical nature submitted by the class, and she felt that mine needed clarification. "I was originally going to discuss it with you in my office," she said, "but on second thought it might be better if we did so in a less constrained atmosphere. I have an errand or two not far from Gibson's, so let's you and I meet there for a nice cup of tea and a chat."

Inasmuch as Miss Cronjager had honey-colored hair and a figure evocative of the coryphées portrayed in cigarette pictures, I saw no reason to gag at the proposal and turned up well ahead of time. Before long, I began salivating as waitresses ran to and fro bearing charlotte russes, schnecken, and gooseberry tarts to the women shoppers about me; at last, tortured by the rich aroma of hot chocolate and spicy fruitcake, my will power collapsed, and I ordered a portion of jelly roll and a coffee float. The question of payment for the snack did not concern me. After all, I reasoned, since Miss Cronjager had initiated the conference, it was her obligation to pick up the tab.

Half an hour passed without any sign of Miss Cronjager, and, fearful that the management might deem me a stiff loitering in the premises to keep warm, I ordered a butterscotch ice-cream soda and a slice of angel cake topped with hazelnuts and chocolate sauce. What with the surrounding turbulence, I succeeded in remaining persona grata for another thirty minutes, but then panic overtook me. My repast thus far totalled one dollar and eighty-five cents, and all I had on me was my carfare home. Fantasies began multiplying wherein Miss Cronjager had broken an ankle en route or been run down by a streetcar. The consequences—a hullabaloo of exposure, arrest, arraignment in juvenile court—were too horrid to contemplate. Moreover, and as if to intensify my qualms, a busboy materialized and polished the table to a high gloss while the manager, arms folded behind his cash register, surveyed me menacingly.

Luckily, before I could throw myself at his feet and plead for mercy, Miss Cronjager appeared, flushed and rosy from the biting cold. She was wearing a Russian pony coat, and every woman in the place immediately turned sick with hatred. "I hope I haven't kept you waiting," she apologized. "You should have had something to eat." I mumbled some gallantry of a Spartan nature, which she brushed aside. "No, no—order some cinnamon toast or buns, whatever you'd like. I'll just have tea." Feigning elaborate reluctance, I studied the menu, torn between mocha layer cake and a walnut sundae with ladyfingers.

Rather than be categorized as a glutton, however, I checked myself and settled for an eight-inch segment of poppy-seed strudel and a vanilla freeze.

"Now, then," Miss Cronjager began, as lethargy from an excess of carbohydrates stole over me, "very likely, you wonder why I chose to hold our discussion here instead of at school. The reason is that the essay you wrote about your past . . ." She hesitated. "Well, it raised some personal questions that I felt could be better answered in a heart-to-heart talk."

My pulse skipped a beat, a hot blush rose to the roots of my hair, and a mixture of anxiety and guilt churned in my breast. Had I willingly divulged some dark corner of my psyche, visible only to an adult? Had Miss Cronjager, reading between the lines, sensed with her feminine intuition the fantasies I sometimes cherished about her, particularly before falling asleep?

"Eh—sure, Miss Cronjager," I said. "What would you like to know?"

She reached under her chair and withdrew my theme from her briefcase. "Well, let's go over it in detail. Your earliest boyhood memory, you say, was of a village on the rocky, fogbound coast of Maine, of rough but kindly fishermen hauling lobster pots and mending their nets. Occasionally, when they voyaged to the Grand Banks in their schooners, they took you along, because you recall men in dories detaching codfish from hand lines. Now, on one of these voyages you made the acquaintance of an English lad, who had accidentally fallen off a transatlantic liner and been rescued by your vessel, with whom you became fast friends. Tell me"—she broke off—"did you ever read a book by Rudyard Kipling called *Captains Courageous?*"

"Not that I remember," I said. "Why?"

"Oh, I was just curious," she said. "One other point. Not far from the village, you state, there was an isolated tavern named the Admiral Benbow Inn, frequented by suspicious characters who clinked gold coins when they roistered and sang nautical chanteys. Together with the boy whose mother ran the tavern— his name, you believe, was Hawkins—you hid in an apple barrel and ascertained that these men were mutineers. How large was this barrel that it could accommodate two boys?"

"It was more of a keg—a hogshead, like, with iron hoops," I explained. "They used them for rum and molasses, too. The inside was real sticky."

" 'Sticky' is a good description," agreed Miss Cronjager. "I felt that when I read the passage. All right, we come next to the stage in your narrative where your folks have moved to a cotton plantation in Dixie. Your account of their huge pillared mansion, with a family retainer named Uncle Cudgo, Southern belles waltzing with their escorts, and field hands strumming banjos, is very colorful, but you neglect to mention where the money for all this came from. I was under the impression that your parents' livelihood derived from catching finny denizens."

"It came about through a legacy, I believe," I said. "I remember a lawyer bringing us some stocks and bonds in a hamper, but I was too young to understand."

"Besides, you were rebellious," she reminded me. "As you point out, you soon tired of all the fussing, the endless coddling of nurses and tutors, and you ran away to the Texas Panhandle, to live the life of a cowboy. You must have been the youngest cowhand in the West at that time."

I nodded. "I was, but if you read *Riders of the Purple Sage* or *The Winning of Barbara Worth*, there were lots of young fellows seeking their fortunes out there. I mean, it was the frontier, and it took plenty of vim to rope and tie the dogies, brand the mavericks, and stave off attacks of the marauding red man."

"From which you didn't flinch one iota, I'm sure," she said warmly. "Was that how you became a rustler?"

"A rustler?" I repeated. "Not a rustler, Miss Cronjager—a *wrestler*. You see, the family objected to my life on the range and packed me off to Lawrenceville, where I made the varsity team and hung around with ginks like your Doc Macnooder, the Tennessee Shad, and so forth."

"What a privilege to have known those fabled characters of Owen Johnson's personally, rather than through the printed page like the rest of us," she observed enviously. "However, at that juncture, I confess, I was mystified. Why didn't you go on to Yale thereafter?"

"Gee, I thought I made that clear," I said. "Dink Stover was the big man on campus there, and I was afraid that our rivalry —well, I hate to say it . . ."

"No, go on," she urged. "You're much too self-effacing."

"I felt there wasn't room for us both," I said. "And, besides, I had those two projects I couldn't decide between."

"Oh, yes, I forgot." She consulted my pages. "Whether to track down the insidious Dr. Fu Manchu or to join Allan Quatermain in the Mountains of the Moon. You really were on the horns of a dilemma, weren't you?"

"Worse than that," I said. "The Yukon was calling, too, and the South Seas. One minute, I saw myself skimming over the frozen wastes in a dogsled driven by some laconic sourdough; the next, I was piloting a longboat manned by seven bronzed Kanakas through the surf at Rarotonga."

"Now, that's the part of your reminiscences that puzzled me most," said Miss Cronjager. "With all these clashing impulses, what finally brought you back to Providence and the Classical High School? For one whose history is so colorful, don't you find existence here a bit prosaic—humdrum, in fact?"

"Well, it's not as exciting as some places," I admitted. "I remember one time when I was a supercargo aboard a Swedish tramp bound from Mombasa to Tientsin. It was typhoon weather in the South China Sea, and we were scudding along under bare poles—"

"Wait a minute," she interrupted. "When did this take place? There's no indication here that you ever shipped before the mast."

"Look, Miss Cronjager," I expostulated. "When you assigned us this subject, you said to make it brief—to just emphasize the salient points. If I put down all the adventures I've had, it would read like *The Arabian Nights' Entertainments*."

"It does even now," she said. "That in a way is what I'm driving at. Tell me, how old are you?"

I replied that I had recently celebrated my fifteenth birthday.

"Well, you certainly have led a life jam-packed with incident. And," she added, with an enigmatic smile, "you've managed to squeeze in quite a lot of reading, haven't you?"

Stupefied though I was by my sugar intake, some instinct warned me at that moment that the question was loaded, and in a flash the truth dawned on me. In my innocence, I had accepted the teacher–pupil relationship at face value, only to fall victim to the third degree. Miss Cronjager, for all her silken benevolence, sought to trap me into admitting that my past was a tissue of falsehoods—a collage, or mosaic, of the great books that had enriched my youth. Instantly, I was on the qui vive. In the next breath, this woman might very well demolish me with charges of plagiarism, forever ruin my credibility. Luckily, if the hours I had spent with Leatherstocking, with Sax Rohmer's Nayland Smith, and with Craig Kennedy, the Scientific Detective, had taught me nothing else, they had honed my sense of caution to razor sharpness. I had learned that destruction lurked behind the snap of a twig in the forest path, that a trifling cigarette ash could doom even the most cunning individual and bring his house of cards crashing down on his head. It may seem incredible that a mere fifteen-year-old should be capable of so complex a chain of reasoning, yet it hurtled through my mind with the speed of an express train, and in the next instant my foil parried Miss Cronjager's thrust with lightning swordsmanship.

"Why, yes," I returned, my lips curving in the exact Oriental smile that Sydney Greenstreet was to popularize several decades later. "I occasionally like to while away the idle hour with a book, as who does not? However," I went on, rising, "I fear I detain you. If you have no further questions, Miss Cronjager, it is incumbent on me to scoot. The Y.M.C.A. gymnastics team, which I captain, is competing tonight for the Horace Dooley silver cup, and I must insure that everything in the way of sweatshirts and similar gear is in apple-pie order."

Had Miss Cronjager known that far from being captain, or even a member, of any gymnastics team, I could not vault over a sawhorse without sustaining multiple fractures, I would not have escaped so easily. For whatever reason, though—possibly out of sheer ennui—she interposed no objection, and I beat a hasty retreat. Several days later, I was chopfallen to discover that I had received a mark of D-minus for my handiwork. To this day, I can think of no adequate explanation. Perhaps, aggrieved by the staggering bill she paid at Gibson's, Miss Cronjager revenged herself by flunking me—a disheartening instance of the Dickensian cruelty prevalent at that time in New England high schools. Nonetheless, and by what rare gifts of forbearance in my makeup I cannot say, I never bore her a grudge. Maybe it was that stern upbringing in the Maine fisheries, mellowed by plantation life in the old South and matured at Lawrenceville and in the South Seas, that made me incapable of vindictiveness. Or maybe it was that honey-colored hair and exquisite figure I still remember, particularly before falling asleep. ¿Quién sabe?

One of Our Stagecraft Is Missing

In these days when rock stars hatch one evening and perish the next with the mortality of mayflies, how many of those who, like myself, idolized him ever give a thought to Liberace? All of us were spellbound by his meteoric rise, hungrily followed his career, and kept his picture under our pillow, but I suppose that essentially we looked upon him as a great, gorgeous peacock who shed enchantment on our lives and then flapped off into obscurity. So it was a signal for rejoicing when the night-club page of *Variety* blossomed forth recently with a review of his new act at the Las Vegas Hilton, the essence of which was that he had once more breathtakingly demonstrated his virtuosity. Said the account, "Liberace outdoes himself on each return with a more spectacular wardrobe (this time it's a dazzler whipped up by young designer Jim Lapidus), more expensive automobiles to deliver him onstage, more colorful supporting acts (the Little Angels of Korea are aboard currently), and more surprises. The surprise this trip is not his entrance, which is surprising enough, but his exit—he literally flies off the stage and into the wings suspended by wire à la Peter Pan. It adds up to a fine funfest bursting with extra flair by the master showman."

My initial reaction, understandably, was one of awe; it must have taken an engineering genius like Isambard Kingdom Brunel, the wizard who built the Great Eastern, to whisk someone of Liberace's girth into limbo before the audience's eyes.

27

Yet that was only half the problem; after he described his parabola, how had they cushioned his descent? Was he pitchforked onto a hair mattress or feather bed, a firemen's net stretched by half a dozen stagehands? The report cast no light on such technicalities, and perhaps it was just as well. Coruscating and effulgent in his jewelled finery, Liberace had again flashed across the firmament like Halley's comet, creating a moment of theatrical magic. To equivocate about the phenomenon would be as idle as analyzing a moonbeam.

Keen though my pleasure was at Liberace's resurgence, I was nagged by a feeling that somewhere in the past I, too, had assisted in the lightning disappearance of an actor. It couldn't have been connected with *Peter Pan*, since I never saw Barrie's play and my only association with him was that pipe smoker's bible, *My Lady Nicotine*, in some freshman dormitory when heated disputes raged about the relative merits of Barking Dog and Imperial Cube Cut and people used to rub Dunhill briars along the side of their nose to bring out the beauty of the grain. No, my imbroglio had some reference to show business, but stap my vitals if I could pin it down. Just as I was chastising myself for an amnesic old pantaloon, a chance encounter provided the clue that resurrected the whole thing.

I was combing the kitchenware section of Macy's for a prosaic enough appliance—an hourglass gauging how long to boil an egg. All I could find was a Swiss monstrosity (a tiny glass cathedral filled with blue plastic beads) and a nine-dollar automatic timer that switched on lights to deceive burglars. The salesgirl, a Mexican Indian from Mazatlán who had not had my advantages, was unable to grasp what I sought.

"An hourglass," I pleaded, sculpturing a figure in the air like Lillian Russell's. "You know, the same on top as on the bottom. . . . For boiling *huevos*—like the one Father Time carries with his scythe."

Irked by her utter incomprehension, I threw up my hands and flung off, nearly capsizing a middle-aged woman burdened with shopping bags. Before I could apologize, her face brightened. "Why, hello, stranger!" she said, chortling. "Don't you remem-

ber me? I'm Noreen Cannister—have you forgotten? I played
Gloria Kramer in *One Touch of Venus*."

Well, her features evoked no memory of any in the cast I
treasured, but after a struggle I succeeded in placing her. Her
married name was Breastbohn, she disclosed, and her husband
had an automobile agency in Plainfield, New Jersey.

"Now, promise me," she urged as we parted. "If you ever
should pass through Plainfield—"

I pledged I would stop by for the clam fritters or shoofly pie
or whatever delicacy Plainfield was renowned for, and left.
Almost an hour later, the full significance of our meeting hit
me. But of course! This was the party—this selfsame Noreen
Cannister—whose inexplicable fate I had been groping to re-
cover from the past.

In the autumn of 1943, the company of *One Touch of Venus*
was in New York, girding itself for its Boston tryout under the
direction of Elia Kazan. The libretto Ogden Nash and I had
fashioned for Kurt Weill's score was an intricate one, but,
stripped of its details, as it was by Kazan doggedly, it concerned
the goddess's infatuation with a barber. One of the key scenes
dealt with a quarrel in the latter's shop between his fiancée,
Gloria, and Venus, at the climax of which the incensed divinity,
with an imperious gesture, caused her rival to disappear on the
spot.

"That may take a little doing," observed Kazan, who had had
some small experience in amateur theatricals.

Luckily, we had foreseen his objection. There was, said Nash,
a person named Cubbage, a member of the Society of American
Magicians expert in such illusions, who had signified his readi-
ness to tackle the problem if a proper quid pro quo was forthcoming. Skeptical at first that anyone could be made to evaporate
in full light, Kazan finally agreed to run the scene for the
magician. Cubbage, a lanky stringbean of a man resembling Pee
Wee Russell, watched the action, pondered awhile, and assured
us he could work it out.

"That's what we call a mid-stage vanish," he explained. Then scrutinizing Gloria, he asked, "Tell me—do you have to use that actress again?" Kazan replied that she was indispensable, and Cubbage sighed. "It's a shame," he said. "I could have given you a really spectacular trick. Anyhow, don't worry. I'll get back to you. I have to measure a few barber chairs for what I have in mind."

The solution he returned with was brilliant in its simplicity. A conventional barber chair would be altered in but one respect —its back to consist of a hollow replica five inches deeper than the original, masked by a roller curtain of simulated leather. During the altercation, Venus would advance on Gloria with arm upraised so that the girl staggered backward into the seat, drawing up her knees in terror. As the goddess majestically consigned her to oblivion, the chair would begin revolving. Gloria would jackknife into its hollow in her fetal position, and within two and a half quick revolutions she would effectively vanish into thin air.

Despite managerial outcries at the expense of Cubbage's device and forebodings from Kazan that Gloria might suffocate inside it, majority opinion hailed the idea as sensational. Word was dispatched to the scenic studio to ready the chair for the Boston tryout, now less than a fortnight distant. In the attendant frenzy of preparation, none of us alluded to the subject again; while the fate of the show was unpredictable, Gloria's mid-stage vanish was a cinch. We could already hear the cheers of the opening-night audience as it gave the scene a standing ovation.

At the dress rehearsal in Boston's Colonial Theatre, costumes ripped, scenery buckled, and tempers frazzled, but the illusion worked superbly. The two principals and the chair performed with brio, spiriting away Gloria like a puff of smoke. There was only one imperfection—a drawback, to put it mildly, that nobody could have anticipated. On Gloria's scheduled reappearance in the plot, she failed to turn up on cue. The rehearsal ground to a stop as emissaries scouted dressing rooms, the lounges, adjacent lunchrooms in vain. Saddled with a vast company of mummers, dancers, singers, and musicians frozen into inactivity, not to mention nineteen stagehands drawing overtime pay, Kazan tore out handfuls of hair—an action that threatened to leave him as bald as an egg. But the search was unavailing; by whatever agency, human or divine, the girl had in fact disappeared and divil a bit if anyone had seen her go.

At the première the following night, Gloria's understudy took over the role, playing the scene without the use of Cubbage's prop. Instead, Venus wrought her magic on a stage aquiver with thunder and lightning, and the girl stole off through the murk. The audience, inured to displays of thunder and lightning, failed to respond with a standing ovation. Nash and I, draped over the orchestra rail, were embittered by the thought of what might have been. To further lacerate our self-esteem, Kazan, whenever he beheld the two of us thereafter, would sardonically comment, "There go Cubbage and Burbage."

I t followed as the night the day, hence, that, having collided with Noreen Cannister, I was avid to quiz the lady about her untimely disappearance, and I hastened to phone her. However, since I had stupidly forgotten her married name of Breastbohn, this presented a difficulty; I remembered it as something like Sternum or Midriff, but no such person was listed in Plainfield. Ultimately, I sequestered her through her husband's car lot, and we met for lunch in an Italian restaurant in the Village whose ambience I felt would encourage confidences. She was, as I expected, reluctant at the outset to yield up particulars, but three Side Cars and a quantity of Verdicchio loosened her tongue. It was a bizarre story.

Six months before joining our musical, Noreen had met a wealthy furrier named, if I recall, Max Bibulous, who fell madly in love with her. She described him as magnetic rather than handsome, adding that, though overweight, squat, and brusque, he radiated a sense of power. He was also the soul of generosity; he lavished jewels and clothes and flowers on her without stint and sought to install her in a Park Avenue garçonnière, which she found unacceptable. He, on his part, drew the line at marriage, claiming that his insanely jealous wife would drink iodine if he left her. Their friendship grew ever more tempestuous as his ardor increased, and on the eve of her departure for Boston he proposed that they run away to Brazil and start life anew. She derided the idea, a fierce quarrel ensued, and the evening ended with her vow never to see him again.

To boil down her rather diffuse narrative, she recalled that on the night of the dress rehearsal she felt giddy after her spin in the barber chair and had gone out the stage door for a breath of air. In the alley, she was accosted by a burly individual—a sailor, seemingly, for he had on a peajacket—who said that Bibulous, in a limousine outside, wished to speak to her. Foolishly unsuspecting, she started toward the curb, suddenly felt herself overpowered and smothered by a cloth exuding some noxious liquid, and knew no more. When she regained consciousness, she was in a hopeless predicament—a prisoner aboard a yacht, chartered by Bibulous, steaming for Brazil. So overcome was she by rage at his perfidy, by agitation at the ruin of her career, that her sanity almost gave way. No amount of supplication or of appeals to his finer nature produced the slightest effect; he countered with word pictures of their future together on vast *estancias*, of the carnival gaiety of Rio and journeys up the Amazon. Drained of emotion, corroded with bitterness, she locked herself in her cabin, resolved to starve herself to death.

"I don't know how long I was in there," she went on tragically. "I was so weak that time ceased to exist for me. Then the boat stopped moving, and in my delirium I thought we were in Rio, till Max forced the door and told me."

"Where were you?"

"In Camden, New Jersey. Max was crying and blubbering like a little boy. His whole world was in pieces. He had just been handed a cable by the harbor master—I forgot his name—"

"Never mind his name," I interrupted. "What was in the cable?"

"It was from his accountant, Irving Previne. It said that his wife and his partner had cheated him out of his share in the business and eloped together. He didn't have a dime—only enough to pay the mooring fee. He begged me not to desert him —he was going to open a small fur shop in Mount Holly and begin over again if I would stick by him."

"But you were free," I objected. "Why didn't you come back to the show?"

"What, and be cooped up in that chair eight times a week?" she scoffed. "Listen, I was a nervous wreck, but I had some sense left. I hitchhiked as far as Plainfield, where luck smiled on me and I ran into Nels Breastbohn. Today, I have three darling kiddies, a devoted husband, and a lovely ranch-style home. So I guess I should be grateful."

Especially, I thought, to a man named Cubbage, who was more of a magician than he knew. "Still and all," I said, "don't you sometimes miss the glamour of show business?"

"Oh, *that*." She shrugged. "I can get all of that I need from a copy of *Variety*."

Which, considering what that journal's review of Liberace had done for me, took the words right out of my mouth.

The Frost Is on the Noggin

I once asked the retired fly cop Dashiell Hammett, a former Pinkerton employee who'd switched to writing for the pulps, a technical question about surveillance. In his experience as a sleuth, I inquired, was a person under suspicion ever conscious of being shadowed? Hammett responded with an anecdote. It seems that a certain New York jewelry concern had a drummer named Finsterwald—a Teutonicism for "Darkwood"—whose honesty it had reason to question. Finsterwald was about to go South on a sales trip, bearing two cases of valuable samples the firm believed he was planning to steal, and Hammett was detailed to keep an eye on him. Conspicuous for his height, emaciation, and snow-white thatch, Hammett was an unlikely choice for the job, but, as it happened, all the other operatives were out breaking strikes or retrieving gold falcons or whatever gumshoes of that era busied themselves with.

Finsterwald, closely followed by Hammett, entrained for Philadelphia and on arrival there checked into a hotel. Hammett got a room two doors away, ate dinner at an adjacent table in the coffee shop, and yawned in concert with him in the lobby until bedtime. The next morning, the salesman took off for Hagerstown, where he and his shadow went through the same uneventful routine. In the ensuing five days, the pair progressed in succession to Richmond, Raleigh, Knoxville, Columbia, and Macon. Nowhere in his zigzag pattern was Finsterwald ever out of Hammett's sight for a moment during waking hours, nor did he call on a single prospect. His manner was unhurried and devoid of the slightest hint of furtiveness. Not once by word or deed did he exhibit any awareness that he was under scrutiny.

Midafternoon on the eighth day of the trip, according to Hammett, he was sitting in a park in Savannah, idling through a newspaper and observing Finsterwald as the latter dozed on a bench nearby. Distracted by some item of unusual interest in the paper, he forgot his quarry for an instant. Suddenly a voice sounded at his elbow. Finsterwald, a diffident smile on his face, was addressing him.

"Excuse me, but you look familiar. Haven't I seen you somewhere before?"

"Why, no—not that I recall," Hammett returned blandly.

"Strange," mused the salesman. "Oh, well, probably a resemblance . . . Mind if I sit down here?"

Hammett bade him do so, exchanged profundities about the beauty of Savannah, and, upon mutual agreement that its climate, while balmy, aroused thirst, accompanied him to a tavern. After several beers, Finsterwald began oozing bonhomie. He deemed Hammett a capital fellow, one who knew a hawk from a handsaw and could be relied on in a pinch. It was only a guess, but he felt intuitively that his companion might not be averse to making a little easy moola. Affirming that his pores were ever open for a proposition, Hammett asked what he had in mind. The drummer thereupon unfolded a complex scheme that involved stowing the jewelry samples in a Miami railroad checkroom and mailing the claim tickets to Hammett, who would convey the cases to a fence in Zanesville and rendezvous with him in Altoona to split the swag. Amid much cackling, the bargain was sealed over a couple of boilermakers, and they parted—Finsterwald to visit a Turkish bath and Hammett to turn him in at the nearest police station for conspiring to commit larceny.

"And if I know what goes on in stir," Hammett concluded, "that bird spent the next couple of years scratching his head and saying to himself, 'Jeez, it was foolproof—how did they ever catch on? What did I do wrong?' "

Any likelihood that I was about to be drawn into a similarly bizarre situation was farthest from my mind when, several weeks ago, I read a striking report in the London *Times*. "The West Germans are rapidly becoming a nation of shoplifters," it said. "One prosperous businessman stole, over a long period, all the food he wanted for a party he was giving. A titled woman, wearing a fur coat worth thousands of marks, was found to have the lining stuffed full of stolen food. . . . One man shopper took a fancy to a frozen chicken, and went to the extraordinary length of concealing it in the crown of his hat. He was detected at the cash desk, but only because he fell unconscious while waiting to pay for those goods he had decided to declare. The frozen fowl nesting on top of his head had slowed down the blood circulation to his brain."

Not long after I read the foregoing, I happened to notice in the Third Avenue supermarket where I shop a remarkable person contemplating the showcase of frozen foods. Gaunt, well over six feet tall, and chin-whiskered, he was clad in a rusty Prince Albert set off by a silk hat of the type known as a tile. Whether it was his expression of deep melancholy or his posture as he stood grasping his lapels, he reminded me of someone, but I could not remember who. Clearly oblivious of my gaze, he opened the showcase door and withdrew two packages—a Stouffer's beef pie and a Sara Lee cheesecake. At that juncture, some old gaffer maneuvering his wagon jostled me. I stepped aside with an apology, and when I turned back the tall stranger had vanished into the detergents and soap powders. I assumed I had seen the last of him, but no—on reaching the express checkout lane I beheld him directly ahead. The clerk was bagging his sole purchase, a Teflon scouring pad, and, mystified, I watched him exit through the automatic doors. Where were the foodstuffs he'd selected, the beef pie and cheesecake? And who in tarnation was he? There was an enigmatic quality about the man, an elusiveness, apart from his identity, that unsettled me.

Had I consulted my astrological forecast, as I should have, it would have told me I was entering a period of suspense, which shortly became apparent. Three days thence, the counterman of a delicatessen on Nineteenth Street was slicing a quarter of Novy for me. The ambient air was heavy with the fragrance of whitefish, Maatjes herring, and freshly minted bagels, and, crowded around me, a bevy of dynamite chicks, each lovelier than Faye Dunaway, awaited their turn with nostrils flaring. All of a sudden, like a chill wind, I felt an alien presence, and there stood the same wraithlike figure by the frozen food locker, clasping an icy carton of wonton soup atop two packets of Chinese snow peas and water chestnuts. I stared at him for what must have seemed an eternity, because the counterman loosed an enraged bellow.

"What next, Mister, what next?" the counterman cried. "People are waiting!"

"Yes, and they're famished!" echoed one of the beauties. "What's eating you, chum? You look like you seen a ghost."

She was right, in a sense, for in that instant I had witnessed an uncanny sleight-of-hand performance—the disappearance of all three eatables into the man's uplifted hat. By the time I squirmed through the press, clutching my Novy, his only visible selection, a bar of halvah, had been rung up on the register and he was speeding down the block. Burning to ascertain whether the refrigeration would fell him as it had the kraut shoplifter, I took off in hot pursuit. Our contest was unequal; the gelid ice cap seemed to act on him like adrenaline, though possibly he may have raised his sugar level with the halvah. Whatever the cause, I lost him somewhere near Gramercy Park, but the chase was not wholly unproductive. In one of several buildings where he could have gone to earth, I found a mailbox reading Eban Locnil. It didn't promise much at first, but, thanks to a pipeful or two of Latakia and an aptitude for cryptography, it rearranged itself into Abe Lincoln, and I knew a moment of elation. So that was why the chap had seemed familiar. Well, I resolved grimly, *ruat caelum*, I was going to discover how this dishonest Abe had flouted the most elementary laws of physiology.

The opportunity came that Saturday, in the hurly-burly of

weekend shopping. Poring through the bins of Nussbaum's Gourmeteria, on Second Avenue, for a breakfast kipper, I overheard a woman railing against the rudeness of a customer who, she asserted, had practically wrenched a broiler out of her hand. "He's some kind of a poultry freak, the muzzler!" she shrilled. "He's there right now at the meat counter! An old-fashioned weirdo in a high hat."

Sparse though it was, her description warranted a rundown, and I tiptoed into the next aisle. The sight that met my eyes was well-nigh past belief. Disdaining easy choices like goose liver and chicken wings, my Presidential doppelgänger was about to execute a *coup de théâtre* by forcing a butterball turkey into his headpiece. Providentially, he did not see me, and I ducked back. That was all to the good. If there was to be a confrontation, I wanted it on my own terms.

"Reach for the sky, Locnil." The words I had rehearsed since quitting Nussbaum's sounded less puissant at the entrance of his brownstone, but they gained menace from the briar pipe I jammed into his back. He stiffened, and before he could resist I herded him into the foyer. Then I did some quick thinking. If he lamped a Dunhill in my mitt instead of a police special, the jig was up, so I shifted it to my coat pocket. I wasn't sure if he'd buy it, but he bought it. All the way up in the poky little elevator, he spoke only once.

"You the fuzz?"

"Uh-uh, just someone who knows his way around the circulatory system and needs a few answers. This your pad?"

He nodded, fiddled with the locks, threw on a switch. Then, as the room flooded with light, he swung around, his eyes twin clouded agates. "All right, what's bugging you?" he snarled. "Talk fast. I've got a turkey melting on my head."

"Boohoo, you're breaking my heart," I growled. "Sit down, Lincoln, and keep your hands on your lapels. That way nobody gets hurt."

His face fell apart. "How did you know me?"

"I wasn't born yesterday. Anyway, there aren't too many gees around that look like rail-splitters. Once I ruled out Raymond

Massey and Arthur Miller, there was only one other person you could be."

"Listen, you," he said, his twin agates narrowing. "I got a hunch you've been tailing me. I'm positive we've seen each other in the past."

"Maybe you were a king in Babylon and I was a Christian slave," I chaffed him. "But enough with the yocks. Where did you get the idea?"

"I don't read you. What idea?"

"Of wearing a heated wig on your sconce for insulation—to counteract the deadly frost that you knew would cause syncope, from cerebral anemia."

He figured the odds a long moment, decided I had him. "You win, Doc," he said. "But how did you tumble? Tell me where I goofed."

"For one thing, at the meat counter in Nussbaum's. You stepped out of character, my friend. The Great Emancipator would never have snatched a broiler from a lady."

"Yeah, I guess I overplayed my hand. What else?"

I flicked aside his muffler, exposing the electric cord leading under his hat. "At first, I thought you had a can of Sterno up there, or a small hibachi. Then I spotted this when you were heisting the gobbler. That cinched it, Locnil."

Rarely have I seen such desolation on a human countenance; staring out at me, all pretense flown, was a mute hunted animal. He silently extended his wrists. "O.K., I'm ready. Let's go."

I extracted my pipe, tapped out the dottle, and rose. "Smarten up, fellow," I said. "I told you—I'm not a lawman. Nor am I, in spite of your awed expression, that implausible creation of Jacques Futrelle's, The Thinking Machine."

"Then who are you, in God's name?" he whimpered.

"Merely an insomniac," I said. "A reader of the London Times who can't rest until he solves their news reports." And went out the door.

Zwei Herzen in die Drygoods Schlock

"Everyone else is talking about me," said Diane Von Furstenberg, the 29-year-old princess turned dress designer whose fashion empire grossed $60 million last year. "So I figured, why don't I?"

Not content with just being one of the most successful designers to make waves in the recession/inflation fashion economy, Miss Von Furstenberg has now set her heart on literary acclaim. Her next project is a book. It will hit the stores in September and will be titled "Beauty" . . .

"I'm not beautiful—I'm interesting looking. But I've done a lot of work on accepting myself. . . . I've never been a designer," she says. "I was just a woman who walked into her closet one day and realized that everything was out of date."

Ron Talsky, 41, the Hollywood costume designer whose main claim to fashion fame has been designing for Raquel Welch, says they've split.

"I no longer want to be considered by Hollywood as Raquel Welch's designer," says Talsky, who is Oscar-nominated this year for his Welch wardrobe in "The Four Musketeers."

It's not sour grapes. "I'm proud of changing Raquel's image from a young sexpot to a sexy actress," says Talsky, "but I'd like to work with Streisand, Faye Dunaway, Candice Bergen now." —*Los Angeles Times*

SCENE: *A closet in Los Angeles. As the curtain rises, Charisma von Ausgespielt, a breathtakingly beautiful twenty-four-year-old woman no longer in the first bloom of youth, stands before the door, racked with indecision. After a moment, the door opens and a young man emerges.*

CHARISMA (*startled*): Mercy! Who are you?

MAN: What do you mean who am I? Can't you see? I'm a person who's just come out of the closet.

CHARISMA: I realize that, but it still doesn't explain what you were doing in there.

MAN: That's between me and my shrink, nosy. I don't feel obliged to account for my life style to every Tom, Dick, and Harry. (*He exits.*)

CHARISMA: My goodness, what a pepper pot. You can't hardly rummage through your own schmottas nowadays without some ignatz snaps your head off. (*She enters closet and begins sorting dresses, disillusion writ large on her countenance.*) Ugh, to think I ever wore such anachronistic frocks—I must have seemed a frump indeed in these habiliments. However, thanks to a clever needle and the shrewd midwifery of *Women's Wear Daily, Burke's Peerage,* and the *Almanach de Gotha,* I am now on easy street, a biggie in the garment center, and almost finished scrivening my forthcoming smash autobio, *She Spins to Conquer.*

(*Unbeknownst to her, Ricky Tickitavsky, a divinely handsome Hollywood designer, has entered the closet. He is twenty-seven, soigné, and Oscar-rejected for his inept costuming of Anatole France's* Jocasta and the Famished Cat.)

RICKY: Excuse me, Miss—can you tell me the price of these rejects?

CHARISMA (*confounded*): Eek! Where did you come from?

RICKY: Well, it's a long story. My father was born in Lithuania—

CHARISMA: I daresay. Nevertheless, that hardly entitles you to march in here as bold as brass.

RICKY: I don't get you. This is a thrift shop, isn't it? Look at all the schmottas on the rack.

CHARISMA (*icily*): I'll have you know these are all Charisma von Ausgespielt originals.

RICKY: Right, and they've got just the tacky, old-fashioned

quality I need. I'm costuming a revival of *Charley's Aunt* at the Pasadena Senior High School.

CHARISMA: Young man, do you know who you're talking to? I'm the designer of these gowns.

RICKY: So what? I'm a designer, too—Ricky Tickitavsky. You probably read about me in the newspapers.

CHARISMA: Yes, I seem to recall something to the effect that you had just split with Sally Rand.

RICKY: Not Sally Rand—Talleyrand. I changed his image from a sexy young statesman to a sexy older statesman, but it didn't fulfill me. Now I'm thirsting to work with Metternich, Lord Rosebery, Kissinger—the power élite.

CHARISMA: Of course, of course. You mean you want to burst forth from your pupa.

RICKY: What pupa is that?

CHARISMA: Why, your chrysalis—that dull husk which it has heretofore imprisoned your personality. You want to soar out on great golden butterfly wings, to express your potential, to dazzle the onlookers.

RICKY: You know something? You have a way with words. Given the right training, you could be a terrific salesman.

CHARISMA: I sense that in you, too—you have a flair for verbs. Bugging you, though, is the one hurdle: can you accept yourself?

RICKY: (*miserably*): I hate myself. I'm only a—what did you call me before?—a pupa. Sometimes, laying awake in my lonely condominium in Brentwood, I ask myself what behooves it that Vidal Sassoon styles my hair and Yves Saint Laurent makes my cologne, that I drive an Audi Fox. My whole ego is in shards. I feel I'm, like, living a lie.

CHARISMA: *Selbstverständlich*—that's because in your heart's deep core you know yourself to be a pushcart peddler. Now, I was born to the purple, sprung from the proudest loins in Europe, so I don't have these hangups.

RICKY: Forgive me, Highness, but could we sit down maybe? It's kind of close in here.

CHARISMA (*wounded*): Well, after all, it *is* a closet.

RICKY: I'm not criticizing it—I just thought we'd be more comfortable on these shoeboxes. . . . There, that's better. You were saying you sprang from a pride of loins?

CHARISMA: Yes, I mingle with crowned heads as naturally as a duck takes to water, like a baby loves its rock-and-rye. Is there a pheasant drive across the Tweed, a boar hunt in Styria, a gala at Bad Ischl, a champagne party aboard a dahabeah on the Nile? Wherever the *jeunesse dorée* convokes, wherever fun is at its maddest, look for me there, the cynosure of all the men, the envy of all the women. Tell me—do you find me attractive?

RICKY: No, you have something that transcends mere beauty. You have flaring nostrils like a horse, which you never see them on these babes in the five-and-ten-cent stores. Plus a patrician instep that bespeaks five hundred years of breeding.

CHARISMA (*bursting into tears*): Oh, I'm so tired of adulation! Do you know what it means to have men constantly shooting themselves for love of you, slavering over you, pawing you? I loathe the smell of their cigars in the curtains. Hence I became a writer.

RICKY: But you said you were a designer.

CHARISMA: Labels, badges! What are they but rotten little handcuffs that society fastens on the creative to strangulate their genius? Were I to meet someone with the divine afflatus, be he poet, painter, or dustman, then, by my halidom, I would flee with same to the ends of the earth.

RICKY: Take care lest you fling your cap over the moon. If you met them in a closet like this, they might be an exterminator —a dry cleaner.

CHARISMA: 'Twould matter not a groat, by my maidenhead. Anyhow, getting back to basics, what do you think of my book so far?

RICKY: What book is that?

CHARISMA: Why, *She Spins to Conquer*, which, albeit unfinished, has already reduced Virginia Kirkus to superlatives and netted a tidy four hundred Gs for the paperback rights. You've submitted it to a perusal?

RICKY: (*uncomfortably*): No—only browsed it—the first forty pages—

CHARISMA: But you must have a gut reaction. Even the lowest of the low—my podiatrist, the vegetable man in Gristede's—has a gut reaction.

RICKY: Well, I'll level with you. The characters are well drawn, you have a nice sense of plot, but I miss the infrastructure. Who are we rooting for?

CHARISMA: The girl. The part I want Telly Savalas for.

RICKY: Then who plays Cyprian, the boy?

CHARISMA: Telly can play him, too.

RICKY: You don't foresee a collision of identities?

CHARISMA: Well, I'm not wedded to it, but it's a challenge to the designer in me. I'd like to use heaps and heaps of écru satin for the scene where the two of them capture Bryn Mawr.

RICKY: Charisma, did I ever honeyfogle you? Name me one time when I ever sold you out for a lousy commission. You're my ace client—right?

CHARISMA: We've always enjoyed a good working relationship, yes.

RICKY: Then I'll give you my gut reaction. To me that scene is not believable.

CHARISMA: You feel it strains credulity?

RICKY: I didn't say that—

CHARISMA: You did so! (*Sobbing*) I worked over it for weeks. It was the capstone of the arch, the linchpin of the whole story!

RICKY: No, no, the linchpin was the scene with the St. Bernard puppies climbing on Dr. Volk! Listen to me, honey . . .

CHARISMA (*recoiling*): Take your filthy hands off me. How dare you touch someone with my imperious aquiline features, a lineal descendant of the Orlovs, the Potockis, the Poniatowskis?

RICKY: I was carried away. A drop too much vodka . . .

CHARISMA: Goose that I was, all my governess's warnings went for naught. In my father's vast estates in the Crimea, the overseer's whip would have wiped out such an affront.

RICKY: Excuse, Gräfin. I just heard a knock on the door. Should I answer it?

CHARISMA (*acidly*): I'm quite capable of looking after my own closet, thank you.

(*Revealed in the doorway is a soldierly figure, fainting and half exhausted, clad in a military greatcoat. His astrakhan shako has slipped back to disclose a bloodstained bandage.*)

MAN: Is there a Monsieur Tickitavsky here?

RICKY: I am he.

MAN (*saluting*): Sire, I am Michael Strogoff, courier of the Czar; I bear important dispatches from the imperial court. Forgive my appearance, but I have driven many versts. Ricky Petrovich—

RICKY: Enough with the patronymics. Make with the dispatches.

STROGOFF: Here they are, Altesse.

RICKY (*exultantly, as he reads*): Charisma! Sweetheart! Where are you?

CHARISMA: Right here by your shoebox. Is it good news?

RICKY: You better believe it. The thrust is that, following lengthy investigation, it has come to light that Count Boris Przystalski, the wealthiest landholder in the Crimea, and I were switched in our cradles by a scheming quadroon. As the real Count Boris, I now possess twelve thousand serfs, a goodly sum in cash, and his entire fief.

CHARISMA: Oh, Ricky, how super. We always dreamt of having our own fief.

RICKY: Yes, it's magic. Only in an American closet could such a thing happen, a baseborn Litvak winning a shiksa of royal lineage.

STROGOFF (*impatiently*): Is there any answer for the Czar? I can't stand here cooling my steeds all night. They're flecked with foam.

RICKY: How do you like that? A greenhorn, an apple-knocker, and already he's burning up the freeways. Where's the fire?

STROGOFF: I'm huddling with Francis Ford Coppola, Norman

Lear, and Swifty Lazar in the Polo Lounge to lens a thirty-nine-week spinoff from my sensational X-rated *Nudity in Varsovie.*

CHARISMA: Who's doing the clothes, if any? Ricky and I just conceived a thrilling new line of see-through jumpsuits yclept Schmottas Polonaises.

STROGOFF: Then you got yourself a deal, Countess. Follow me!

(The three link arms and hasten excitedly toward the Polo Lounge.)

CURTAIN

The Joy of Mooching

To Mombasa, Mogadishu, and Modesto I have been; to Montecatini, Montenegro, and Monaco; but never, wide-ranging *Wandervogel* though I pride myself on being, have I set foot in Monza. A town northeast of Milan and slightly northwest of Gorgonzola, on the road to Bergamo, Monza has as its chief industry, as far as I can make out, the export of curiosa to the world press. Here are born those strange and often lunatic fillers that piece out the news stories one reads, such as the paragraph that filtered into the *Times* a while ago: "Monza, Italy (AP) — Ambrogio Bacis, 69 years old, does not like dentists, so to pull an aching tooth he fastened a cord to the tooth and the other end to an automobile bumper, and started the car. Mr. Bracis's head collided with the bumper, and he wound up in the hospital, with the tooth still in his mouth." To my way of thinking, the classical Tom Sawyer extraction—the silk thread tied to the bedstead, the hot coal brandished in the patient's face—remains unsurpassed in home dentistry, but obviously Bacis, in his anxiety to be up to date, opted for a fifteen-hundred-pound Imbroglio. Ah, well, *autres temps, autres mœurs.*

Another and even more seductive item emanating from Monza turned up in *The Jerusalem Post* recently; to wit: "It must rank as one of the strangest cocktail parties ever—and it was thrown by well-dressed Sebastiano Amara, of Monza, Italy, to boost sales of a book he's just published, *How to Make*

47

48   S. J. Perelman

Begging Pay. The suave author and man-about-town received his guests, doled out liberal Martinis, then begged to be excused. In a few minutes he returned—disguised as a crippled beggar, his face contorted with agony as he hobbled in on crutches. Guests in cars then followed 25-year-old Sebastiano to Monza's main shopping street, watched as he laid his crutches on the pavement and started weeping. In ten minutes he had collected the equivalent of $15. In his book he claims he never collected less than $100 a day, and says, 'I did it as a part-time job, mainly for aesthetic pleasure, and only partly for pocket money.' "

My initial response to Signor Amara's exploit was, I must confess, one of jealousy. Myself a suave author and man-about-town, I was piqued that I hadn't conceived so original a method of publicizing my own books. As envy subsided, though, one phrase of his kept pestering me like a caraway seed embedded in a tooth (a dental metaphor doubtless arising from Mr. Bacis's predicament): that he had acted thus "mainly for aesthetic pleasure." Now, among various paragons on whom I have modelled myself from time to time—the Scarlet Pimpernel, the Earl of Rochester, Baruch Spinoza—one of the more influential was Des Esseintes, the hero of Joris Karl Huysmans' *Against the Grain*, who ceaselessly sought artistic stimulus in drugs, perfumes, and vice. Was it possible that this scribbler on the road to Bergamo had experienced in mendicancy a psychic release overlooked by Des Esseintes and me, deftly fattening his royalties meanwhile? Unimaginable, I told myself, but still I ought to lose no time in emulating him, and I fell to work.

As a neophyte in the world of beggary, I decided that the role best suited to me was traditional. Accordingly, I purchased a ragged shawl and a size-12 gingham dress from a pushcart on Rivington Street, and issued invitations to a half-dozen friends for cocktails at my hotel on Gramercy Park. At the height of the party, while my guests were feverishly consuming Martinis and bandying epigrams, I excused myself, retired to the bedroom, and transformed myself into a waif. The conversion was not

wholly successful, as the little match girl in the fairy tale of
Hans Christian Andersen is rarely depicted with a mustache, but
nonetheless I resolved to brazen it out. To my gratification, the
effect on the assemblage was volcanic. Everyone literally stood
rooted to the floor.

"*Voyons!* A supreme master of illusion!" I heard people exclaiming. "Another Lon Chaney! Can our eyes be deceiving us?
In a few expert strokes, this *arbiter elegantiarum* has, as it were,
metamorphosed himself into a vag."

Like Sebastiano, I would have liked my intimates to follow
me in their motors, but, as none of them owned any, I bade
them go on drinking—a somewhat empty gesture, since the
bottles were exhausted—and took my leave. Crossing to the
south side of Gramercy Park, I stationed myself with my tray of
matches outside The Players Club. The circumstances, I saw
at once, were unpropitious. Ideally, it should have been snow-
ing; instead, it was a hot, sultry evening, beckoning the passerby
to Baskin-Robbins for an ice-cream cone rather than to contribute alms. After a while, a gentleman came out of the club,
placing his feet with great deliberation, in the manner of one
who has dined well on glazed Virginia ham with sweet potatoes.

"Please, sir, buy my matches," I whined. "Owing to a con-
spiracy among the reviewers, my latest book is already on the
eighty-nine-cent table at Barnes & Noble. Have pity on me—
don't let them recycle it. Also, I write by gaslight, and Con-
solidated Edison is threatening to cut off the gas. Support the
arts, even if, as I suspect, you can barely support yourself."

My prospect gaped at me incredulously and, muttering to
himself, went back into the club. An ashen-haired model in
three shades of denim, leading an ashen-haired borzoi, approached; as they neared me, the dog sat down growling and
she pulled him past with an apologetic "Sorry, he hates beggars"
that at least certified that my disguise was valid. Then two
character actors, their brows furrowed by unemployment,
emerged from The Players. Sucking in my cheeks to simulate
the ravages of hunger, I bore down on them.

" 'A benison, playgoers, a cornucopia! A feast for the intelligence!' " I snuffled. "That is what the New York critics wrote about my last play—amateur rights now available from Samuel French, Incorporated. And how many scripts have they sold? Three lousy copies! How am I to sustain myself, to wield my pen in the tradition of Congreve, Sheridan, and Wilde, without your philanthropic assistance? Buy my vestas, I implore you."

"Beat it, chump," the elder of the pair countered roughly. "Save those hard-luck stories for the Bowery. Write yourself a soap for Procter & Gamble, or go on relief, like the rest of us."

Crestfallen and perspiring from the heat of the shawl, I shambled back to the hotel and sat down to rethink a modus operandi. Could it be, I asked myself, that the persona I had chosen was too depressing, that people would be more generous if the nature of my plight were bizarre or offbeat? To the fiery temperament, decision is consonant with action; in a trice I divested myself of my rags, slipped into a dinner jacket, and, faultlessly arrayed in black silk hose but no slippers, shot uptown in a taxi. Dismounting between two expensive Park Avenue apartments in the Sixties, I took up a stand near the canopy of the more opulent. Several cabs arrived bearing couples and parties, but I ignored them. At length, one discharged a jovial, fortyish individual with a worldly air, smoking a Perfecto. I accosted him furtively.

"Excuse me, friend, but I'm in a bit of a jam. Might we have a word?"

His eyes encompassed my garb, widened at my stockinged feet. "What is it?"

"Well," I confided, chuckling in hearty man-to-man fashion, "the fact is, I was having a slap and a tickle with a certain married lady in this building whose identity must be protected at all costs. I mean, we're all human, what? As the fellow said, who's to cast the first stone?"

"Yes, yes," he said impatiently. "So her husband came home

unexpectedly and you left just in the nick without your pumps. Where do I fit into this?"

"Wait. I was coming to that." I swallowed. "You see, I'm a writer by profession, and I'm supposed to autograph my new best-seller at Doubleday's for admirers, but I can't let them see me like this. Unfortunately, though, I forgot my wallet upstairs, too. If you could lend me the price of a new pair—"

He cut me short with a paternal hand on my sleeve. "Shape up, brother," he said. "You're not a writer—you're a schmo. Anyone that leaves their shoes and their wallet in a lady's boudoir is a butterfingers. Take my advice—if you want to play Lothario, go join the Actors Studio." He shook his head commiseratingly and melted into the foyer.

Dashed though I was by his rebuff, I was not minded to give up so easily, and I squared my jaw. Of the next two arrivals, the first rejected my appeal on the ground that no shoe stores were open at that hour; the second derisively demanded the name of my inamorata. In nineteen years' residence in the house, he said, he had yet to see a female worthy of pursuit. As if to make matters worse, it shortly came on to rain, and by the time I reached home in my wet socks I had such a cold that laryngologists skyed in from as far away as Mayo to study it.

During the long, slow convalescence that followed, I stewed over my inability to equal Sebastiano's receipts or to glean even a mite of aesthetic pleasure from the process. At last, I hit on the reason. The identities I had chosen, match girl and philanderer, were too foreign to my nature. Temperamentally a dreamer and a rover, I was trying to be a schnorrer, too, which was altogether alien, for *au fond* I was prouder than a Spanish hidalgo and would accept alms from no man. It was out of character—as if Lord Olivier were to impersonate Pecksniff and then pass the hat. Ergo, I must not dissemble; I must boldly admit myself a genius whose wares were unsalable, a drug on

the market, and if that shamed an apathetic public into shower-
ing me with gold, I could with dignity accept my rightful due.
Immediately a weight lifted from my shoulders. Donning the
velvet jacket, Windsor tie, and beret I normally wear when
writing, I hurried to the Marboro bookshop on West Eighth
Street. Rapture—my suspicion was confirmed; an unsold pile
of my most recent opus, reduced to fifty-nine cents, loomed up
higher than a ziggurat. Folding my arms, I took up a position
alongside it and waited to be pitied.

Half an hour passed and nobody appeared—not even a klepto-
maniac. Finally, a heavily bearded man in a filthy Confederate
tunic, who looked like Colonel Mosby but proved to be a youth
of seventeen, materialized and asked the clerk for a primer on
flagellation. A couple of teen-agers with schoolbags came in,
leafed through Eberhard and Phyllis Kronhausen's *Pornography
and the Law*, and left, sniffing disappointedly. A stout yenta in
picador dress but minus leather chaps exchanged a copy of Sara
Kasdan's *Love and Knishes* for a poster of Donatello's David.
With that, all activity halted, and I grew hot under the collar.
My patience was ebbing fast.

"Hey, General Guderian, what gives here?" I queried the
uniformed guard sporting a nightstick. "Where are the
browsers?"

"Nobody gets up before noon in the Village," he said. "Takes
a while for the marijuana fumes to clear."

In due course, the pace altered; shoppers, most of them
somnambulists, started drifting through the aisles, languidly
fingering the bargains and striving to read the erotica sealed in
cellophane. Posed by my works, I assumed an expression at once
dismal and haughty, insouciant yet despondent, that would have
wrung the stoniest heart. But naught booted me, truth to tell,
for as the illiterate swine neared my books their faces hardened
and they sheared off, burying their noses in the fescennine pages
of Harold Robbins and Irving Wallace. Resolved that those who
had died for literature should not have fallen in vain, I determined to speak out.

"So the philistines have triumphed again, have they?" I

began, raising my voice. "What price now Kafka in his garret, Melville eking out his days as a customs inspector? Was it for this that Keats—"

Suddenly the words died in my throat; a Lincolnian figure I recognized as—or took to be—Philip Roth's had entered the door and was scanning the counters for remaindered copies of his books. He did not have to scan long, because adjacent to mine stood another ziggurat, even taller and likewise discounted, of *The Great American Novel*. In the same instant, his quick novelist's eye discerned what I was doing and he strode angrily toward me.

"Scab! Cut-rate fink!" he exploded. "So this is how you dispose of your overstock, by appealing to the sentimental side of your non-readers!"

"For shame, mealymouth!" I flung back. "Who are you to criticize? You were just sneaking in to push your own remainders. I at least was bent on deriving aesthetic pleasure from my humiliation."

"Oho!" he jeered. "Uncontent with being a dreamer and a rover, you're a masochist, too. My psychiatrist has an ugly name for that!"

"You don't say," I returned, interested. "What is it?"

"Well, I forget, actually," he said, "but I'll give you his phone number—you can ask him."

"Gee, that's nice of you, Roth," I said. "Look here, I'd like to inscribe one of my books for you."

"And I for you," he said, doing so and handing it to me. "Listen, if you're going uptown, why don't we split a cab? After all, between us we sold a couple of books this afternoon."

And that, plus a talk we had about girls over a glass of tea at the Belmore Cafeteria, is the sum total of what I gleaned from patterning myself on the author of *How to Make Begging Pay*. Well, I hope his manual sells like hotcakes in Monza and never gets remaindered. Because if the silly beggar comes around to me for sympathy, I'll tell him a thing or two.

Recapture Your Rapture,
in One Seedy Session

Loath though I am to bring *The New York Review of Books*, *The Times Literary Supplement*, and the academics buzzing down around my ears like a cloud of hornets, I'd like to ask a simple question. Why is it that in the torrent of acclamation, exegesis, and criticism which has gushed forth during this century about Proust's monumental *Remembrance of Things Past* we find not so much as a mention of the Steinberg theory? It may come as a surprise to those who regard him as merely a gifted artist to learn that Mr. Saul Steinberg has thought long and deeply about the catalytic agent of the novel. (I do not refer to Gaston Farblondget, the playbroker who first brought it to the attention of Grasset, the original publisher, but, rather, to the pastry, the *madeleine* soaked in lime-flower tea, that evoked the author's recollections.) Nevertheless, Mr. Steinberg has, and it is his contention, iconoclastic if you will, that Proust deliberately falsified what he had eaten as being too plebeian. In Steinberg's judgment—and he buttresses it with a formidable array of interior evidence from the work—Proust's *madeleine* was in reality a matzo ball, and the past unfolded itself to the Master as he sat hunched over a bowl of chicken soup in Flambaum's, the famous kosher restaurant in Paris.

Absurd, you say? Improbable? Yet scientific researchers, people like L. Ron Hubbard, Jeane Dixon, and William Safire, who have spent years studying the intricacies of the human brain, tell us that one's own skein of memory often starts unwinding under similarly mundane circumstances. Such was undeniably the case with me several months ago in the basement workshop of a bootmaker in London's West End, twenty feet below the surface of Cork Street. I had crawled down there on a rainy afternoon to pick up some shoelaces he had rehabilitated for me, and, as was his habit of late, Mr Bloodroot launched into a gloomy discourse on the decline of his calling. In the best of times, Bloodroot has never displayed a tincture of optimism, and today his wrinkled visage was more doleful than a basset hound's. Vanished forever, he declaimed, were apprentices willing to school themselves in the discipline of shoecraft, vanished the client with discernment and the means to appreciate superb workmanship. Was this subterranean badger hole we stood in an adequate reward for his years of unremitting industry? Apprehensive lest the man disembowel himself with an awl before my eyes, I appealed to his *amour-propre*.

"But think of the clientele you've had, sir," I protested. "Sir Winston, Duff Cooper, the Sitwells—"

"Oh, aye, I've made for them all," he agreed sombrely. "And the actors, too. Olivier, Gielgud, and Redgrave—the lot."

"Yes, and what about the American film stars? I daresay you've known plenty of them, like Clark Gable and Douglas Fairbanks, Jr."

From his instant disdain, I saw that his pride had been touched. "Fairbanks? He was a nobody compared to some of my customers. Look here." He fumbled out a battered cardcase, shuffled the contents, and handed me a creased and yellowed letter. "You've heard of *him*, I expect."

I had indeed. Dated March 14, 1921, the note was addressed from North Roxbury Drive, in Beverly Hills. "Dear Mr. Bloodroot," it read. "I trust that this finds you well. I would like at this time to order another pair of the patent-leather shoes with gray cloth tops, buttoning on the side, which you supplied me in the past. Will forward international money order on receipt. With kindest regards, Rudolph Valentino."

Valentino the incomparable—the immortal Rudy, with his glittering snake eyes and hair ebony as the raven's wing, his feline grace; the image of those shoes brought him surging across the gulf of years as nothing else could. Dazzled, I toiled back to sidewalk level from Bloodroot's den and, over a pint of Guinness to offset the bends, gave myself up to memories of the Sheik of Araby. Certainly the most vivid, if not the first, was that of his performance as a torero in *Blood and Sand* about 1922, when he twirled across his dressing room like a teetotum to gird himself in a silver sash held by an attendant. His leading lady, of course, was the divine Nita Naldi, and, by a nice coincidence, light had been shed only recently on the reason for her choice. Reporting on a Dublin film festival, David Robinson, the movie critic of *The Times* of London, told this story:

The exotic Latin vamp of the 1920s, Nita Naldi was, it appears, really called Anita Dooley. She first encountered the literary lion of the day, Blasco Ibanez, at a party, and as a good Irish Catholic girl upbraided him roundly for his treatment of the Church. The argument became so heated that the great man's false teeth flew out and straight down Miss Naldi's corsage [which, Mr. Robinson unaccountably neglected to add, was unrivalled in the Western world save by Aileen Pringle's]. Without pausing for breath, Ibanez plunged his hand into the crevasse, retrieved his teeth and clapped them back into his mouth. Evidently the experience had made an impression on him, however, for he insisted that Miss Naldi should star opposite Rudolph Valentino in the film of his novel "Blood and Sand."

Nita Naldi, Wallace Reid, Olga Petrova, Owen Moore, Priscilla Dean, Beverly Bayne, Dustin Farnum, Rosemary Theby, Valeska Suratt—a kaleidoscope of faces swarm up from my early moviegoing to tighten my throat. And, bathed in a flood of sweet melancholy underscored by the throb of violins, I was struck by an awesome thought: I was probably the only surviving member of the Rhode Island audience that witnessed the original screen version of *Anna Karenina* in 1916. This cinematic douche, my baptism in the medium, took place in a malodorous nickelodeon in Providence, the seats of which bore cassettes that ejected Tootsie Rolls with an explosive force like gunfire. The production starred a Danish actress of surpassing loveliness named Betty Nansen—unrelated to the Arctic explorer, except that her beauty froze me in my chair. That Anna's romance with Count Vronsky was star-crossed was apparent to me even at the age of twelve, but when she threw herself under the wheels of the locomotive in the last reel, I fell apart. Blubbering piteously, I stumbled homeward in a mist of tears, and lay between life and death for weeks. Eventually, thanks to nourishing soups and the delicious humor of Octavus Roy Cohen in *The Saturday Evening Post*, I regained my zest for life, but it was a narrow squeak.

Figure to yourself, then, how spooky I felt when, several days after my visit to Bloodroot, there fell into my hands at a curio shop in St. Martin's Lane a magazine for British movie exhibitors published in 1913. By and large, the trade gossip in *The Cinema News & Property Gazette*, the advertisements for pipe organs, ticket machines, and similar embellishments were nothing to quicken the pulse, but the suggestion column did offer one method of attracting summer patrons which was worthy of note:

The man with the screen at one end of a vacant lot and a projection room at the other [will be] in the ascendant. . . . A rockery need not cost £2, and yet it will be worth a hundred times that in the suggestion of coolness that it affords. Tap the water pipe, and put in a small hose nozzle. Build a concrete basin. Even a galvanized washtub with an overflow pipe will do. Some Saturday afternoon get in half a dozen small boys, and promise them tickets for the entire opening week if they will gather up the stones in the lot. They'll work like grownups if you pick the right sort of boys, and by night you'll have a fine pile of stones. Mask in the basin and pipe with these, adjust the nozzle so that some of the spray strikes the rocks, and you'll have a tiny fountain that will splash musically.

How to dispose of the pile of small boys left over after the opening week was unclear, but I assume the stiffs could be paid off in stones and the brighter ones used as ushers. Where the publication really took wing, though, was in its listing of films marketed by various European and American studios, synopsized in language even the most beef-witted exhibitor could comprehend. Included were some with juicy titles, like *The Blind Composer's Dilemma* (Kalem), *While She Powdered Her Nose* (Vitagraph), *The Newest Methods of Coaling Battleships at Sea* (Edison), *Tony's Revenge, or Castor Oil* (Elite), *Cub Reporter's Temptation* (Kalem), *Oh! You Unbreakable Doll* (Lux), and *Saved from the Grip of Alcohol* (Lux). Of the plots furnished in this issue, comedies were preponderant; there were few problem dramas, the producers obviously leaning toward boisterous situations spiced with a dash of sex. Here, typically, was a Selig Polyscope film called *The College Chaperon*, whose ingenious twists were guaranteed to elicit boffs:

The annual college dance is at hand, and the students of the Conserver Military Academy are making their arrangements for this famous function. Jack Carter and Ned Graves invite two out-of-town girls to be their guests at the festivities. The girls, Maude and Alice, accept the boys' invitation, with the understanding that Jack's Aunt Nellie will act as their chaperon. It is so arranged, and preparations made accordingly. Shortly before the eventful day, Jack is notified that Aunt Nellie cannot be present. The boys are much put out at this bit of news, and are about to call the engagement off, when suddenly a bright idea occurs to them. They arrange with Sammy Stone, the college janitor, to impersonate Aunt Nellie. Sammy consents, and plays the part. Outside of several embarrassing situations that arise, the scheme works out all right until Sammy, in his elaborate ball gown, attempts to dance with one of the professors. His identity is discovered, and he lands in the guard house. Here the boys visit him, and offer their condolences to "one of our best little chaperons."

Judging from the background of two other pictures. *The Story of Lavinia* (Selig) and *Luggage in Advance* (Barker), dormitories, and, above all, female ones, pullulated with comedy; both these divertissements featured clandestine chafing-dish parties, pillow fights, male intruders concealed in laundry baskets, and similar low jinks. *The Thief and the Porter's Head*

(Milano), however, classified as a blithesome comic melodrama, proved in the end to be a quite different bouillabaisse:

Mr. and Mrs. Jones are suddenly called away, and leave their son, Percy, alone in the house. Left alone, he helps himself to his father's cigars, and reckons he is quite a nut, until, overcome by the strength of the smoke, he lies down on the sofa. Meanwhile a thief, seeing the departure of Mr. and Mrs. Jones, breaks into the house and frightens Percy, who beats a hasty retreat, being chased from room to room by the thief, until at last he is cornered. . . . Percy slings a pot of paint after him which alights on his head. The thief pulls it off and bangs it down over the head of the porter, who has rushed out to find the cause of the row, and decamps. Mr. and Mrs. Jones return at this point, and Percy rushes down and says he has caught a thief; they catch hold of the pot to pull it off, and succeed in also pulling off the head of the porter. The unfortunate man rushes round with his head, still encased in the pot in his hand, to the doctor, and the rest of the party follow. The doctor succeeds, by the aid of electricity, in sticking his head on again, and upon the pot being smashed, they discover not the thief as they expected, but the porter, and at once proceed to inflict their wrath on Percy. The doctor, getting sick of the rowdy crowd, throws his electric plug into the mob and disperses them.

Surrealism, I had always naïvely supposed, was fathered during the twenties by Max Ernst, René Magritte, Pierre Roy, and like effervescent spirits, but revelations of headless porters in 1913 and doctors welding heads back on with electricity are certain to ruffle the weathers of art historians. I wonder if moviegoers in that distant epoch, torpidly gnawing their Tootsie Rolls, dreamt they were watching the birth of a new art form. Or did they accept weird fantasies flickering across the screen as part of its incomprehensible magic? However glazed, their eyes must have bulged at an Essanay feature titled *Lady Audley's Jewels*, a succulent ragout of show biz and crime detection:

Augustus Pompleton and his wife, Clarice Deveraux of the famous McNight's Celebrated Repertoire Company, are stranded in the small village of Jayville. Pompleton, at the suggestion of his wife, enters the railroad station and asks the ticket agent where they can find the nearest and cheapest hotel. The star leading lady of the noted company drops her lavaliere, made of plate glass and paste, on the floor. The station agent picks it up and asks her how much she will sell it for. The lavaliere is sold for three dollars. Jed Perkins, a would-be sleuth of the town, receives a badge, belt, handcuffs and the regular paraphernalia used by town constables from a detective correspondence school. A five hundred thousand dollar jewel robbery adorns the front page of a New York newspaper. Having secured enough money to hold them over at the hotel for a couple of days, Augustus Pompleton and his wife register and go to their room, to determine how to reach New York. During the absence of the porter, Perkins volunteers to take some ice water up to them. He discovers the performers sorting out some stage jewels. He immediately comes to the conclusion that these two are the thieves wanted in New York in connection with the big robbery. The actors carry out the misunderstanding, and are taken to New York by the correspondence sleuth. Having arrived at the police station, the Captain discharges the couple and has the would-be detective locked up.

The one perplexing aspect of the story—apart from the puzzle of where the producer promoted the funds to make it—is the identity of Lady Audley, who never once surfaces in the summary of the action. Presumably, she is the owner of the gems heisted in New York, a detail whose concealment somebody evidently figured would add a touch of mystery to the script. The practice of withholding information from the audience still persists, by the way; I frequently emerge from movies convinced that some vital ingredient that would explain the whole tzimmes has been deliberately suppressed.

The more one samples the fare offered the cinemagoer in 1913, the greater one's admiration for his ability to endure punishment. Dazzled as he undoubtedly was by the witchery of the new medium, he must have staggered under the impact of some of the lunacies it generated, such as those in *In a Gambler's Clutches* (Atlas Feature Films). Its story line, for want of a better phrase, went as follows:

Rigo Seriesky, a famous violinist, fascinates Marie, the daughter of Baron Schulbert. He asks for Marie's hand in marriage, but the Baron, who has been warned that Seriesky is a common adventurer and card-sharper, refuses his consent. Rigo sends a message to Marie by means of her dog, asking her to elope with him.

This novel deputy, by the way, may be the very first appearance of that folkloric figure, the talking dog, which inspired a host of anecdotes to come. But go on with the narrative:

She agrees, and at midnight they run away and are secretly married. A year later Rigo forces Marie to accompany him to a gambling saloon. He makes her cheat by using cards concealed in her handkerchief, and the fraud being discovered, Rigo is challenged to a duel by one of the gamblers. During the duel Rigo is wounded in the arm, and when the wound is healed he finds to his horror that his arm is paralyzed and useless.

You spring to attention, foreseeing that they are about to use the classic dreidel wherein the hands of an executed strangler are grafted onto a concert pianist—but no, this was long before the era of Tod Browning and Robert Siodmak. Slowly, relentlessly, the story unwinds like some anaconda in the Amazon rain forest:

Ruin stares him in the face, and Rigo, in desperation, forms a dastardly scheme. At the revolver's mouth he forces his wife to telephone to her father, telling him that she is ill, and imploring him to visit her. Without hesitation the Baron drives to Rigo's house, where the adventurer shows him into a room, saying he will bring Marie to him. Whilst the Baron is waiting Rigo creeps up behind him and binds him to the chair. Then he prepares to set fire to the house, telling his prisoner that in a few hours the place will be in flames. Taking the Baron's keys, the villain leaves the house, returning in the waiting motor, disguised as the Baron. It is his intention to rob the Baron's safe. Unknown to him, however, Schulbert has protected his property by a new electrical contrivance. Unconscious of the danger he runs, Rigo approaches the safe and places the key in the lock. There is a sudden flash, and the schemer falls to the floor electrocuted.

What with the Wagnerian pianology that accompanied these
didos and the percussion of the candy machines, I now readily
understand the recurrence of nightmares in my youth. Sleeping,
I relived all the fantasies at the matinée and I was in constant
flight, obsessed by undefinable guilt. Today, so many decades
afterward, *The Cinema News & Property Gazette* provides the
key, and I know how the guilt originated—from close identification with chimeras like *Sammy and the Chicken Run*
(Urbanora):

An extremely clever picture, in which Sammy scores a great
triumph. He, in company with two pals, starts out to steal their
dinner. They enter a poultry yard, and catching half a dozen fowls,
make off with all speed. The owner, disturbed by the cackling of
the chickens, soon discovers the theft, and informing the mayor of
his loss, persuades that pompous gentleman to join in the chase.
But Sammy and his accomplices are too smart for their pursuers,
and get away every time, after allowing themselves to be nearly
caught, and in the end turn the tables neatly on the injured citizens.

And yet, you know something? I've just been struck by
another awesome thought. That isn't such a bad plot after all;
you could update it a little, switch the locale, stick a name or
two in the leads, and make yourself a bundle. Just to spitball
for a second, say that Robert Redford and Paul Newman are
a pair of merchant seamen stranded in the Middle East, at Abu
Dhabi or Dubai. They steal a couple of chicks out of the emir's
harem and take off on his yacht for Israel. A hue and cry in the
U.N., the Third World's on fire, and Kissinger (Rod Steiger)
takes off after them to avert a confrontation. Do you buy that
so far? Right! . . . Operator! In Beverly Hills, please, the phone
number for a catalytic agent on South Beverly Drive by the
name of Irving Lazar. Yes, thank you, I'll wait.

Under the Shrinking Royalty the Village Smithy Stands

The oval anteroom of Diamond & Oyster, my publishers, had been refurbished since my last visit with a large bas-relief plaque of their logo, a diamond-studded oyster bearing the motto "*Noli unquam oblivisci, Carole: pecuniam sapientiam esse*" ("Never Forget, Charlie: Money Is Wisdom"), and under it a blond, oval-shaped receptionist strikingly reminiscent of Shelley Winters. As thirty-five minutes ticked away without any word from Mitchell Krakauer, the editor I was calling on, I began to develop paranoid symptoms. Heretofore there hadn't been any hassle about seeing him; what was amiss now? Had some stripling in patched denim fresh out of Antioch whispered into his ear that I was *vieux jeu,* old hat, *nye kulturny*? Or had Krakauer learned in some devious way that Shelley Winters was in a 1941 play of mine, *The Night Before Christmas*, and deliberately planted her double here to taunt me as a slippered pantaloon? I felt myself inflate like a blowfish at the veiled insult. Surely nobody could be so base, and yet in this carnivorous age of four-hundred-thousand-dollar sales and instant remainders worship of the bitch goddess Success overrode a decent respect for the aged. I got to my feet, cheeks flaming.

"Try Mr. Krakauer's line again, Miss. I can't understand why they don't answer."

The receptionist's eyes rolled upward in martyrdom. "Look,

sir, do I have to keep on telling you? If you'd only state your business—"

"My dear young woman," I said, gripping the edge of her desk to steady myself. "Since you were in amniotic fluid when I first signed with this house, let me enlighten you. Diamond & Oyster have published eleven books of mine. If I have to undergo a Rorschach to discuss a twelfth, maybe it's time I peddled my papers elsewhere."

"Oh, you're one of our *authors*!" she squealed. "Why didn't you mention that before? Who did you say you were?"

"Well, my real name is Travis Nuthatch, but I write under the name of Israel Zangwill."

"O.K., Mr. Zangwill. You have a seat there, and I'll see what I can do."

She busied herself with her apparatus, and I sat down, mollified and refreshed by our interchange. More time passed. Messengers innumerable arrived laden with proofs, drawings, and office lunches. Three or four lovelies from Vassar and Bennington, job applicants hugging postgraduate degrees in Middle English and Georgian poetry to their enchanting bosoms, passed through to be interviewed and dated by lickerish subordinates. A whole decrepitude of writers—Sudanese, Lapps, Bosnians, Trobrianders—appeared and were hustled in on their own recognizance, and still I sat there, a pariah excluded from the temple of letters he had helped erect. Then a sobering thought struck me. In all justice to Krakauer, he had no appointment with me; I'd come by on an impulse, without phoning, and perhaps he was in a meeting, or, more likely, on the bridle path. Krakauer's passion for horsemanship was a byword—he was besotted with the sport. His office was filled with stirrups, snaffles, and trophies attesting to his equestrian skill; he wore riding breeches to work, swished a crop against them as he conferred. Still, wherever he was at the moment, I thought sullenly, it ill behooved his secretary to keep a celebrity like Israel Zangwill, dead *or* alive, cooling his heels in the anteroom.

"Hello there!" a familiar British voice exclaimed. "What in the world are you doing here?" The owner of the voice was a

florid, dapper gentleman with a Guard's mustache, clad in a
short warm. "Remember me? Arthur Maybrick, of Edouard &
Russell, your haberdashers in Clifford Street?"

"To be sure," I said, rising. "How are you? I heard you
retired when the firm closed down."

"Couldn't stand the inactivity. I'm with Tautz nowadays—
you recall, the sporting tailors who used to be in Grafton Street.
Matter of fact, that's why I'm here. Just had a word with
Mitchell Krakauer. Do you know him?"

Curious to ascertain what publishers buy one half so precious
as the thing they sell, I clamored for details. In a recent sale at
Parke Bernet, it emerged, Krakauer, after fierce bidding, had
acquired a pair of breeches made by Tautz for John Huston
when he was M.F.H. of the Galway Blazers in Ireland. As
Krakauer was two feet shorter than Huston, substantial alterations were necessary crotchwise, and Maybrick had been flown
overseas to superintend them. "What with my fare and hotel
expenses, it'll come to a neat eight hundred quid before we're
done," he told me, "but I must say I haven't heard a peep out
of the man."

"Neither have I. I've been waiting here over an hour."

"I say," remarked Maybrick, voice lowered. "Rather weird
setup he has in there for a publisher's office, don't you think?"

"How do you mean—the horse brasses and so forth?"

"No, no, the other stuff," he said mysteriously. "Ah, well, I
daresay you'll see for yourself."

"Ready for you, Mr. Zangwill," the receptionist fluted. "You
can go in now."

With a handshake and an injunction to knock him up on my
next visit to London, Maybrick left and I went down the hall.
Calpurnia, Krakauer's secretary, rose from her typewriter as I
entered. She was wearing not only a bowler and a stock but a
riding apron that seemed excessive for the amount of mud
kicked up on the twenty-eighth floor of a skyscraper.

"Oh, it's you," she said, and added, puzzled, "Where's Mr.
Zangwill?"

I shrugged. *¿Quién sabe?* That's one of those metaphysical

questions." I nodded toward the interior. "Is Mitchell free now?"

"He will be in a jiffy. He's just finishing something."

I subsided, and, reaching for a copy of *The Field*, buried myself in its pages. Halfway through an article on the paucity of oasthouses in East Anglia, I stiffened. A deep repeated wheezing, like giant inhalations of breath, was proceeding from Krakauer's sanctum, followed by the clang of metal being struck. Alarmed, I turned toward Calpurnia, but she was typing away, visibly undisturbed. Moments later, her phone buzzed and she motioned me inward.

So startling was the transformation I beheld that my mouth fell open. The burled-walnut desk, the luxurious easy chairs and sporting prints, the equestrian memorabilia—all had vanished, and in their place was a scene straight out of Longfellow: a miniature nineteenth-century blacksmith shop. Garbed in a leather apron, Krakauer was bent over an anvil, his hammer busily tapping a horseshoe. Spread all about were the traditional accoutrements of the smith—the forge heaped with glowing coals, the bellows, pincers, a workbench strewn with tools, and bundles of iron bars.

"Come in, man, come in!" Krakauer hailed me cheerily, laying aside his hammer. He wiped the honest sweat from his brow with a bandanna, extracted a square of cut plug. "Have a chaw?"

I shook my head, still overcome. "Jiminy, what's happened? Nobody told me—I mean, where am I?"

"I know," he said. "Everyone was stunned when I made the change, but I guess you've been away, eh? Well, sit down somewhere—do you mind this soapbox?—and I'll put you in the picture."

"Before you do, though," I asked, "what business are you in?"

"Oh, I still publish, but in a different way. I take it you know who Gaston Gallimard was?"

"Sure, the famous French publisher. Didn't he die last year?"

"Right. He brought out Proust, Gide, Sartre, Malraux—you name it. Well, just prior to his death, at ninety-four, here's what he said." He handed me a newspaper clipping encased in plastic. "This was his obit in the London *Times*. Read the last paragraph."

" 'If I could have my life over again,' " it ran, " 'I would choose as a first occupation something having nothing to do with publishing, say a pharmacist's or plumber's business. There the income would allow me to publish on the side only all that pleased me without having to think in the slightest about the commercial side.' "

"And you've actually realized his dream," I marvelled.

"I've tried. Of course, pharmacy and plumbing take years of study, but spending half my life in the saddle as I do, all this"— he gestured about—"is practically second nature to me. And you'd be surprised the income I make from horseshoes. Not to be sneezed at."

"But how many good noncommercial books have you discovered?"

"None so far," he admitted, folding his arms. "But just look at my biceps. You won't find brawny arms like these over at Knopf or Viking. Anyway, enough about me. Do I sense you have a new book in the oven?"

"Mitchell," I said. "I don't want to crow, but this is going to be the biggest thing since *Les Misérables*—it'll yield three printings before publication. The central character is another Jean Valjean. I can see Jack Nicholson in the part—"

"For Chrissake, I told you I'm through with best-sellers. I want something doomed, with an aura of failure."

"It's got that, too," I said urgently. "It's got lust, brutality, compassion, foreign intrigue, suspense—the entire gamut of human emotion. The notion came to me in London last summer."

He retrieved his hammer. "Mind if I go on working while you tell it?"

"No, just so long as you stay in the room. O.K., here's how I latched on to the idea. Back in July, I'm stopping at Brown's Hotel, in Mayfair, and in their house organ, a sheet called

Chandelier, I read that Colonel Sanders, the founder of Kentucky Fried Chicken, has also based himself there. During his last stay, he opened the hundredth Kentucky Fried Chicken store in the U.K., held major press conferences, visited Windsor Castle, lunched at the House of Lords, and picnicked at Woburn Abbey. This cat is a real celebrity in Britain, like—well, like Israel Zangwill."

Krakauer blinked. "Odd you should mention him. I just got word he was coming in to see me."

"Fantastic. But what happened then was even stranger. As I step into the hotel lift an hour later, who's riding down but Colonel Sanders himself—white goatee, string tie, the whole shtick—and another guy, a business associate like. And this bird is strenuously urging the Colonel to buy a bunch of shares in Frank Perdue's chicken empire—and force him out of the field. But it's no dice. The old boy keeps shaking his head, and finally comes out with a slang phrase—a British expression they never heard south of the Mason-Dixon line. 'No, suh,' he says. 'That's all my eye and Betty Martin.' Do you see it, Mitchell? Do you get it?"

"Get what?" He stopped hammering. "He meant it was a lot of blue sky, of bushwa."

"Holy Moses, do I have to spell it out for you? The old guy was a *Limey*—a fake! In a flash, it all dawned on me. Ten to one the real Colonel Sanders was trussed up like a fowl upstairs while these two highbinders were scurrying off to manipulate his stock in a power play netting millions! *Voom*—right away, before we hit the ground floor, I've got my whole novel blocked out. The main story line, the two Colonel Sanderses, is a piece of cake; I can life the plot of E. Phillips Oppenheim's *The Great Impersonation*, weaving in actual real-life characters, like Robert Vesco and Meyer Lansky, the way Doctorow and Capote do. Narrating the action is yours truly, a brilliant young crusading journalist—a combination of Inspector Javert and Leslie Howard—who brings the malefactors to book and wins the Colonel's pulchritudinous niece, Cicely Mainwaring."

"Is any of this on paper yet?"

"Are you out of your living mind?" I snorted. "I should leave a gilt-edged yarn lying around where some goniff from the Authors League can filch it?"

"Yes, that's wise. But there's a better reason not to write it down. It's too commercial, kid, too *much* of a cinch. Yes, it'll make a bloody fortune, but if that's what you want, you're barking up the wrong tree. A new wind is blowing through Diamond & Oyster, my friend."

"That's not what it says on your logo."

"That thing? I'll let you in on a secret. Max Oyster's nephew is a sign painter—he made it for a seafood restaurant in Queens, but they went bust." He wiped his hands on a bit of cotton waste and draped a paternal arm over my shoulder. "Now, pay close attention. Your next book should deal with your profound mystical revelation in India."

"Did I have one?"

"You must have, in some cockamamie ashram or other you saw—everybody does. Unburden yourself. Write a series of poetic epiphanies about death and copulation with wide margins like Kahlil Gibran—something I can sink my teeth into. I could get stuck with ten thousand copies of a work like that if it were done right."

"But you can't guarantee a book will bomb. Barbara Walters is apt to read a passage by mistake and overnight a million listeners will be yelling for a copy."

"Hmm, you're right. We can't afford to run a risk like that. Look, maybe it shouldn't be on the adult level at all. What about a tender love story between a little girl and a pony, told from the pony's point of view? You know, like *Watership Down* or *Salar the Salmon?*"

"Wait, Mitchell, wait!" I cried out, inspired. "I had a notion a while back—how did it go? I had a title and everything. Now I remember! *Smokey and the Millionaire: The Saga of a White-fish.*"

"Smokey the whitefish." He rolled it over on his tongue. "I

like it. It smells right, you know what I mean? I can see a whole warehouseful of copies ready to be pulped. Where does it take place?"

"At Barney Greengrass the Sturgeon King, on Amsterdam Avenue. It begins the night before Christmas, and all through the house not a herring is stirring, not even a bloater or a side of Novy. The store is empty of stock except for one lone white-fish, Smokey, shivering in this cold showcase. He's plunged into misery—everyone's home decking the halls with challah, trim-ming the tree with kosher macaroons, and what does the Yule-tide hold for poor Smokey? Refrigeration in a dark store, with a hungry cat leering at him."

"Masterly!" exulted Krakauer. "You know who we'll get to do the jacket? Salvador Dali! Each little bone in Smokey cunningly delineated—"

"What is this—a production meeting?" I interrupted. "I'm trying to tell you a *story*. Well, so, carried along by Smokey's stream of consciousness, we retrace his past—his birth in Lake Superior, spawning with girlfriends, a narrow escape from being devoured by a pike, bilge like that. Then, all of a sudden, a long-forgotten incident comes back to him. A wealthy Grosse Pointe sportsman, while angling there, accidentally hooked into a barrel of cement and was in danger of being pulled overboard."

"What was a barrel of cement doing in the lake?"

"Search me," I said impatiently. "Somebody was standing in it—some hoodlum from the Dion O'Banion mob. Anyway, Smokey realized the sportsman's peril, swam to his rescue, and snapped the line with his teeth. Naturally, the sportsman caught only a glimpse of him, but, eternally grateful, vowed that if it was ever in his power he'd repay his debt to the little fellow."

"Now, then," I continued fluently. "We dissolve to the forty-second floor of the Waldorf Towers, where tuxedo-clad Daniel Mariana Trench, powerful Midwest utilities tycoon and world-famed sportsman, sits alone and desolate on Christmas Eve. All his millions, his forty Rembrandts, the superb specimens of fringe-ear oryx, greater kudu, and Mrs. Gray's lechwe that have fallen to his gun frowning down from the walls are as ashes in his mouth, for he is friendless. The four women he's espoused, the children they've borne him care merely for his money; nowhere is there a soul to whom he can turn for companionship. Finally, with a heavy heart, he summons his motor; *faute de mieux*, he will celebrate the Nativity with a midnight snack. As the superbly appointed Daimler glides through Central Park toward Barney Greengrass's—"

"Stop!" commanded Krakauer. "I'm way ahead of you, I can already hear Trench's hoarse cry of recognition: 'Smokey! Is it really you?' I also know where you stole the plot, but in Shaw's version Androcles never ate the lion."

"Neither does Trench eat Smokey," I said firmly. "We squeeze on the two at the Waldorf Towers before a blazing hearth—maybe with Smokey in a little brown tuxedo—clinking glasses in a toast as the bells usher in the Yule."

For a full five seconds, Krakauer stood immersed in thought. "Nope," he said at last. "It's another Pollyanna story and it'll sell like hotcakes, but I regret we're forced to turn it down—it's too joyous, too upbeat. You created a marvellous mood of despair with Smokey brooding in the showcase—almost like Louis-Ferdinand Céline. I was hoping the cat would get his tongue as well as the rest of him. But you blew it with the bubba-meiseh about Daniel Mariana Trench. It's not for Diamond & Oyster, kid. I'm sorry."

I left him standing by his anvil, an idealist from whose deeply furrowed face the last remnants of a dream had drained away. Then, turning up the collar of my trenchcoat, I trudged out into the rain and went across town to Harcourt Brace Jovanovich.

To Yearn Is Subhuman, to Forestall Divine

"But you have to eat *somewhere*, man." Roland Portfolio's voice over the phone, wheedling until now, simmered with impatience. "All I'm asking is meet the boy, have a sandwich with him, listen to his ideas. Is that such a hardship?"

"Roland," I said, struggling for self-control, "will you for God's sake get off my back? I've just finished telling you—this Friday night I'm due in Istanbul to catch a Turkish boat bound for Iskenderun and I'm not even packed yet. I've got a million things to do—convert my air ticket, close up the flat, buy a hot-weather fez—"

"Yes, yes, you sound frantic—"

"I'm not *frantic*," I said, and pounded the desk to prove it. "But the last thing I need right now is a kaffeeklatsch with some dropout from that cinema course at N.Y.U."

"Strobe Fischbyne is not a dropout," he snapped. "He graduated Antioch in three years and he won the top award at the Beaver College Festival for his two abstract films, *Blossomings* and *Mosaic in Bubbles.*"

"And he's also your nephew, I reminded him. "O.K., here's what you do. Tell him to send me a nine- or ten-page letter written in longhand, on both sides of the paper, outlining the film he visualizes."

"Why in longhand?" he asked suspiciously. "He can type."

"Because it's harder to read that way," I said. "But it'll help me gauge his personality while I'm scrambling around the ruins of Ephesus. He needn't seal the envelope, because the Turks'll open it anyway looking for coins. Well, Roland, thanks for ringing up—"

"So that's all friendship means to you." Now I was in for it—a jeremiad on my inhumanity, selfishness, and basic triviality, "Look, think back to your own career. When you were a nobody, a punk kid just starting out, didn't anyone ever lend you a helping hand? Didn't anyone, out of the goodness of his heart—"

"Stop!" I said wildly. "All right—O.K.! I can stand anything but that rabbinical intonation of yours. Where is this golden boy?"

W hich, in essence, was how I came to be in the Village one day at nightfall, combing the purlieus of Bleecker Street for a coffeehouse named the The Loony Bin. At long last, I found it, a dank, tenebrous tunnel wedged between an Italian social club and a leather shop catering to bondage freaks. Roland's nephew, predictably, was forty-five minutes late, and by the time he appeared I was so numbed by the sickly-sweet odor of hash and the hard rock blasting out of the jukebox that my choler had wilted. Strobe Fischbyne's dark, hollowed eyes, the wisps of beard depending like Spanish moss from his greenish-white face, and his expression of patient suffering instantly verified what I had foreseen. I was straddled with a Raskolnikov.

"Did you have trouble locating this place?" he asked. "The Village is sort of confusing for strangers."

"Isn't it?" I agreed. "It sure baffled me in 1925, but after thirty years or so on Washington Square I managed to get the hang of it."

He was clearly startled. "You mean you lived here that long ago? What was it like?"

"Oh, mainly fields, a few buildings. Not much virgin forest, though."

"Did you know Eugene O'Neill when he was hanging around those waterfront saloons, and E. E. Cummings?"

"Well, he may have hung around E. E. Cummings, but I think on the whole he preferred women. I believe he married a couple of them."

"I don't understand something," Fischbyne observed, perplexed. "My uncle said you spent most of your time in California. That you worked in Hollywood during the Golden Age."

"Which Golden Age was that?"

"Why, the *thirties*," he said, enunciating as if to a deficient child or someone hard of hearing.

Chagrined that I hadn't brought along an ear trumpet like Foxy Grandpa's, I bade him particularize.

"You know, the era when Thalberg and Scott Fitzgerald, Josef von Sternberg, and all those greats were turning out their classics."

"What about it?"

"Well, there was a tremendous burst of creativity in those years—or weren't you aware of it? The same thing that was going on here at the Round Table in the Algonquin."

The temptation was strong to take the lad on my knee, dry him behind the ears, and correct a few misconceptions, but at my back I seemed to hear a Turkish steamer hurrying near, and I desisted. "Just what did you want to see me about, Fischbyne? Your uncle said you had a brainstorm about a film."

He frowned. "Yes, I've got the overall concept, but the skeletal framework is still nebulous in my mind, so to speak. I thought you might help me come to grips with it." Rummaging in his Zouave regimental jacket, he produced a crumpled bit of newsprint. "This piece in last week's *Variety* kindled my thinking. I'd like your reaction."

Tobe Hooper, young Texan who directed the cult favorite 1974 horror film, "The Texas Chain Saw Massacre" [the item reported], is now at work on his first Hollywood film, "Death Trap," about a

Texas psychopath who feeds people to his pet crocodile. Neville
Brand plays the lead role in Mardi Rustam's indie production. . . .
Hooper, who seems amused while directing the blood-and-gore
antics of Brand stabbing girls with a pitchfork and dumping them
into his crocodile pond, compares the film to a horror comic book
but also feels that it resembles "Chain Saw" in being "a commercial
film that I feel good about. It's much more complex than it seems,"
says the 33-year old director. "I tried to establish some kind of motif
that carries throughout the show—sometimes that's more important
than what you're actually showing."

"Man, that's cool," I said, clutching at the only bit of jargon
that seemed applicable. "I wonder if the flick'll still be around
when I get back from the Aegean."
   "Why, how long are you staying there?"
   "Well, I planned on only two months, but I may take up
Turkish citizenship now. However, that's beside the point.
What's your problem, son?"
   His fingers toyed with the tendrils fringing his mouth.
"Would you say Hooper's theme is valid?"
   "You mean of a psychopath feeding girls to crocodiles?" I
shrugged. "O.K. for the raincoat brigade, but rather bland for
the longhairs. Still, I daresay he'll beef it up—lay in a couple of
shrinks and so forth."
   "No, I meant his statement that the motif is more important
than what appears on the screen. You agree with that?"
   "Emphatically. In my experience, the public is sick and tired
of watching actors hugging and kissing. What they're hungry for
is motifs."
   "Right!" he said warmly. "I was thinking along those lines,
too, but I couldn't formulate it until Hooper put it into words.
It's a totally new concept in modern cinema."
   "Oh, I wouldn't go quite that far. I remember once, during
the Golden Age, overhearing three ace directors discuss this
very point—William (Wild Bill) Wellman, Billy (Wild Billy)
Wilder, and William (Wild Willie) Wyler."
   Strobe Fischbyne's eyes, insofar as they were capable of

glistening, glistened. "They were the immortals," he said reverently.

"Well, not altogether," I said. "Two of them aren't dead yet. Anyhow, there they were, Academy Award winners all, but their current productions, as it happened, were bombs. Every man jack of them was covered with flop sweat, and you ask why? Because not one—I repeat, not one—had a motif."

"But that's precisely why I needed to see you! I mean so I could like steep myself in the residue, the effluvia, of your experience." He drew a deep breath. "I've decided to make a full-length documentary about jeans."

"Genes?" I asked dubiously. "DNA, mutations, all that stuff?"

"No, no—*Levi's*." He leaned toward me, his expression rapt. "The symbol of youth's sixties revolt against the crassness and stupidity of the Establishment. How does that grab you for a motif?"

"Fischbyne," I said after a moment's reflection, "every once in a while somebody comes up with an inspiration so dazzling that it leaves one speechless. The last time it happened to me was back in the Golden Age when Hunt (Wild Hunt) Stromberg told me his production plans for *Naughty Marietta*, with Nelson Eddy and Jeanette MacDonald."

His face grew radiant. "You really like it?"

"It's a winner, kid. It's got everything—heart, lungs, liver, and twice the box-office appeal of *Chain Saw Massacre* and *Death Trap*. Furthermore, you can bankroll the whole production with one phone call—to Levi Strauss in San Francisco. They'll flip. Think of the pants potential."

His face stopped radiating. "Wait a minute," he objected. "You and I seem to be on two different wavelengths—the commercial and the artistic. It's true I've only made a couple of films, but both of them lost money, and I don't intend to compromise now."

"Holy cow, no—never compromise!" I enjoined him. "But don't you want—I mean, would it hurt if your picture got back its negative cost?"

"I'd much rather it didn't, so I can go on being a young film-maker," he said earnestly. "Now, the technique I have in mind occurred to me while I was watching some glue being melted. It would be a slow, dreamy montage of abstract shapes endlessly weaving in and out, underscored by sitar music and gourds."

"The jeans," I ventured, seeking to lure him back to reality. "I'm trying to envisage how they'd fit in with the abstractions."

"Well, I'm not sure whether I'll show them at all. They might detract from the purity of the concept."

"Yes, it might easily be a false note. Tell me, will the audience —assuming there *will* be an audience—be able to grasp the motif?"

"Actually," returned Fischbyne, "I'd much prefer if they didn't. You see," he explained, "in a sense, a director like me is a magician. I enchant and delight the public, but I also mystify them. And I do that by withholding little things from them— motifs, bits of plot, et cetera. But I also give them something in return—the feeling that we're communicating, that through the witchery of the lens we've established a dialogue."

"A *viable* dialogue," I corrected, and arose. "Well, Strobe, if I may address you by your first name—What *is* your first name, by the way?"

He reddened. "Stanley. I haven't used it since I turned professional."

"A good name, my boy. Wear it proudly, for it belonged to one who, aided by a merciful God and infinite courage, won eternal renown on the Dark Continent—"

Simultaneously, with a report that clove the skull, a rock group exploded on the jukebox, blotting out the remainder of my sentence, which ran: "—and let us hope, Stanley, that one day the same merciful God will wrest the megaphone from your hands and consign you to the shipping department, where you belong." Fischbyne, meanwhile, was mouthing something inaudible that I took to be gratitude, but I wouldn't bet on it. Could be he was reviling me.

Thus, then, our brief and seemingly fruitless colloquy in bohemia. Nevertheless, it had an unexpected sequel. Six weeks afterward, at Lindos, on the isle of Rhodes, I received the following cable:

"PROFOUND THANKS INVALUABLE ADVICE NEPHEW STOP STANLEY FORMERLY STROBE ABANDONING FILM CAREER STOP COMMENCING MERCANTILE DITTO KORVETTES SHIPPING ROOM MONDAY EXCELLENT SALARY STOP WHOLE FAMILY ECSTATIC BLESSINGS AND BON VOYAGE ROLAND PORTFOLIO."

All Precincts Beware
Paper Tigress Loose!

Saturnine, tweedy Gabe Hammerschlag, head of the N.Y.P.D.'s Confidence Detail, struck a match on his desk top and, sucking the flame into the bowl of his pipe, eyed me meditatively. Gabe and I had known each other ever since 1953, when I had helped him straighten out a rather nasty copyright mess among the Kachins of Northern Burma, and I knew that when Hammerschlag sucked flames meditatively into his pipe bowl the unexpected could be expected.

"Sir Herbert Lopretni phoned me from London the other night," he said abruptly. "His name mean anything to you?"

I frowned, the loose skin on my forehead corrugating into parallel ridges. "There are those who think it could stand for Interpol spelled backward."

"I wouldn't know about that." His face was a mask. "But this I do know—we've a crisis on our hands, and it's going to take a pretty special type of chap to sort it out. Passive to the point of stupidity on the surface, yet keen as mustard underneath. Only one man in this city answers to that description."

Despite myself, I blushed at the compliment. "Why, thanks, Gabe."

"Good. Then here's the drill—we're going to use you for bait, as a decoy. The way shikaris stake out a goat in India."

"Oh? And just who is the tiger, pray?"

"Say, rather, the tigress. The wiliest, most dangerous feline ever to stalk the world of wholesale stationery."

"That's a metaphor of some kind, I gather."

"No, I'm being quite literal." He produced a file from his desk and opened it. "Early last May, ten men were convicted in London's Central Criminal Court of participating in a huge carbon-paper fraud. Immense quantities of the paper were sold at inflated prices to the purchasing agents of a number of British companies. Get the picture? Then let me read you the Crown prosecutor's account of how the gang operated, as reported in the London *Times*: 'Company buyers, known as "dupes," were bribed with champagne, cigarettes, or cash and then threatened with exposure to their employers once they succumbed to the stationery salesmen, he [the Crown prosecutor] said. . . . An Exeter store, Bobby and Company, paid out £70,000 in 18 months and was invoiced with 3,750,000 sheets of carbon, enough to last the typists 3,000 years, he added. The Northern Ireland firm of Ulster Carpet Mills were invoiced with enough for 400 years and the Coöperative Society in Bangor, North Wales, got 438,900 sheets, enough for 290 years.' "

"But the perpetrators—or paper traitors, so to speak—were caught," I objected. "Whence hence this tigress of yours?"

"Precisely—that's what has baffled the police of two continents, causing us to scratch our polls in bewilderment. Obviously, these men were puppets, fuschers, boneheads. Behind them there had to be a cold, diabolic intelligence akin to that of a Fu Manchu or a Professor Moriarty—housed, as Lopretni and I believe, in the body of a supremely beautiful woman. From Cesare Lombroso to Craig Kennedy the Scientific Detective, sleuthdom has clung to one cardinal principle—*Cherchez la femme.*"

"Then are you implying," I queried, "that somewhere in this puzzling affair there lurks a she-devil, maddened by who can say what dark neurotic compulsion, dedicated to undermining the very foundations of stationery as we know it today?"

"Yes, yes," he said fretfully. "I just *told* you that. Well, it only remains to add that somehow Mademoiselle L'Inconnue—her name is unimportant; she changes it at will—has either slipped through the immigration net into Manhattan or not. Where or when she will strike nobody can predict, nor is a description worth a plugged nickel, she being a past-master at disguise." He dusted his hands. "Look, go hang around a few stationery stores and see what happens. Right now I got a million other things on my mind."

"Gabe," I pleaded. "Give me at least a hint of what to anticipate—"

"For Chrissake, am I a magician?" he shouted. "I sit here day after day in this crummy office worrying how to get up the rent, the insurance, my alimony payments, and now I'm supposed to be Mr. Answer Man! Who Killed Cock Robin? Who was the Dark Lady of the Sonnets? What was S. S. Van Dine's real name?" He beat clenched fists on his blotter. "I can't stand it, I tell you! I'm up to here!"

"O.K., Gabe, O.K.," I placated him softly, sidling toward the door. "I'll get back to you the second anything jells."

A chill gust sent fragments of newspaper eddying up the gutters of East Twenty-third Street as, weary in spirit, I crossed Lexington Avenue and headed toward Third. Since nine that morning, I had doggedly checked every stationer's along lower Madison and Park Avenues, hoping to espy one woman resembling the criminal genius Hammerschlag had postulated. All their salespersons, without exception, tall or short, slim or fat, had proved to be vapid boobies devoid of any sinister charisma, and now, with only one such store in the district left to investigate, instinct whispered that I might be pursuing a phantom. Approaching the shop, I cast a mechanical glance over its windowful of cut-rate diaries, staplers, pencil sharpeners, and ball-points, and peered past them into the interior. In the next instant, I stood transfixed.

What was Faye Dunaway doing in this unlikely place? And *working* in it, moreover, judging from the delft-blue smock she was clad in. She must be involved in a film or an upcoming television special. . . . Still, where were the cameras, the generator, the technicians? Perhaps in the rear, where I couldn't see too clearly, a director with cordovan leggings, reversed tweed cap, and a suède whistle was outlining the shot. Simultaneously, another possibility presented itself. Back in the days when she was a struggling drama student, had she worked here part time, returning today out of sentimentality to schmooze with the boss? But in that case a Camargue or a Fleetwood Cadillac befitting a star would be idling at the curb. . . . The devil take these hypotheses; chance had thrown a mystery in my path, and it was incumbent on me to sniff it out.

No sooner was I inside the door than I realized my identification was faulty—the plate glass, ashimmer with worry birds and assorted novelties, had distorted the lady's image. Rather than Dunaway, this was another cupcake, equally a goddess. The face was a pastiche combining elements of Corinne Griffith, Olga Baclanova, and Mary Astor; the smock concealed a figure, lithe as that of a great tawny cat, that owed nothing to Lauren Bacall or Lilyan Tashman. By that I mean she was rangy. Withal, so husky was her contralto voice, so reminiscent its lisp of Kay Francis, that when she asked me what I wanted shivers coursed up and down my spine.

"Why—er—catch pads," I faltered. "You know, for scratching on."

"For scratching?" she repeated. Her hazel-brown eyes clouded in perplexity. "But this isn't a drugstore. Do you speak English?"

I stared at her wordless, wondering why her eyes evoked hazelnuts, except that they reminded me of October and woodsmoke and lovers wandering hand in hand down forest lanes. Poignancy welled up in my throat, and, with an effort, I recovered my tongue.

"Sure, I'm native-born," I said defensively. "You see, I'm by profession a writer. I'm always jotting down thoughts, ideas, aperçus—fleeting impressions and insights. So this is why I'm needing pads rather than match covers and pieces of Kleenex. You can understand that, can't you?" I implored.

"You're a real *writer?*" Her eyes widened in admiration—a phenomenon I could hardly credit, for already they were wider than even Joan Blondell's. "We don't get many in this neighborhood. They're mostly west of here, over around the Hotel Chelsea, but their beards and jeans are scruffy, whereas you—well, you look as though you stepped out of a bandbox." My heart melted. Before I could mutter some self-deprecatory phrase, she had plunged on, dispensing further catnip. "Is that coat genuine Harris Tweed? You must have got it in England; doubtless you have all your clothes made in Saville Row. . . ."

Divine as I found the harmony of her words, I couldn't help but notice a blue-jowled citizen in shirtsleeves behind the counter, a cigar clenched in his teeth, regarding me with suspicion. "The scratch pads, Miss," I said nervously. "You're stocking them in various sizes?"

"Oh, yes, indeed. They're on the shelf back there." She preceded me through two narrow aisles packed with office supplies, paused before an assortment in different sizes and colors. "Which did you have in mind?"

"This little one with the gray cover—how much is that?"

"Fifteen cents. A dozen in a package for a dollar sixty-seven."

"I don't need a package. I just want one, for like scribbling down an apothegm or so that pops into my mind."

"But supposing more than one apothegm pops in—five or six?" In the constricted area of the aisle, forced into proximity as we were by ledgers, ring binders, and jars of mucilage, her scent of Mitsouko and those extraordinary eyes were creating a hypnotic effect on me. "You'd kick yourself if you ran short of paper. Doesn't it make sense to buy a dozen and save thirteen cents on the price?"

"Well, I . . . all right," I said weakly. "I'll take a package. Could you wrap—"

"On the other hand," she pursued, "two packages, at three dollars and seven cents, would be real thrifty, a saving of twenty-seven cents."

"I know, but I can only use—"

"You certainly can use twenty-seven cents—everyone can. As

a matter of fact, the intelligent thing is to buy a gross, ordinarily seventeen dollars and forty-eight cents, but, lucky for you, we're taking inventory and we can let you have it for sixteen fifty-two."

The faint drumming sensation in my ears grew louder and my legs felt incapable of sustaining my weight. "Lady, who's got space for a gross? I'm living in two small furnished rooms. It's like the Collyer brothers' in there!"

"But space is never a problem," she whispered, though here, with lips a hairbreadth from mine, it was rapidly becoming one. "If, for example, we invoiced you for a carload, we could keep it for you on a siding. The pads would be only six cents a unit, and they'd last you two thousand years. So you will—take a chance!"

"I can't—I mustn't," I choked. 'I'll think it over—I'll give you a commitment in thirty days—"

"Goodness me, it's lunchtime!" she broke in, with a surprised glance at her watch. "Listen, there's a cute little tearoom around the corner where we can discuss the whole thing, away from all this noise and frenzy. Come on, it's my treat."

While our present locale struck me as more suitable for a business talk, I deemed it graceless to cavil and, albeit reluctantly, acquiesced. The Persian Kitten, when we arrived there, sported a façade more bar than tearoom, with a tiny slit window and a heavily armored door. Its interior, lit by a few amber bulbs, was so crepuscular that I at once fell over a rock-maple chair and skinned my knee. Fearing it might lead to tetanus if neglected, I strove to examine it by the light of a match, but my companion pooh-poohed the mishap and bade me choose an apéritif. After consideration, I agreed to a little white wine and seltzer.

"Rats, you sound like a sorority pledge at Sophie Newcomb College," she said contemptuously, and called off into the gloom, "Hey, Paddy, crack a bottle of Dom Pérignon—and put aside a couple more for my guest to take home." She turned back to me. "How are you fixed for cigarettes? . . . Only that pack? Paddy, are you there? Send out to the smoke shop for three cartons of straw-tipped Melachrinos." She pulled her chair closer. "Why, your hand's like ice," she said, patting it. "And your teeth are chattering. What's the matter? Don't you trust me?"

Simpleton that I was, I did. It would have been less than human not to, seated there in the cozy darkness with champagne warming my stomach and hands enclasped with so luscious a creature. Yet imperceptibly a nameless terror began to pervade me as her endearments gave way to a brutal, unashamed sales talk.

"What are you—a pantywaist?" she scoffed. "You're going to rest content with a measly carload of scratch pads? Where would the Wizard of Menlo Park have wound up if he'd quit with the prototype electric bulb? Or Haldeman-Julius with the first of his Little Blue Books? I know where you can pick up an entire *warehouse* of memo pads—better still, a whole forest to make them! You could be a greater novelist than Trollope, a bigger paper tycoon than Weyerhaeuser! Here, precious," she raced on, extracting a roll of greenbacks from her stocking, "accept this as an earnest of friendship between the two of us. Not a bribe, mind you—"

Cra-a-ck! Suddenly the rear door of The Persian Kitten buckled under the hammer blows of Gabe Hammerschlag's emergency squad, and forthwith ensued a melee punctuated by harsh commands to freeze and the crunch of fists on bone. When it subsided, and the squad members felled by one another, owing to scanty illumination, were hoisted to their feet, Gabe finished manacling my would-be seductress and dispatched her, snarling and unrepentant, to be booked under Section 4-B—vending wholesale without even a retail license.

"A close call, that," he commented, as we quaffed the balance of the wine. "Fortunate for all, the blue-jowled proprietor of that store phoned us your whereabouts so we could intervene in time. Well done, old chap. Thanks to you, local and international stationery can sleep peacefully tonight."

Yes, I thought ruefully, but, try as I might, I could not rid myself of the memory of a pair of hazel-brown eyes. If I was the goat and she the cupcake, why had I denied myself the privilege of a nibble? *Basta!* Hammerschlag's characterization was only half right. Passive to the point of stupidity on the surface I was, but dull as a hoe underneath.

Methinks the Lady Doth Propel Too Much

W hat red-blooded male of my generation, unless he has spent his life immured in a Nepalese monastery or footloose in the Empty Quarter of Arabia, has not heard of toothsome Alma Mahler? For those who haven't, Alma Mahler was the foremost sex kitten in Central Europe in the first quarter of the twentieth century, a lady whose fame rested on the fact that four headliners rested on her—the eminent composer; the poet and novelist Franz Werfel; Walter Gropius, of the Bauhaus; and Oskar Kokoschka, the painter. She was, successively, if not in that order, the wife and/or sweet patootie of the quartet, and the veracity of the anecdote that follows was sworn to me by a stateless Bukovinan in Rhodes. And for anyone who has ever known a stateless Bukovinan in Rhodes, nuf sed.

It appears that, in the period she was rooming with Kokoschka, Alma became infatuated with a celebrity in the world of science—a biologist named Pitzel. Physically, Professor Pitzel was unimpressive; a troglodyte just over four feet in height, he was myopic, ill-favored, and snappish, but he was engaged in a wondrous experiment. From deep in Lake Titicaca, on the Peru-Bolivia border, he had retrieved a family of salamanders, creatures that had been sightless for two hundred million years, and was grafting eyes onto them. Day after day, Alma hung around his laboratory breathlessly watching the

Professor amid his retorts and Bunsen burners, and at nightfall she would hustle back to rhapsodize to Kokoschka.

"A genius, Oskar—*ganz unglaublich!*" she bleated. "While you stand here schmiering on canvas, over there is a wizard creating miracles. Professor Pitzel . . . Professor Pitzel . . ."

Naturally enough, her bedfellow's amour-propre was not increased by such hosannas, and he sometimes became so jealous that he broke his maulstick over his knee. The episode reached its climax on the afternoon she raced into his studio with her face aglow.

"Oskar, Oskar!" she exulted. "Glorious news! Today, for the first time in two hundred million years, the salamanders opened their eyes!"

"Yes," said Kokoschka through his teeth, "and the first thing they saw was Professor Pitzel."

The story obtruded itself on my memory last year, when I read about someone who seemed to have accomplished a feat quite as remarkable as the Professor's. "A Brooklyn woman," the *Times* announced in its weekly tally of recent inventions, "has invented a suit designed to convert a female swimmer into a mermaid. Mrs. Chloe Grilli, a professional pianist, was granted Patent 3,344,449 this week. Her garment covers the body and legs from the waist down, with a pair of fins, or flippers, over the feet. . . . The patent explains that the wearer gets propulsion by kicking and manipulating the fins. It is said that the swimmer can dive gracefully, and on land can maneuver along, caterpillar style." Evidently on the assumption that if the invention flopped a buck could be made elsewhere, the item added, "Mrs. Grilli has written an Off Broadway show, 'The Very Gay Prima Donna,' and hopes to have it produced soon."

No sibyl, not even the most gifted astrologer, could have foretold that Mrs. Grilli's oceanic doodad was fated to touch my life, yet early in July, commencing a fortnight's vacation on Martha's Vineyard, I shortly became aware that complications were in store. The manager of Breinig's Market, where I bought a sizable order of groceries, refused to honor my New York check. I explained I was a longtime visitor to the Island, currently staying in a nearby efficiency that I rented from Herman Moulmein.

"You mean the Herman Mealman who's the mailman?"

"No, Moulmein, as in Kipling. You know, the old Moulmein pagoda in 'Mandalay.' "

"What about it?"

"I'm only trying to tell you how the name is spelled. His family have lived here for generations—they made whaling history."

"The one I mean made deadbeat history." The grocer was a leathery old crab, with eyes of pure flint. "We're a cash-and-carry operation, friend. It'll cost you thirty-one dollars and eighty-seven cents cash to carry that bag out of here."

Well, you can't argue with a mentality like that, so I shelled out the money. Moulmein was reading the *Vineyard Gazette* on his piazza when I got home.

"Look, this is a nuisance," I said. "They always took my check up-Island, at Chilmark and Menemsha. Why are they so suspicious down here?"

"Not suspicious, just careful," he said, with a cold little smile. "We get a lot of riffraff in the summer."

I chewed that over, wondering how he classified me, and decided to skip it. "Thing is"—I cleared my throat—"I'm going to run short of cash very soon. Maybe you could vouch for me over at the bank."

His wattles froze as if someone had applied an ice collar to them. "Are you asking me to stand good for your checks?"

"No, it's just that I come from a long line of eccentrics. I like to have a fiver or so in my pocket in case of emergency."

"Then do what I do." He hiked up his sweater. "There's two thousand berries stowed in this money belt at all times. That way, I don't have to go around begging folks to vouch for me."

"I see. Well, I'll get one, in case I ever come back here."

"But keep it a secret from your family," he warned. "I don't even tell my wife. Women gabble."

For someone raised, as I was, in New England and weaned on the works of Joseph C. Lincoln, I had forgotten how salty the

natives were. I tried another tack. "By the way, could you recommend a good barber in town?"

Moulmein scratched his nose reflectively. "I could, but I
won't," he said finally. "If you complained, he'd probably give
me a rotten haircut next time I go in."

"Yes, that makes sense," I agreed. "Hmm. Well, guess I'll
drive over to Edgartown and buy a can opener. I *was* going to
borrow one locally, but I imagine people are wary about lend-
ing them."

The hush that ensued, plus Moulmein's absorption in his
paper, confirmed my fears. I went upstairs, parked the groceries,
and, assembling the gear I needed for the beach, bore it down
to my car. Moulmein had vanished, and, to insure against depre-
dations by the riffraff, had taken his rocker with him.

Unpropitiously as the day had begun, though, an hour later
I was in as paradisaical a situation as any mortal could wish for,
recumbent in a sheltered nook on the beach between West
Tisbury and Chilmark. The sky was cloudless, and zephyrs
fanned my brow as I lay there, my head supported by Motley's
The Rise of the Dutch Republic, watching the majestic combers
boom in from Portugal and thinking equally majestic thoughts.
Why not gather a few kindred spirits in a poets' commune right
here? We could subsist on cranberries and fish cunningly netted
from these waters, wax our own batiks, and betweentimes play
the lute and recite the georgics that must inevitably spring from
such halcyon surroundings. By Jove, what a crackerjack idea!
I sat up, overcome by the brilliance of the inspiration. It was
then, despite vision dazzled by the noonday sun, that I caught
sight of the phenomenon crawling toward me along the shore-
line.

She was incontestably female, and she was moving ahead like
an inchworm, using elbows for locomotion—her only recourse,
inasmuch as her trunk ended in a fishtail. Unable to credit my

senses, I stared at her transfixed, and at last, satisfied that she was no chimera, approached for a closer look. How to describe her loveliness? She was rapture personified, a naiad whose olive skin, blue-black hair, and green eyes would have captivated the most embittered misogynist, and from the instant her lashes fluttered upward at me I was hers, body and soul.

"Uh—excuse me, Miss," I stammered. "I hope I'm not being forward, but who are you?"

"What do you mean who am I?" she demanded pertly. "Haven't you ever seen a mermaid before?"

"Oh, come on," I retorted. "I wasn't born yesterday. Do you see any green in my eye?" Then, as the words left my mouth, I hurried to make amends. "I mean, I see plenty in yours—and they're very beautiful, may I say—but everyone knows mermaids are fabled creatures who lure sailors to their doom."

She bridled. "Why, that's hateful—*I* never have. Some of my best friends are sailors."

"Right, right," I agreed quickly. "Where would we be without them, plowing the deep and reefing the topsails and all? But what I'm driving at is, can I assist you in any way, me being well acquainted in these parts and you a stranger? You've evidently crept a long way, judging from the amount of sand in your hair."

"Yes, I have." She fingered her locks self-consciously. "Goodness, I must look a perfect fright. You wouldn't happen to have a comb, would you?"

"Sure, in that grocery bag over yonder. Can you reach it O.K.? If not, I'll be glad to carry you."

She signified there was nothing wrong with her—a diagnosis I had already made—and cumbrously wove her way there. I sat by, munching a Goldenberg Nut Chew while she untangled her tresses and shook them luxuriously over her shoulders.

"Listen, why don't you pile your hair up in a knot the way the Gibson girls used to?" I suggested. "You know, in what they call the *guiche*, or concierge, style. It may be a trifle sexy, but we older chaps go for it."

Typical of womankind, whether terrestrial or marine, she knew better. "No, it's more becoming around my face. It softens the features."

"Golly, nobody's could be softer than yours," I protested. "You haven't got a wrinkle I can see. Oh, yes, maybe a crow's-foot or two, but that's undoubtedly from the strain of creeping."

"And hunger, too—I'm starved. What is that you're eating?"

"It's a candy bar, invented by a little professor in Central Europe. People had been eating plain chocolate for two hundred million years until he grafted peanuts onto it. Do you care for some?"

"It sounds horrid."

"No, it's quite yummy, in fact. But I suppose you generally subsist on briny foods like plankton and mollusks, what?"

"Yes, and salads. I adore salads—I often make a whole meal off them."

"I shouldn't wonder. These waters around the Vineyard teem with salads. By the way," I broke off, "we haven't introduced ourselves properly, have we? My name's Henry Knifesmith. It used to be Hans Messerschmitt in the old country, but we Anglicized it when we came over."

Her eyes clouded with suspicion. "I think you're pulling my tail."

"No, really. When my brother Fritz and I were boys—we were known as Hans und Fritz—we were two little devils, always up to some mischief. We used to tease our father, der Captain, unmercifully, and as for his best friend, the Inspector, he used to cry '*Was ist los?*' and jump up and down on his tall beaver hat."

"But why are you telling me all this?" she asked, echoing a line I recalled having heard in a play.

"Oh, I don't know—I guess it's because I feel so drawn to you." Assuming a shy expression compounded of equal parts of James Stewart and Glenn Hunter, I dug my toe awkwardly in the hot sand. "Gee, Miss, you're the most beautiful lady I ever saw. I'm crazy about you, but I know that if I reached out to touch you you'd vanish."

"Listen, Buster." Her face hardened. "If you reached out to

touch me, you'd get a blow from these flukes that would send you reeling. You don't know what strength we mermaids have in our tails."

"Ah, yes, you mermaids." Suddenly my face hardened to twice the rigidity of hers. 'I was just getting around to that. Tell me, did you ever hear of a Mrs. Chloe Grilli, in Brooklyn— a pianist-playwright who invented a suit designed to transform a female swimmer into a mermaid?"

"I—I've no idea what you're talking about." Olive an instant before, her face had gone white.

"Don't play the innocent with me, sister," I said roughly. "You knew all about that suit, *didn't* you? And you lusted for it with every fibre of your being, *didn't* you?" I drove on remorselessly. "And finally you found one at a garage sale, mayhap, or a students' and misfits' clothing store. And you saw in it a way to ensnare the unsuspecting, first borrowing their combs, then graduating to saltwater taffy, shore dinners, joyrides—"

Defenses crumbling like sand castles, she burst into sobs. "We meant no harm," she blubbered. "It was a thoughtless schoolgirl prank, devised between I and others at Miss Madeira's School over a Welsh rabbit in our dorm. Ere I knew what possessed me, I was inching up here from Oak Bluffs, elbows sorely enchafed. Please, please don't squeal on me."

"I have no wish to, my dear," I said generously, and arose. "Good day, and leave us hope this experience will be a salutary lesson in eschewing false plumage. The environment is bleak enough without phony mermaids lousing up the strand."

$\mathbb{M}$oulmein was again seated on his piazza when I returned. He looked up from his paper. "Get your can opener?"

"Well, no, but I saw a very strange thing up-Island."

"What's that?"

"Never mind," I replied, and shut up like a clam. I knew what kind of response I'd get out of him.

Scram! You Made the Pants Too Short

W̓hen an Englishwoman named Victoria Glendinning—whom I somehow conceive of as a tall, radiant beauty clad in a Laura Ashley dress, and with that marvellous complexion they have over there, no matter how grasping the unions are—sat down a while ago to review a book of photographs called *Lady Ottoline's Album* for *The Times Literary Supplement*, she little dreamt that her first sentence would take the words right out of my mouth. Those words, already masticated to the consistency of Wheatena, read, "Bloomsbury has been over-exposed in the past few years, as the biographies, memoirs and collected letters have rolled off the presses." Man, was that ever British understatement. Nothing, but nothing, has been left unsaid about Virginia and Leonard Woolf, Lytton Strachey, Aldous Huxley, T. S. Eliot, Duncan Grant, Henry Lamb, Dora Carrington, u.s.w. Every reader, chick or child, knew by now what fantasies had stoked their neuroses and tickled their libidos, what subterranean fires lay banked under their imperishable works, who had frolicked with whom in what daisy chains. It was high time, in short, that the gossips stopped beating their gums.

Nonetheless, Mrs. Glendinning saw in *Lady Ottoline's Album* a chance to wring a few more drops of elixir out of these talents and the hostess under whose roof they congregated, and she rolled up her sleeves. A good many of the male celebrities snapped by Lady Ottoline at Garsington, her country house, were apparently chosen as much for their dimples as for their brain power, and there is more than an imputation that she cavorted in the supercales with machos like Bertrand Russell and Augustus John. Mrs. Glendinning girlishly admits to being turned on by Siegfried Sassoon's "dark, nervy, attractive face," Lord David Cecil's "elegant profile," and as for T. S. Eliot, "a sweetness in his face for which one was not prepared." In contrast, she disparages André Gide's "sharp, narrowed eyes . . . long, rather cruel mouth" and shafts him with the icy comment "Besides, he was bald, and one bald intellectual looks much like another." Mrs. Glendinning is nobody to talk about cruelty in mouths, having taken the words out of mine, but such naked prejudice against naked pates verges dangerously on Fascism. Let one whose hair is thinning on top urge restraint, lest she start burning books instead of reviewing them.

As for the chatelaine of Garsington herself, the reviewer's tone alternates between the syrupy and the astringent. "Plain at sixteen, Lady Ottoline was magnificent at twenty," she says in one breath, only to sear her in the next with an allusion to "the jutting chin and what Augustus John called her 'bold baronial nose.' " (Still, this is kinder than if he had called it a bald baronial nose.) An insipid marine view of the noble lady later in life does excite her compassion, but she exculpates her: "There is another surprising picture of Lady Ottoline at the seaside, in a bathing suit, in much the same pose as she assumed in bed [in Venice], but vertical; if it is less alluring, it is probably the bathing suit's fault. Those woolly garments which gave no support to the bosom and terminated at the cruellest point, just above the knee, would have been too much even for Aphrodite." Cruelty in mouths, cruelty in bathing suits—what is this with Mrs. Glendinning? I started to get all shivery, like the first time I read the Marquis de Sade.

Truth to tell, not one jot or tittle of the foregoing could possibly be deemed momentous except for a throwaway line near the end of the review. Smack on the heels of a discontinuity about men's wide-brimmed hats, some alterations in W. B. Yeats'

physique, and similar trivia comes the sudden pettish demand
"And why did E. M. Forster wear his trousers three inches too
short?" I fell back into my Barcalounger, utterly flummoxed.
For whom were the trousers too short? The elegant company at
Garsington? For Mrs. Glendinning? Or for E. M. Forster himself? The longer I thought about it, the more convinced I grew
that here was an enigma that hungered for explication. The
belletristic role of pants, after all, could not be minimized. It
was through a member of this very Bloombury circle that they
had achieved poetic significance: T. S. Eliot's "I grow old . . . I
grow old . . . I shall wear the bottoms of my trousers rolled."
And, more recently, what about James Joyce's legal involvement
with a pair of pants in Tom Stoppard's *Travesties*? Yes, by
George, this was literary research tailor-made, you might say, for
me, but it posed a dilemma. Where could I promote the funds
to back me in such a work of scholarship?

The answer—a dismal one—was speedily forthcoming. Re-
plying to my application, an official of the National Endowment
for the Humanities wrote that he remembered me as the recipient of a Litt.D. he had conferred when president of Brown
University. "As I recall, however, you still lack three points in
the freshman trigonometry you flunked in 1921," he reminded
me. "You ought to do something about that—people are
talking. . . . *Re* your inquiry into Forster's pants, wd. say that
chances for a handout don't seem hopeful. We have a Mt.
Holyoke grad overseas sifting Thomas Hood's 'The Song of the
Shirt' and a Yalie here digging into Senator Vest's 'Tribute to a
Dog.' Consensus is your project wd. put too much emphasis on
matters sartorial." The National Institute of Arts and Letters
took a stronger line. "A fine one you are to beg for a subsidy,"
snarled the Award Committee for Literature in its letter. "Investigate your own pants, you schnorrer. Your pockets are full
of the stamps you peel off from our prepaid envelopes. A trolley
car should grow in your stomach." The situation, in a word, was
bleak. There was no patroness like Joyce's Harriet Shaw Weaver
to put the bite on, and whatever rich society woman I
approached would, I knew, inevitably exact payment too horrid

to contemplate. The prospect of fluttering like a tiny wounded bird in their boudoirs sickened me, so I chose the only other alternative. I put up my passbook as collateral with the Usurers & Defalcators National and bought myself an economy flight to London.

The first order of business, clearly, was to determine what had become of Forster's wardrobe after his demise, and I hastened to King's College at Cambridge, where he had resided. Though most gracious, the warden was unable to aid me, but I did elicit that the writer's former servitor, one Fred Pauncefoot, was still extant and working at a fruiterer's in Petty Cury Street. Thither I repaired and found him, a wrinkled oldster, polishing a tray of pippins. Over a pint of bitter at the corner pub, I conveyed the nature of my quest.

"Aye, his bags," Pauncefoot quavered. "Well, now, that's easier said than done. All his cronies and relations were in there at the finish, jabbering away and snatching up mementos. I remember Coleridge took the spoons and Cavafy stole a quilt—"

"Are you quite certain of that, sir? Coleridge died in 1834 and Cavafy left England almost a hundred years ago."

"Ach, who can remember their names, the spongers?" he said fretfully. "Anyhow, there wasn't a drop of port left when they cleared off. The carpets and the andirons—let me see—oh, yes, they went to Sledgehammer's, the furniture people."

"But his clothes, his suits, I said impatiently. "What happened to them? Did he leave them to anyone?"

Pauncefoot stared at me. "How could he? He was dead at the time."

"No, no, *before*." I signalled for another pint of bitter to jog his memory. "Try to think—when was the last time you saw them?"

"Why, when Goldberg put them in the van. . . . Goldberg. You mean to say you don't know Goldberg?"

His incredulity that I didn't stunned him, or maybe it was the bitter, but I finally wormed out the information that the aforesaid's gentlemen's resale shop had acquired the clothing.

Half an hour later, thanks to my powers of persuasion, Goldberg and I were seated in a café next to his store. Actually, my powers of persuasion had little to do with it. Business, he confided to me, was rotten.

"Sure I remember what I bought from the estate," he said, sipping his glass of lemon tea. "Two sports coats, a herringbone and a pin-check, and three pairs of slacks. The rest they gave to charity. The coats and two pants I sold to a student from Nigeria."

"Did you get his address?"

"In Nigeria? Why should I get his address in Nigeria? He paid cash."

"O.K., then what about the third pair of slacks? You wouldn't still have them, by any chance?"

"What do you think I have there—a museum? No, those a lady took. A couple in an Aston Martin—tourists."

"You mean a woman bought the garment for herself?"

"Of course. We sell girls, old ladies, everybody. She tried them on and they were too short, but she said she would make alterations."

I reacted as if to a blow in the solar plexus. Could the purchaser have been a certain reviewer for *The Times Literary Supplement*—a tall, radiant beauty in a Laura Ashley dress? "Look, Mr. Goldberg, this is important. I'm a detective—a private eye—and this may be a vital clue. What did she look like?"

"Who knows?" He shrugged. "A young woman, pale, in a Victorian schmotta. With long hair and those aviator glasses they all wear."

Victoria—that was Glendinning's Christian name. I was on the right track. "Was she tall, would you say? With that marvellous English skin?"

"Tall, yes. The skin—I didn't notice where it came from. The man with her, the driver of the Aston Martin, had a red beard."

I nodded. "I know—the kind that conceals a weak chin. Did

you have the feeling they were from London? I don't suppose you copied down their license number?"

"Listen, my friend," he said with dignity. "That only happens in *Kojak*, on the telly. I'm conducting here a gents' resale business."

"'To be sure, Mr. Goldberg," I soothed him. "I wasn't implying you were snoopy. Er—one more thing. Did the jackets contain a label of any kind—some bespoke tailor's in Savile Row— whereby they could be traced?"

"No, strictly off-the-peg merchandise—Austin Reed, or one of those other chains." He tapped his forehead. "A brilliant head, Mr. Forster, but a Beau Brummell he was not."

Checkmate. I had reached a dead end, and, what was worse, had plainly aroused the dealer's suspicion. For all I knew, he might tattle to the police and create untold embarrassment, so I decided to transfer my search to London. Someone at Forster's publisher's there, Edward Arnold, was bound to recall details of his attire. In any case, they would certainly welcome an effort to restore lustre to his image. The very next morning, over elevenses outside a snack shop in South Kensington's Bute Street, I hit on a better scheme: the agony column of the London *Times*. Unfolding a serviette, I began constructing an advert for the purchaser of the third set of slacks. "Information Wanted. Will tall, smashing bird owning trousers acquired Cambridge circa 1970 please contact . . ." No, that was too static. I must galvanize readers, excite public attention. "Missing— E. M. Forster's Pants!" I trumpeted. "American collector, scholar, Litt.D., urgently requires whereabouts—"

The screech of automobile tires braking to a halt petrified me, and I spun around. A scant twenty yards away, in the Old Brompton Road, a silvery Aston Martin piloted by a girl in aviator goggles had paused at a light. So striking was her resemblance to the person I had imagined that I shot out of my chair and raced toward the intersection. Just as I neared it, the traffic surged onward, but, blessedly, a cab headed in the same direction materialized, and shouting "Follow that car!," I leaped inside. Away we whizzed past the V. & A. and the

Brompton Oratory, into the turbulence of Knightsbridge, through the underpass at Hyde Park Corner, and along Piccadilly, alternately sighting and losing the fair scorcher. When her vehicle swept north from Leicester Square up the Charing Cross Road, I was ready to abandon the chase, but by then my jehu had concluded I was a member of the Special Branch and held to the trail like a bulldog. Careering wildly around St. Pancras Station, we hurtled through Camden Town and within minutes were ascending the hilltop maze of streets in N.W. 5. Finally, in the upper reaches of the Dartmouth Park Road, the Aston Martin pulled up at a semi-detached villa, rich in curlicues, of the type immortalized by Osbert Lancaster. From a discreet vantage point, I saw with exultation that my quarry, clad in trousers and roll-neck sweater, was seemingly unaware of our presence. The moment she was indoors, I paid off my cabby and rang the bell.

A bulky, fortyish party whose red beard obviously concealed a weak chin answered the door.

"Look here, do forgive this unwarranted intrusion, but I'd appreciate a word with the young lady who just came in here. It's a matter of the highest importance, I assure you."

"Oh?" He was definitely a hollow man; I knew who wore the pants in this household. "May I ask who you are?"

"Professor Gideon Titmarsh, of Rexall College, in Ohio."

He hesitated, motioned me in. "She's changing, but she'll be down in a minute."

I followed him into a tiny, disordered living room.

"Join me in a sherry?"

I declined, and while he busied himself with his drink studied my plan of action. Useless to employ subterfuge or duplicity; I would be open, forthright, gusty, a contrast to this shuttered room.

After a few moments, footsteps sounded on the stair and the lady appeared. She was a lulu, a peachamaroot, and if her figure was less opulent than the Jersey Lily's, my standards were less rigorous than the late monarch's. And whoever had designed the dress, Laura Ashley or Pablo Picasso, sure knew how to make women look willowy.

I arose and sprang to the attack at once. "Pray, let us dispense with formalities, Madam. The trousers you had on a moment ago—are you aware they belonged to E. M. Forster?"

"Indeed." Not a trace of emotion ruffled her perfect composure. "I was under the impression they had no previous history."

"Didn't Goldberg tell you?"

"Alas, Goldberg tells me nothing."

"He never intimated that they were used by the author of *Howards End, A Passage to India, Two Cheers for Democracy,* and *Aspects of the Novel?*"

"Not even by word or gesture."

"Yet knowing you were in a gentlemen's resale shop, a stone's throw from where he had composed those works, the idea never occurred to you?"

"I suppose I was a blind little fool."

"Excuse me," I said coldly. "I did not come here to discuss your deficiencies. Perhaps it would save time if you handed over the pants."

"For what purpose?"

"So I can measure them. I quite realize they were altered, but the old stitch marks should reveal their original length."

"And if I were to refuse?"

"I should be compelled to demand of the authorities that you submit forcibly."

"Just one moment, please." She drew herself up. "Do you imply that I'm harboring or otherwise withholding someone else's property?"

"You and Victoria Glendinning," I said aggrievedly. "You put words in my mouth and she takes them out. All I meant was, if you haven't got the pants, where are they?"

Her answer was as upsetting as it was unexpected. She turned to her red-bearded companion. "He's the one, all right, Vivyan. I'd recognize his voice anywhere."

"Well done, Gillian." He stepped forward, his fists doubled menacingly. "So you're the blackguard who's been making obscene phone calls to my wife and pursuing her in cabs."

"Hold on, my dear sir—"

"And now you have the impudence to storm in here and accuse her of being a transvestite. I ought to thrash you within an inch of your life. What do you have to say for yourself before I hand you over to the police?"

Well, dog my cats, I don't mind telling you I was pretty frightened, but I said it as best I could—told them the whole story—and you know what happened? By the time I finished, they were nodding sympathetically and circulating the sherry. And all of a sudden the most extraordinary coincidence emerged. It turned out that Vivyan's uncle, who'd been a don at Cambridge in Forster's time, was at White's Club at that very moment. They rang him up, roused him out of his drunken stupor, and we all met for lunch at the Connaught. And he told us that once, during the May Bumps, he had borrowed a pair of trousers from Forster, since the two men were the same size, and they fitted him perfectly, breaking just over the shoes—which, I hope, forever disposes of that balderdash about their being three inches too short. So then, to round things off, we signed Victoria Glendinning's name to the luncheon check, in care of *The Times Literary Supplement*. Perhaps that will teach her to keep mum on matters she knows nothing about.

Meanness Rising from the Suds

I used to pride myself on being impervious to the sentimentalities of soap opera, but when that loveliest of English actresses, Rachel Gurney, of *Upstairs, Downstairs*, perished on the *Titanic*, I wept so convulsively and developed such anorexia that I had to be force-fed. Hovering between life and death for weeks, I sat in a Bath chair on the great dappled lawns of my country house with my favorite collie at my feet and an alienist, until one of them—I can't recall which— recommended that I watch a few other soaps to palliate my anguish. So I did; I watched *Another World, Days of Our Lives, As the World Turns,* and *Somerset,* and in less time than you could say "Dr. Gregory Zilboorg" I was whole again. Compared to the torment their characters underwent, Rachel's fate was a piece of cake.

I usually avoid such personal revelations, reserving them for my diary and a few copies for friends, but not long ago a paragraph on this subject, in a periodical called *American Film*, horrified me anew. It said that *True* had examined the treatment of men in daytime soap opera and recoiled in shocked indignity. "Shows like 'Another World,' " it complained, "portrayed men as 'gutless and/or villainous boobs.' Moreover, [*True*] found that most male characters on daytime serials suffer from something, and listed the embarrassments that are visited on the stronger sex: 'sterility, stupidity, amnesia, alcoholism, impotence, night sweats, acne, acrophobia, senility, insecurity, and outright lunacy.' " The item continues, "An editor of a soap opera newsletter told *True* that some actors have quit in protest at the 'shambling fools' their characters were reduced to. Worse, some even found their characters so emasculated that their offscreen sex life was affected."

Hardly able to credit the evidence of my eyes, I swiftly dug up the relevant issue of *True* for confirmation. Every word was gospel. One actor, John Colenback, who has played Dr. Dan Stewart in *As the World Turns* for many years, charged, "The writers I worked with always managed to turn the men on the show into either evil or totally weak characters who were manipulated by women. . . . I was trapped in an extremely paranoid position. I was really vicious when I was working at the hospital, screaming at the nurses and patients like a little Hitler. But at home I had to be the biggest of boobs, pushed around unmercilessly by my wife and my mother." (And, judging from that adverb, Colenback's travail also fractured his English.) Furthermore, *True* pointed out, these shows were not alone in their castrating complex, and gave more examples of male *faiblesse* gleaned from *Days of Our Lives*: "A man turns out to be the father of his brother's child. A husband ruins his wife's career by refusing to let her sing in public. . . . A man shaves off his mustache because a girl tells him that she doesn't trust men with face hair." All of them, I was forced to acknowledge, were unspeakable bounders—the husband in particular. Rather than wicked, actually he was a dolt. The craftier way to ruin his wife's career would have been to *compel* her to sing in public.

The second dent of soap opera on my consciousness had barely faded to a purplish bruise when out of left field came another—this time, though, more in the nature of a soft nudge. A ravishing friend of mine who, by a coincidence, had won her acting spurs on *Another World* and was now starred in a network show called *Millionaire Pauper* rang me me up one evening from the Coast. Not for nothing had Kathleen been called the Zuleika Dobson of Hofstra University; in addition to green eyes, honey-colored hair, and a figure that capsized the senses, she had a brain stored with more knowledge than

Chambers's Encyclopædia and a gaiety unequalled since Carole Lombard's. But tonight she was in a sombre mood. "Look, baby, I've got to come up for air," she confided. "I'm skying into town for a couple of nights. Do you know a real person that a person could spend an evening with—not a chauvinist pig or a garter-snapper?"

I tried to think of one, and, failing, timidly nominated myself.

There was a curious pause, and a crackling akin to chuckling, as though we were disconnected. Then I heard her voice. "You?" she asked dubiously. "Yes, you're sweet. But, frankly, dear, I've always felt there was—how shall I say?—something lacking in you."

I bristled. "You mean that I'm kind of weak? Gutless? A boob?"

"No, just ineffectual—sort of Pre-Raphaelite. A bush-league Dante Gabriel Rossetti, so to speak. You'r not really *evil*, like the men on my show. The trouble with you, darling—"

"Listen, this call is costing you an arm and a leg," I broke in, forgetting that she had reversed the charges. "I'll meet you at '21' tomorrow at eight. No, wait—you don't want to be bothered signing autographs. Let's make it the corner of Fifty-eighth and Fifth, and if I'm late you can look in Bergdorf's windows."

The realization that Kathleen conceived of me as a sheep rankled throughout the night, and by morning I decided to change my image. Fie on the funereal lounge suit from Brooks I had worn hitherto, the discreet neckwear, the bespoke shoes; I would transform myself into a swinger, one of those breezy, jovial loudmouths around the Americana Hotel, and sweep her off her feet. At a quarter to seven, I stood aghast regarding my alter ego in the bathroom mirror. The peacock-blue safari suit, the Tibetan prayer beads encircling my neck were disastrous. All I needed was a little tin can on my head to look like Happy Hooligan. Eyes aplenty popped at the Golden Noodle subsequently as the headwaiter ushered Kathleen and me to our table, but they were riveted on her Celtic beauty rather than on me. Understated my old Brooks number may have been; still, it didn't glow in the dark.

Our faces were greasy with egg rolls and spareribs before I mustered up courage to pose the question gnawing at my subconscious. "Kathie," I demanded, "why do you women in soap opera detest my sex?"

"Hate your sex?" The widened eyes turned on me were as lambent as a jaguar's. "My dear, you talk like a sausage. We don't at all."

"You do, you do!" I drummed my fists on the table. "We're always being portrayed as drunkards and eunuchs and fatheads —greedy, lascivious morons without one redeeming virtue."

"But you *are* swine, you can't deny," she said, palms outspread. "Look at Verdun, the Huguenot massacre, the annual statistics on rape."

"And women are angels, I suppose," I retorted. "What about Messalina knocking off her lovers? And Catherine of Russia, Madame Defarge, and Lizzie Borden?"

"Oh, we've had a few hotheads, sure, but if you dig into it, you'll find men were usually to blame. Remember the breakfast Andrew Borden had served up that blazing Fall River morning? Warmed-over mutton soup, leftover mutton, and bananas. No wonder the poor thing went berserk."

"Don't try to squirm out of it," I said roughly. "You and your ilk are helping to perpetrate a lie. How can you accept money for blackening the opposite gender?"

"Well, money is the only thing they give us. I guess it's better than nothing."

"Really. I'm surprised you can sleep nights with that on your conscience."

"I did have trouble at first, until I switched to Compoz. You should, too—it's great for the kind of indignation you're suffering from." She shovelled in a second helping of subgum chow mein with water chestnuts. Typical feminine behavior. They eat a spoonful of yogurt when they're alone, but when you're

buying, man, it's like Thanksgiving. "Now, shape up, honey—
you know better than to bad-mouth my profession. We just
speak the words you writers give us."

"Then we're traitors to our sex," I snapped. "We ought to be
horsewhipped for maligning ourselves."

"Hyperbole," Kathleen dismissed. "Those scribes out there are
merely using soap opera as a confessional. Believe me, I speak
from experience—I lived with one a couple of months last year.
He was a gorgeous animal. Body by Mark Spitz, hair like the
raven's wing, pearly teeth, Byronic profile; the man was a
veritable collage. And clever, too—not a speck of talent, but he
knew exactly whose work to plagiarize. So we're in paradise as
envisioned nowadays by Erica Jong—though, between you and
me, I was brought up on Andrew Lang's *Orange Fairy Book*
and I like to do a little sewing betweentimes."

"What ever attracted you to a bullock like that?" I asked,
repressing a shudder. "Sheer physical perfection is abhorrent to
me. Lacking nobility of mind, love is a barrel without hoops."

"You don't say," she commented. "Would you mind dis-
engaging your foot from mine? There, that's better. . . . Well,
one day I was seated in front of my checkbook, as Sir Arthur
Sullivan's song has it, weary and ill at ease. Not only did it not
balance but, chancing to glance through the cancelled checks, I
discovered that, unbeknownst to me, I was supporting a household in Redondo Beach. I taxed Wolf, my lover, with it, and
learned the place was tenanted by an orphan—a wistful, flaxen-
haired call girl to whom, out of compassion, he had also given
a charge account at I. Magnin."

"Whereupon I imagine you sent him packing."

"Yes, in my white Mercedes 450-SEL, which, blinded by
tears of remorse, he drove into a stanchion on the San Diego
Freeway. The shock to his psyche might have been irreparable,
except that he embodied our idyll in his soap opera and then
wrote it off as a deductible business expense."

"Kathleen mavourneen." I reached over and took her hand—
the one that was not busy spooning up water chestnuts. "How

can you allow yourself to be endlessly exploited by such para-
sites, trapped in an environment so alien to you? Need I remind
you that with each passing day you grow older?"

"Oh, remind me, do," she begged. "That's why I flew three
thousand miles—to be warned I was becoming a raddled old
crone."

"Well, it isn't too apparent yet," I comforted her. "And anyway there are lots of old-crone parts you'll be able to play. No,
what I'm trying to convey is that however stupid or clumsy your
past has been, I'm big enough to overlook it."

"Then nothing else matters," she said warmly. "As long as
you think I'm straight and clean and fine—"

"I didn't say that," I interrupted. "Let me finish. Now, I'm
not very rich in this world's goods, but I know where there's a
tiny cabin in a bee-loud glade just large enough for two. Can
you guess what I see there?"

Like so many of your Hibernian persuasion, Kathleen is more
than a bit psychic, and, after a moment's reflection, she told me.
She saw herself bent over a washtub humming contentedly as
several chubby youngsters played around her knees and I sat
indoors writing paperbacks that I hoped to sell for four hundred
thousand each so as to put meat on the table.

"Yes, yes, go on," I encouraged. "Is there anything else you
want to tell me?"

"Just one thing, lambie," she said, and patted my hand.
"Fearing you might become sleepy after these Chinese dinners
you consistently feed me, I availed myself of a backup date with
a person staying at the Americana."

"Some loudmouth in a safari suit and prayer beads, no
doubt," I said, stung to the quick.

She nodded. "Poor in spirit but not in this world's goods—he
owns forty-one per cent of the Texas Panhandle. Hence," she
said, rising, "that's why I'm rushing off precipitately, because he
can't bear to be kept waiting at '21.' " She imprinted a light kiss
on my ear and was gone in a rustle of silk.

Temperamentally, I'm an easygoing, philosophical chap stimulated by rejection, as I've often noted in my diary and a few copies for friends, and within a month the entire episode had faded from memory. Then, one afternoon, as I was watching *Millionaire Pauper*, the soap Kathleen appears on, I was taken aback by a new character introduced as comic relief—a bespectacled writer hopelessly besotted with a glamorous young actress. Torn between satyriasis and parsimony, he insists on conducting her to substandard Chinese restaurants, where he fondles her over the less expensive choices on the à la carte menu—but why should I compound the humiliations? The whole thing is a cowardly slur on the masculine sex, and any male voluntarily tuning in on the show should be horsewhipped. Still, don't let me influence you. That's just one viewer's opinion.

Is There a Writer in the House?

Some fifteen years ago, I began harboring a suspicion that the individual writer as such was obsolescent and would soon become as extinct as Battenberg insertions, Pluto Water, and Ayvad's Water Wings. Behind more and more of the craft, it struck me, there was becoming visible a corps of assistants, catalysts, technicians, and *accoucheurs*, but, at the same time, these incubators, these keepers of the flame who had breathed on the vital spark, were being denied screen credit. My conviction was shortly verified by a 1965 dispatch to The *Philadelphia Inquirer* from the Baltic: "Helsinki, Finland—Kati Kidstina's first book comes off the press this fall. A combination of poetry and prose, it will be dedicated to her mother. Mrs. Kirstina is especially proud, since Kati is only 3 years old." The dedication, clearly, should have been shared with Mrs. Kirstina's obstetrician, who had also helped out. Three years later, a prominent English press figure begrudged a similar debt. Alongside his photograph in the London *Times* was the caption "Charles Douglas Home, Defence Correspondent of *The Times*, is 29. He says he entered journalism with the publication of a story in the January 1944 issue of *Lilliput*. He was five years old at the time and had dictated it to his mother." Again, nary a mention of physician, nanny, or wet nurse. I was about to indite a letter to the World Health Organization, urging its obstetrical members to withhold prenatal care unless their names appeared on title pages, when *The New York Times* carried an account of

an even more flagrant omission: "Ahmedabad, India (AP) —
Three-year-old Surjit Shah has published his first collection of
short stories, entitled 'Black, Black Rain.' The book, dictated to
Surjit's father in the Gujarati language, has been translated into
English by 8-year-old Claudia Kohn."

As if I still needed proof of the growing hypertrophy in
authorship, it was afforded me my last summer in London. Like
many another Briton, a friend of mine there named Max
Waxwing is involved in a multitude of enterprises. A partner in
an art gallery, he conducts a health-food restaurant and a wine
bar, deals in vintage cars, imports cork ice buckets from Portugal,
and sells medieval oak furniture to persons avid for medieval
oak furniture. Months before, he had casually mentioned a
book he was writing about primitive and self-taught painters,
and I asked how it was progressing.

"Ah, very slowly, I'm afraid," he said, downcast. "Half the
time, he just sits there."

"Who does?"

"Why, the word man. The chap who's putting down the text."

"But you said you were writing it."

"So I am. I give him all the gen, and he whips it into shape."

"Oh, I see. It's a collaboration."

He bridled. "Not at all. Everything in the book"—he tapped
his forehead—"originates right here. He doesn't know damn all
about primitive painting."

"Then why do you bother with him?"

"Because that's his profession, man," he said, plainly annoyed
at my stupidity. "You expect me to sit down and type out the
whole thing?"

"Wouldn't it be simpler if you just reeled it off to a secretary?"

Waxwing compressed his lips. "That's *his* job, for Chrissake.
I tell him the facts, and he goes off and dictates it to some
wretched bint he's living with."

"Aha, now I get it." Light dawned. "She's the one does the
writing."

"Well, she or her flatmate—a repulsive little worm from
Zaïre or wherever." He dusted his hands. "At any rate, I'll be

finished with the rough draft in a few days, and then I begin polishing. That's going to take plenty of midnight oil."

So careworn was he already at the prospect that I urged him to husband his strength for only vital changes, and we parted.

Emerging from Crown Passage into Pall Mall a fortnight afterward, I collided with him. His usual natty garb had given way to the broad-brimmed black Stetson affected by W. B. Yeats, together with a waterproof draped impresario style over his shoulders. "Just come from my publishers," he said wanly. "Gad, what a nightmare. I've had to fight like a tiger to keep them from castrating my work."

My heart bled for him, having endured a like travail myself, but he waved aside my condolences. "Philistines, that's all they are," he spat. "You spend hours evolving a phrase, a nuance, and slash goes the blue pencil. I tell you, it's enough to make a chap give up writing."

"Now, stop talking nonsense," I reproved. "Where would Eugène Sue and Irving Wallace and Rod McKuen be today if they'd quit?"

"I guess you're right," he said, brightening. "Well, can't stand here gossiping all day. I'm due at Christina Foyle's literary luncheon and then that four-thirty symposium about the book on the BBC."

"Hold on a second—I'm confused. Your book hasn't come out yet, has it?"

He looked around furtively. "Not officially, but remember the worm from Zaïre I spoke of? Her cousin—brilliant tutor at the University of Leeds—is brushing up the rough spots in the tapes as soon as they finish detoxifying him. There aren't any actual copies so far in the shops, but everyone in Paternoster Row is buzzing about it."

While I cocked my ear dutifully for such sibilance the rest of my stay, I failed to hear any, nor have I since. Soon after arrival in New York, though, I encountered another instance of pullulating creativity. Through a mouthful of food at Downey's, Rebecca Earwig, a press agent I know, disclosed that she and one Mumtaz Mahal were writing a cookbook.

"Not the favorite wife of Shah Jehan?" I asked incredulously.
"Honey, she's been dead for three hundred and fifty years."

"No, this one performed in a Bengali dance troupe that was stranded at the Hotel Edison. I and she are penning a book of the favorite recipes of celebs like Olivia de Havilland, Celeste Holm, and Josh Logan, together with their most sparkling show-biz anecdotes."

"Gee, that ought to be a blitzkrieg. How does one go about writing a cookbook?"

"Well, I call up the diverse personalities, and she does the recording."

"On what—palm leaves?"

"Of course not— on a cassette. Then Mumtaz sets up an audition with a publisher."

"You mean she dances while he listens to the recipes?"

"You know," she said, breathing fire, "sometimes you can be a very aggravating person."

"I'm sorry, I expressed myself badly. What you're saying is that you transcribe the tapes—"

"*I* don't transcribe anything," she said haughtily. "My girl Friday handles that kind of thing. When she's through, the result is edited for like grammatical errors and fluffs."

"By you and this Bengali?"

"No, we haven't time. I'm enmeshed with my P.R. work, and she's grading cardamom seeds in a store downtown. There's some cockamamie instructor in the night school at Brandeis revising the script."

"Won't you have to acknowledge indebtedness to him and the secretary for their coöperation?"

"Are you out of your skull?" she snapped. "I and Mumtaz midwifed the idea between us. Nobody can use the recipes or even the jokes without they pay us a fee!"

So incensed was she at my skepticism that she forgot to demand my favorite recipe—upside-down cookies—and, as for the eventual publication party, I stand less chance of being invited than Father Damien's lepers on Molokai.

W ith mass authorship erupting all over the place, I became fearful lest I, too, be shanghaied into some congeries of the sort, and I kept my guard up. Unfortunately, it was down one morning when a telephone caller identified himself as Adrian Luftmensch, of Honeyfogle House, a firm of publishers outside my ken. Before I could tell him to put an egg in his shoe and beat it, the man was entreating me to lunch with him.

"What is it about? I can't seem to place your organization."

"That so? Just look us up in Dun & Bradstreet," he said, sensing that I would as likely possess the Book of Kells. "But never mind that—just answer me one question. Is one hour of your time worth five hundred thousand dollars?"

"Yes, and I've already wasted a bundle on you. I've got a five-act tragedy in reverse about H. P. Lovecraft on the front burner, so talk fast."

"I can't over the phone, friend. It's too delicate. Listen, where can we meet—The Four Seasons, Lutèce, '21'? No, on second thought, that's dangerous. If we're seen eating together, some columnist might squeal. . . . Wait, I've got it. Do you know Esteban's, a Puerto Rican fast-food shop at Columbus Avenue and a Hundred and Fifth Street?"

After five minutes of senseless wrangling, we compromised on a rathskeller off Vesey Street, of fragrant memory in Horatio Alger's novels. Thither I went, where once honest bootblacks rescued flaxen-haired maidens from runaway steeds, and found Luftmensch, a toothy entrepreneur exuding charm as specious as his Donegal tweeds. The *plat du jour*—rinderbrust with brown mucilage sauce—came with a side order of flattery for my past achievements, foremost among which, declared Luftmensch, were those matchless Potash and Perlmutter stories. Having dissipated the illusion that I was Montague Glass, I enjoined him to state his business.

"Reet," he said. "We heard on the grapevine that not long ago you and someone else succeeded in communicating through the Ouija board with a number of famous deceased authors."

So the news had leaked out. "Well, yes. A colleague and I conversed briefly with Booth Tarkington, Rex Beach, Scott Fitzgerald, and Alexander Woollcott. What of it?"

"What *of* it? Man alive, it's a scientific breakthrough!" He hugged himself in excitement. "But first—are you satisfied that they were the McCoy, the actual bona-fide scribes?"

"Incontestably. A Madame Blavatsky monitored the exchange at their end. She attested to their legitimacy."

"Wow-*ee*!" he crowed. "Do you realize what a sensational book—what a paperback, movie, TV series it could make? This is the biggest thing since Isaac Newton's fall of gravity, the landing on the moon!" His eyes protruded so alarmingly from their sockets that for a moment I feared a syncope. "I can get you a larger advance than Mailer and all those crumb-bums put together!"

Frail vessel that I was, I must confess my heart skipped a beat at his words. It was not the prospect of the riches he held forth, though they would have bought me the leisure, as well as the necessary quills and ink, to complete my great work on Lovecraft. Rather, it was the elation at the acclaim that would accrue for having breached the veil to the hereafter—that is, if I could establish that the planchette we had employed was unaffected by vodka Martinis.

Luftmensch, however, must have construed my hesitation as reluctance, for he whipped out a blank check and scrawled his signature on it. "Here—you want evidence of my good faith? Fill in any amount you like—fifty, a hundred dollars—to bind the deal."

"Slow down, brother." I restored the jar of horseradish he had overturned. "I've got a bunch of commitments to meet—a child's life of Vito Genovese, a history of woodworking among the Amish. I don't know when I could get to this book."

"You won't have to—that's the twisteroo!" he exulted. "My nephew Pincus, a graduate of Pace University, has a part-time job at *The Village Voice* sorting those classified ads for cohabitation. In his free time, he could take down your whole story in shorthand."

"It's not as simple as all that. There's a legal problem. We'd have to get clearances from the departed."

"What are you saying, Mr. Perlmutter? How can a ghost sign a release?"

"I beg your pardon." My voice suddenly turned icy. "Incorporeal, insubstantial, even ectoplasmic these revenants may be, but I consider the term 'ghost' a vulgarism and impermissible."

"Right, right," he chattered. "I didn't mean they were spooks —just that their signatures wouldn't stand up in court."

"Well, that tears it, I guess," I said, rising abruptly. "Doubtless some influential firm, like Harper & Row or Random House, can work out these minutiae. Nice meeting you, Luftmensch."

"Wait, wait. Don't be so hasty." Dew speckled his forehead in the uprush of inspiration. "How about this idea? We plant you and your friend on the Johnny Carson show with the Ouija. You contact these—uh, phantoms, or whatever you call 'em. And right there, with all of America watching, they agree for you to go ahead with the book. Is that legal enough for you—seventeen million witnesses?"

"An ingenious solution," I congratulated him, struggling to keep my temper. "We research the material, endure the agony of creation, possibly suffer the contumely of the critics, only to share the billing and royalties with Johnny Carson and the whole NBC network? Why, you little measle, I've a good mind to give you a biff in the snoot!"

So there we were, scuffling away like two demented roosters, when the door opened and who should come in but Herbert Mitgang, Israel Shenker, and John Leonard, all of the *Times*. God only knows why they had chosen to dine in a dingy fleabag off Vesey Street, unless perchance they were holding an Ochs roast, but, skilled newshawks all, they knew a hot story when they saw one, and they sped to their typewriters. Each wrote his version with no reliance on tipsters, tapes, or legmen, and Luftmensch and I shared equal discredit. Granted the entire episode was sordid from start to finish, still there was nobody without whose help it would never have been written.

As I Was Going to St Ives, I Met a Man with Seventeen Wives

Now that the more feisty in our midst have left the table and gone off to Plato's Retreat to loosen their inhibitions, perhaps those of us who have trouble staying awake after eleven o'clock would care to loosen their stays and join me in a toast. This year, friends, happens to be the golden anniversary of a spot where nobody had any trouble staying awake after eleven— a *Nachtlokal* called the Parody Club, on Manhattan's West Forty-eighth Street, at which the team of Clayton, Jackson, and Durante burst into glorious flower in 1928. Since its patrons were packed as tightly as sardines, space there was minimal, but in what was left such disparate connoisseurs of the trio as Robert Benchley, Frank Costello, Edmund Wilson, and John Hay Whitney might have been descried rolling on the floor, overcome by mirth. I myself, a raw youth resolved to learn all of Jimmy Durante's routines by heart, was near-bankrupt from attending the club thrice weekly, while my betrothed sat by aghast, dreams of a European honeymoon fading as I cannibalized her dowry to pay for the research.

Among the three or four dozen songs and monologues the audience never tired of, like "Jimmy, the Well-Dressed Man," "So I Ups to Him," and "Shipwreck," with its valiant last line, "Pull for the horizon, it's better than nothing," was a short recitative about an occasion when Durante innocently came into conflict with the law. He had been out for a peaceful stroll with his wife and twelve children, he recounted, when a policeman suddenly materialized and took him into custody. Durante was transfixed. "Under arrest, Officer?" he stammered. "What for? I didn't do nothin'!" "None of your lip," the cop retorted. "You must have done *something*, with that crowd follying you."

Much the same suspicion flooded into my mind a while ago about the defendant in a Far Eastern trial reported by the *Times*. Headlined "117-year-old Malaysian Guilty in 'Living out of Wedlock' Case," the story, emanating from Kuala Lumpur, read: "A Moslem religious court has released a 117-year-old Malaysian man on probation after he pleaded guilty to living out of wedlock with a 40-year-old woman. It was his third conviction on the same charge with the same woman, court officials said. The court fined Lebai Omar Bin Datuk Panglima Garang $80 at the hearing yesterday. Lebai Omar described himself as a teacher of 'Silat,' the Malay art of self-defense. He had been married seventeen times previously and divorced all his wives."

On the face of it, it seems improbable that anyone skilled in the art of self-defense could have voluntarily married seventeen women, but doubtless the man was an irrepressible idealist, a matrimonial Audubon doomed to wander aimlessly questing the bluebird of happiness. Still, I reflected, one was forced to admire his doggedness. Unlike such amateurs as Tommy Manville and Artie Shaw, who lost heart after a paltry eight or eleven wives, Lebai Omar gamely pressed on, confident that in the next shower of rice and old shoes he would come up with a winner. In an attempt to gauge the length of his individual marriages, I got out my calculator and estimated that if he had started at the age of thirteen, the average union ran six years. On the other hand, he may have been precocious and begun marrying when he was seven, in which case there was an eighteenth wife unaccounted for. How he ever moonlighted three times with that forty-year-old woman staggers the imagination.

Before a hungry mob of feminists, sexologists, and other mullahs descends on the case to extrapolate earth-shaking judgments, I herewith wish to stake a claim to the dramatic rights. In this tortuous, steamy maze of conflicting passions, I believe, repose the seeds of a powerful drama—possibly one like Joseph Hergesheimer's *Java Head*, wherein the lovely Chinese bride of a New England mariner (played, I recall, in the silent movie version by the incomparable Jetta Goudal) is subjected to the bigotry and scorn of his puritan townsfolk. Or it could be something on the order of *Alice of Old Vincennes*, sentimental yet rollicking. I just mention these two extremes to show how widely I propose to cast my net and see what we can scoop up. So if everyone will kindly shove back his chair a bit, we can improvise a little stage and begin. It'll be hours before those hooligans get back from Plato's Retreat.

SCENE: *The conservatory of Mucho Dinero, the Newport mansion of Bonanza and Wolfram Frontispiece, socially prominent leaders of the colony and longtime possessors of old money. A profusion of smilax, exotic plants, bibelots, and objets de vertu. Through the open French doors behind them is glimpsed Cliff Walk, along which occasionally saunter the figures of Mrs. Potter Palmer, Berry Wall, Mrs. Lytle Hull, Laddie Sanford, Mrs. T. Markoe Robertson, and other members of the gratin—an illusion achieved by cardboard cutouts of the foregoing drawn along a groove in the stage floor. At rise, Wolfram Frontispiece, white-thatched and peppery, paces to and fro chewing an unlit Havana, his brow furrowed. After a moment, Farkrimter, the butler, appears on the threshold.*

FARKRIMTER: Oh, excuse me, sir. I didn't realize the consistory was occupied.

FRONTISPIECE: Consistory? This is a conservatory, man. Don't you know the difference?

FARKRIMTER: Not really.

FRONTISPIECE: Then you'd be a hell of a guy to arrange a meeting of cardinals. What is it?

FARKRIMTER: The chauffeur phoned from the airport, sir. He's bringing your daughter Wheatena and her fiancé from

Benares, but there wasn't room in the Cadillac. The rest are coming by bus.

FRONTISPIECE: The rest of whom? We're not expecting anyone else.

FARKRIMTER: The seventeen Indian ladies with Dass Ist Kein Kint, your daughter's intended.

FRONTISPIECE (*taken aback*): Suffering catfish, what kind of fumadiddles is that brat of mine mixed up in now? Bonanza —*Bonanza!* . . . Where the devil's my wife?

FARKRIMTER: She's down in the basement, laundering some thousand-dollar bills.

FRONTISPIECE: Well, go get her—don't stand there like a wooden Indian! (*As there is a wooden Indian standing there, a statue of Massasoit, Farkrimter awaits clarification, but finally obeys.*) Humph, a pretty kettle of fish. I knew no good would come of it when that willful, capricious minx went off to study in that ashram. And then, to agitate us further, came word that she'd fallen in love with some handkerchief head twice her age. However, best not to fly off the handle; the fellow must be a rajah at least, seeing as how he's brought his retinue with him.

BONANZA (*Bursting in distractedly*): Oh, Wolfram, what ever shall we do? Willful, capricious Wheatena has just skyed in from her ashram with a handkerchief head—

FRONTISPIECE: Yes, yes, the audience knows all that. Farkrimter and I planted it in the exposition.

BONANZA: Then why did I burst in here distractedly?

FRONTISPIECE: To cover a stage wait until the couple and their female cortege arrive at our porte cochère below. (*A hubbub of voices ascending*) And here they are now, by Jove. I've a premonition these voyagers from the subcontinent may have a surprise in store. (*His intuition is faultless. Dass Ist Kein Kint, a frail and wrinkled Bengali clad in a dhoti, totters in supported by Wheatena Frontispiece. His face is as deeply seamed as Ramses II's, and he weighs sixty-three pounds soaking wet. Behind them comes a swarm of gaily plumaged women of varying age and hue in saris. Note: These last, in*

*order for the ensuing dialogue to be heard, should be deftly
shunted offstage to the kitchen by Farkrimter.*)

WHEATENA: Well, hello, everyone! My, Mucho Dinero is certainly a sight for sore eyes after that grotty ashram. *(Archly)*
However, I daresay you menfolk have a lot to hash over between you, so Mummy and I will creep away to my old nursery
for some girl talk. (*They exit, arms around each other's waist.*)

FRONTISPIECE (*a pause as he debates whether to clap his prospec-
tive son-in-law on the back*): Hiya, old man. Nice to have you
on board.

DASS IST (*cups ear*): How's that?

FRONTISPIECE: I said—welcome. On Bailey's Beach you will hear
the mermaids singing each to each. Have a cigar.

DASS IST: No, thank you. I am at present munching on some
betel nuts.

FRONTISPIECE: Oh, sure—feel free. (*Nudges brass cuspidor
toward him*) Ah—how are things over there in the sugarcane?

DASS IST: So-so. As the Lord Krishna says, cow dung cannot be
gathered where no cow has been.

FRONTISPIECE: Hmm. This is not a problem we have in Newport,
Rhode Island. (*Abruptly*) Say, how do you manage to chew
that fodder? You haven't got a tooth in your head.

DASS IST: No, I lost my choppers—let me think—soon after the
fall of Port Arthur to the Japanese, in 1905.

FRONTISPIECE: Yes, I noticed you had a bit of mileage on you.
Might I inquire when you were born?

DASS IST: In 1857, during the Sepoy Rebellion. I'll be a hundred
and twenty-two next July, he-he-he.

FRONTISPIECE: What are you giggling about?

DASS IST: Oh, the idea of me and Wheatena and all my ex-wives
living in a spread like this. Boy, the Emperor Aurangzeb never
had it so good.

FRONTISPIECE (*voice rising*): Ex-wives? See here, Clyde, are you
concealing something from me?

DASS IST: Of course not. You saw them just now—the seventeen
ladies that rode in on the bus. Also, I've been mousing around
with a pharmacist in Jaipur, a lulu—

FRONTISPIECE: But I thought . . . (*Roaring*) Young man, you have the impudence to come in here seeking my daughter's hand—

DASS IST: Now, slow down, Pops, you're liable to blow a fuse. You want to wind up with blue lips and a tag on your feet?

FRONTISPIECE: Don't try to sweet-talk me, you insolent puppy! (*Rips open a bureau drawer; extracts a checkbook*) I know your sort. How much?

DASS IST (*dangerously*): Let's get this straight. Are you under the impression you can buy me off—that a scrap of paper could compensate me for the love of a creature as delicate as a startled fawn?

FRONTISPIECE: Money talks. Every man has his price.

DASS IST: In that case, we're in business. Speak up, fat man—how much is the white bird worth to you?

FRONTISPIECE (*his chuckle oilier than Sydney Greenstreet's*): By gad, sir, you *are* a caution. I like a man I can see through. By gad, sir, I like a man who can see through me. Why don't we meet somewhere, like Locke-Ober's, in Boston, and talk this thing over?

DASS IST: All right, but tell that gunsel of yours, Farkrimter, to keep his hands off me or I'll kill him. Also, we're going to need a fall guy—to pay for the lunch.

FRONTISPIECE: I'll bring along Farkrimter. The money he gets in kickbacks from my tradesmen, he could support I and you the rest of our days. And now, shall we join the nineteen ladies?

DASS IST: Frontispiece, I like your style. By gad, sir, you're a man after my own heart—but too many are after it, and the hormones are different. (*As they exit arm in arm*) Listen, how about you and your wife and what's-her-name coming over to the ashram next summer?

CURTAIN

Wanted: Short or Long Respite
by Former Cinéaste

I often ask myself these days as I shell out four dollars, stumble over people's feet in the murk, and gingerly settle down on the slag of their popcorn just what sort of will-o'-the-wisp I'm still pursuing. Surely anyone marinated by sixty-five years' exposure to the silver screen, mile upon mile of acetate etched with the hallucinations of ribbon clerks and debauched waitresses, would be much better off at home sipping hot cocoa and reading Pascal's *Pensées* in his nightgown—they now have nightgowns embroidered with Pascal's thoughts—yet there I sit, slack-jawed, a grizzled prospector still avid for whatever nuggets might turn up in the sludge. To be candid, the only ones I hope to unearth someday were encapsulated, say my informants, in two foreign films of such unrelieved tedium that projectionists fainted away in their booths. The first was an Italian production, laid in ancient Greece, which bumbled along inexorably up to the moment its hero declined an invitation to dinner. "I really would love to come," he assured the host, "but we're having a dialogue at Plato's tonight." The second, a Mitteleuropean strudel based on the life of Mozart, contained a passage wherein the young genius trembling approached his patron, a Herr Mossbach, for an estimate of his latest work. The verdict, alas, was devastating, and Mozart, streaked with tears, tottered out into the snow. Waiting on the corner, his confidant, Bill Eugen-

123

spiel, refused to be daunted by the news. "Courage, Wolfgang,"
he said, clapping him cheerily on the back. "Who cares what that
old mossback thinks? Let us go and compose *The Magic Flute.*"

While treasures as dazzling as these are of a rarity beyond
price, it should be noted that there are equally precious ones
that were never recorded on film but that sparkle in the
memory of graybeards like yours truly, who was once connected
with the cinema. During the spring of 1935, I was briefly employed at Warner Brothers–First National studio in Burbank,
spot-welding the dialogue on a number of its pictures. Among
the dozen or so screenwriters on the assembly line, which included Flotsman and Jetsman, a team that wrote several gangster
classics, was one Winston Finston, a scholarly, withdrawn chap
with a hearing aid, whose deafness, mercifully, shielded him from
our boisterous witticisms. His particular achievement, I learned,
was that he had furnished the idea for *Dr. Ehrlich's Magic
Bullet,* the movie, starring Edward G. Robinson, about the
epochal discovery of arsphenamine, the anti-syphilitic compound
marketed as Salvarsan. Even had Finston and I been marooned
together on a desert island, however, the pallid spirochete would
have been a dubious basis for friendship, and in due course we
left the lot without exchanging so much as an imprecation about
its godhead, Darryl Zanuck.

A decade passed before I heard of the man again, and then in
a context so different that it defied credulity. Shortly after Pearl
Harbor, Finston, despite other seeming disabilities, like flat
feet and membership in the Consumers Union, had applied for
entry into the United States Marine Corps and been accepted.
His experience gained as a screenwriter enabled him to survive
the rigorous training of the Corps. He scrambled through mire,
demonstrated he could eviscerate any opponent, and in general
displayed sufficient barbarity under pressure to qualify him for
jungle warfare. Shortly thereafter, his outfit received a forty-
eight-hour leave, along with the strict admonition to hold itself
ready to be shipped out. Four days later, a couple of burly
M.P.s ransacking the Los Angeles area for strays came abreast of

a renowned delicatessen called Woloshin's, on La Brea just off Wilshire. Through the window they caught sight of a figure in Marine uniform staging a culinary orgy. A cornucopia of smoked salmon, sturgeon, pastrami, corned beef, chopped liver, sauerkraut, dill pickles, sour tomatoes, rye bread, bagels, and seeded rolls ranged before him, Finston sat, chewing blissfully, his eyes closed and hearing aid switched off—a man literally at ease in Zion. His bubble, woefully, burst in a twinkling when the M.P.s yanked him to his feet and branded him AWOL.

"I'm not! I'm not!" he pleaded. "They sent me here!"

His captors gaped at him. "They what?"

"They told me to go to Woloshin's."

"Not Woloshin's, you fool," they cried in outrage. "The *Aleutians!*"

C ame postwar Hollywood, when McCarthy's tumbrels rolled and the mournful cry of the fink—"Bring out your dead heresies"—resounded through the streets. From Azusa to the shores of Malibu, from the throne of Harry Cohn, at Columbia, to the cardboard spires of M-G-M, where Louis B. Mayer and Dore Schary were suzerain, dissent was hushed, and no man gave ear to his neighbor lest Communist henbane be poured in while he nodded. Under the iron heel, the crucible well-nigh cracked, but along with the dross it produced one gem of purest ray serene. Its mineral elements, so to speak, were two—Keenan Wynn, the actor, and an executive at M-G-M named Serge Kolodny. The latter, a porcine type akin to those that root out truffles in Périgord, had been chosen by management to sniff out lurking subversives, and though Wynn bore no taint, he had been observed at meetings of the Hollywood Anti-Nazi League, a supposed branch of the Comintern. Inviting the young man to his office, Kolodny proceeded to massage his ego with chicken fat. Like his immortal sire, greatest of all comedians, Keenan was B.O. dynamite, the most blazing talent since Warren William, and Clark Gable's own choice to inherit his mantle.

Hence it was imperative to inoculate him against insidious foreign doctrines. Could Keenan by any chance, he asked silkily, recall the names of any individuals he had encountered at the Hollywood Anti-Nazi League?

"Jiminy crickets," Wynn protested. "I meet hundreds of people every day, Mr. Kolodny. I never listen to their names, I just autograph—"

"Of course, my boy," his inquisitor soothed him. "Nobody could answer a question like that off the top of their head. Now, why don't you go home, have a couple of highballs and a good feed, and tomorrow, when your brain clears, we'll have another chat—O.K.? . . . By the way," he called out as Wynn was closing the door, "the option of your contract's just coming up for renewal, isn't it?"

A sudden, inexplicable fantasy that he was being drawn up into Kolodny's snout as into a vacuum cleaner seized the actor, and he left hurriedly.

The interrogation resumed next day, with Kolodny using every means short of threat to elicit the identity of the League's conspirators. In vain, he wheedled, flattered, cooed. Wynn's forehead beaded over with perspiration as he lashed his memory to no purpose. All he could recollect, he asserted, was a sea of faces, speeches, applause.

The other man resorted to guile. "The human mind is like a maze," he pronounced, formulating what might be termed Kolodny's Law. "The more you hock away on it, the less you can drain out. Now," he added, with apparent irrelevance, "I understand you're very fond of motorcycling. Is that correct?"

Wynn signified it was.

"Then forget everything we said. Take a carefree little spin on your wheel—go to Vegas, Tijuana, lay in the sun and commute with nature. Remember what Shakespeare said: 'Where the bee sucks, there suck I.' By Monday, you'll be as fresh as a baby, ready to spill out names, dates, all that poison they fed you."

Three days thence, Wynn sat once more in Kolodny's office, oil-stained and travel-worn, fiddling with the helmet and goggles in his lap. "The next night, we went on to Bakersfield," he recounted. "After dinner, I shot some pool there—"

"Yes, yes, must have been a great trip," Kolodny said impatiently. "You look fabulous, Kennan. But, getting back to our little problem—did you at least think of one person you recognized at those League meetings?"

As Wynn hesitated and nodded slowly, Kolodny half rose from his chair. "Who, who?" he fluted like a barn owl.

"Dore Schary," said the actor.

Kolodny's face went livid. "What the hell, kid, you're only human," he sputtered. "If you can't remember, you . . . can't . . . *remember!*"

Among the regrets most of us harbor in common, I daresay, is the wish that we could have been a fly on the wall at some colloquy of the great. I once grew dizzy when Sax Rohmer, the creator of Dr. Fu Manchu, in the course of narrating some trifling incident observed, "At the time, I was strolling arm in arm with E. Phillips Oppenheim at a hotel in Evian-les-Bains." Similarly, what a privilege it would have been to eavesdrop on Dashiell Hammett and Raymond Chandler at the dinner *Black Mask* gave its contributors in the twenties, even though each swore he was unconscious of the other's presence. No less historic was an occasion in 1933 when two celebrated poets converged in Hollywood, giving rise to a line that lit up the sky like Vesuvius. Flies on the wall there were none, but one of the duo, e. e. cummings, generously confided the details many years later.

"God knows what I was doing on the Coast," he said. "Some impresario with a pointy head had read my play *him* and thought it would make a good musical for Jeanette MacDonald and Bertrand Russell, so Marian and I went out to see if there was any catch. There was—he wanted me to play Russell, in a sailor suit. Well, when that fell through, we figured what the dickens, you're only dead once, let's be real Angelenos. So we visited the homes of the stars, watched the grunion run at Santa Monica, drank malted milks too thick for a straw—it was stupendous. Those people really know how to get the marrow out of life." He paused, obviously derailed by a random memory. "Say, who was the fat poet who used to hang around Lee Chumley's place down here in the old days?"

"Fat poet?" I pondered. "Would it be Eli Siegel, who wrote 'Hot Afternoons Have Been in Montana'? He was thin, but his poetry was quite fat."

"No, no, this one wrote light verse. Used to contribute to F.P.A.'s 'Conning Tower' in the *World.* . . . Well, doesn't matter. Anyway, just before we left L.A., some face card in the movie colony invited us to a party, a very stylish affair, in a gorge called Pussy Willow Canyon—or am I making that up?"

I assured him that naught was impossible in the Land of Nod.

"Well, we had a devil of a time finding the place—drove up and down endless ravines, blundered into the wrong haciendas, châteaus, palazzos—and finally got there an hour late. The house was lit up like Versailles. Rivers of champagne, two hundred magnificoes milling around the lawns—it was a floorwalker's idea of heaven." He stopped again. "Look, this fat poet whose name escapes me—you must remember him. He was pretty well known; in fact, he wrote some very sprightly stuff for the old *Life* and *Vanity Fair.*"

"I can't think who you mean. Wait a second—could it have been Louis Untermeyer or Arthur Guiterman?"

He brightened. "Yes, the same *galère,* the W. S. Gilbert school, but it wasn't either of them. Oh, well, it'll come to me. So there we were at this shindig, Maid Marian and I, strutting around with the other peacocks. Eftsoon, some rake like Lew Cody or Lowell Sherman besought her to trip the light fantastic, and away they whirled to the strains of 'There's Danger in Your Eyes, Chérie.' Just as I was heading for the bar, someone grabbed my shoulder, spun me around, and wrapped me in an embrace, drenching my shirtfront with his tears. It was this poet from Chumley's. He'd been out there writing movies for fifteen years— And now I remember his name. 'Look on me, *cher*

maître, and have pity,' he was sobbing. 'You knew me when I was Sam Hoffenstein, a bard. Cummings, I'm a whore!' "
     But, of course, that was just a metaphor. I worked in the place. They never made any of us wear kimonos.

Portrait of the Artist
as a Young Cat's-Paw

The other evening, I was rummaging around in my bureau for a Belmont-style celluloid collar, slightly yellowed by age, that I planned to wear with my pongee suit and a lawn tie when the weather got warmer. This was the same outfit in which I posed for J. C. Leyendecker in those ads he drew for Kuppenheimer and for Hart Schaffner & Marx; you probably remember me also as his Arrow-collar model. Anyhow, during my search I pulled the bureau away from the wall and found a book I'd repeatedly flung there in exasperation while reading it. Its title was *James Joyce: A Portrait of the Artist*, by Stan Gébler Davies, and wild horses—nay, Percherons, Clydesdales, and Suffolk punches yoked together—will not persuade me to confess my lack of admiration for its author. Mr. Davies, a Dubliner, is identified in a biographical note as born in 1943 and "an enthusiastic Joycean since his discovery at the age of thirteen of an illicit copy of *Ulysses*." (It was illicit in Ireland at the time.) Nowhere in his book, sad to say, does he describe his euphoria on that occasion, so we can only imagine him cracking his knuckles and exclaiming "Hot spit!" as he floated down Molly Bloom's stream of consciousness in the final chapter.

Curiously enough, it was this very topic, the once illicit status of *Ulysses* in the United States, that prompted Davies to write the one passage arresting enough to make me cease—if only temporarily—flinging the book against the wall. It read, "Forty copies were smuggled across the Ontario border by Barnet Braverman, a friend of Hemingway's (the Canadians had unaccountably failed to ban *Ulysses*). Mr. Braverman crossed by ferry from Windsor to Detroit once a day with two copies making an alarming bulge front and rear of him, eyed suspiciously by U.S. Customs. But they, as it happened, were more eager in those days to suppress booze than literature."

Mr. Braverman's contraband echoes in memory the account my wife gave me of returning from her maiden voyage to Europe, also during Prohibition. She was accompanied by her mother, who in turn was accompanied by sixteen minute bottles of liqueur— Bénédictine, Chartreuse, anisette, and the like. To get past the lynx-eyed customs inspectors, they were suspended from her mother's girdle in a fringe of sixteen little hammocks the elder had crocheted aboard ship. Apart from tinkling like the Swiss bell ringers then favored in vaudeville, the bottles reached home undetected, as did the copy of *Ulysses* secreted in some silken recess of the ladies' steamer trunk.

I myself bore home a copy of the sacred text from my initial trip overseas, but I also brought back a package that caused me far more inquietude. To put the story into perspective and a nutshell, I undertook the trip because two other marine excursions had bombed. In the spring of 1927, I occupied a wee studio on West Ninth Street in the Village, where I drew cartoons that ultimately lowered the circulation of a weekly named *Judge* to the vanishing point. The studio had a north skylight and the approved décor of the period—primrose-yellow walls, a Roman daybed with slipcover of monk's cloth, and a lamp consisting of a huge glass carboy and a parchment shade that excluded all light. It was on the sixth floor of a building equidistant from the Athens Chop House and a restaurant run by the Siegel brothers, and, what with my meagre sustenance and my constant toiling up those five flights, I became so thin that a Siegel brother inadvertently stuck me in a jardiniere, mistaking me for an umbrella. Realizing that my dream of bankrupting *Judge* was futile unless I recovered my strength,

I went around asking people did they know a place a man could get away for a while.

They vouchsafed that they did indeed. They hadn't been there themselves, but everyone said that Martha's Vineyard was the Garden of Eden, only less crowded. That was what I was looking for—a roomy spot where one didn't have to stand in jardinieres. So I packed up all my gear, the bristol board, the Higgins India Ink, the Chinese white, and the fixative, and, bent double like a Sherpa, caught a train to New Bedford and a steamer down to Vineyard Sound. Well, one look at the salt-water taffy and that merry-go-round in Oak Bluffs—the Flying Horses—and the gingerbread houses in Cottage City, and I pelted back to the vessel. Eighteen years were to pass before I discovered what I'd missed.

My second journey offshore, to Fire Island, was a similar epiphany. Somewhere between the ferry landing and the Ocean Beach Inn, a distance of thirty feet, I contracted a virulent case of poison ivy. For the next six days, snow-white with calamine lotion and more heavily bandaged than Claude Rains in *The Invisible Man*, I sat in a second-floor room of the inn, inhaling the scent of fried clams drifting up the stairway. Desperate for contact with anyone, even the management, I offered to type their menus for free, but they refused, fearing that my touch would infect the bill of fare. Incensed, I determined to emulate Bet-a-Million Gates—to purchase the hotel and fire the whole bloody lot of them. The impulse waned, and the moment my affliction did I took leave of the sandspit pronto.

It was, hence, without any appetite whatever for travel that on returning to New York I strayed by chance into a UFA film called *Variety*. In it Emil Jannings, Lya de Putti, and Warwick Ward composed a troupe of aerialists whose career ends in mayhem when Miss de Putti switches her affections from Jannings to Ward. The key scenes took place in Berlin's renowned cabaret the Wintergarten. Why the picture evoked in me a burning desire to visit the Wintergarten, and, moreover, how I dug up the wherewithal, I cannot fathom, but one month thereafter the S.S. *Leviathan* was bound east for Cherbourg and

I was on her second-class manifest. So were Francesca Wild and Bunny Huggins.

Francesca and Bunny, two lovelies newly hatched from some incubator like Mount Holyoke or Wheaton, were well calculated to ravish the Old World or anyone on his way to it. A frail, blond Angelica Kauffmann type of beauty, Francesca was clad in what seemed to be moonbeams, but I could be wrong about that. Bunny was dark and vivid—lots of eyeshadow and lipstick—with a divine figure, the kind that makes men yearn to wrap its possessor in twenty-thousand-dollar sable coats. (I could not only be wrong about that—I could be talking through my hat.) The voyage had scarcely begun when a turn of fate threw us together. I was quietly sketching away in the bar, unaware that the two were at the adjoining table. Suddenly Bunny leaned over and inquired if I was an artist.

"The reason I ask," she explained, "is that you can't fail to have noticed that I'm wearing a black tailored suit and blouse set off by a bunch of foamy white lace at the chest. My friend and I are at loggerheads anent the correct term for this frizzy accessory. You being an artist, would not ephemera of this sort fall naturally within your purview?"

"Why, yes," I said. "I believe it can be variously described as a jabot or as a fichu or as ruching. Under whatever designation, Mademoiselle," I said, rising and kissing her hand, "it has never been more enchantingly displayed."

"*Tiens*, Francesca," she exclaimed, coloring to the roots of her hair, "I declare, we must have bunked into Monsieur Beaucaire himself! Shall we invite Mr. Valentino to join us?"

From that point on, the three of us were inseparable, the balance of the trip a kaleidoscope of shuffleboard, quaffing bouillon, with saltines, in our deck chairs, wearing paper hats at the captain's gala, and little other activity, since smooching in lifeboats was alien to our moral code, and, besides, impossible when you are three people. In due course, we steamed into Queenstown and were welcomed with a cornet solo of "When Irish Eyes Are Smiling," performed by an alcoholist teetering uncertainly in a dory. At Southampton, amid emotional farewells, the girls debarked and I proceeded onward to the Continent.

The pilgrimage to Berlin's Wintergarten took its place reasonably high on the list of debacles in my experience. There were, of course, no aerialists executing triple somersaults around the rafters of the cabaret. Instead, two dozen Central Europeans sought valiantly with throats, feet, accordions, Indian clubs, playing cards, and magic equipment to demonstrate their crippling lack of talent. Meanwhile, I sat by drinking sweet Tokay that turned to crystals of sugar on my lips. But ultimately there came deliverance. In an American jazz group that headlined the show I recognized a former classmate, and to him I dispatched an SOS. The good man did his best, according to his lights. He and several fellow-bandsmen conducted me on a tour of various bars in the Kurfürstendamm district, where they painstakingly collected the ingredients of a monumental hangover and presented it to me at the railway station. As the milk train crawled back to Paris, every piston stroke of the engine athrob in my brain, I became in fancy that detestable stereotype who has imbibed too freely, the wealthy young rounder cowering under an ice bag applied by his devoted manservant. Such was my relief when the delirium ceased that on arriving at the Gare du Nord I knelt down and promised the stationmaster I would never touch another drop of sweet Tokay—a pledge I have kept to this day.

In the week following, I alternated from the Dôme to the Select to the Rotonde to the Closerie-des-Lilas, eavesdropping on folk I thought might be the originals of Jake Barnes, Lady Brett, and Bill Gorton, and when I found they were eavesdropping on me under the same misapprehension, I decided we were all a lost generation and booked a trip homeward on the *Berengaria*. A couple of days before sailing, I ran into Francesca and Bunny having a pressed citron at the Two

Maggots. With them was an elderly woman, a Mrs. Wolf or Fox, or some such predator. We had a nice reunion, and possibly I took one more thimble of Dubonnet than I usually elect to have.

"So this is your first trip to Paris, Mr. Praline," says this Fox person cunningly. "I suppose you've bought a lot of gifts over here for your girlfriends back in New York, tee-hee."

No, blurts out the wealthy young rounder and authority on the high trapeze, only around sixty dollars' worth. It's a wonder I didn't hand her my watch and chain and billfold, too, while I was at it.

"Oh, you don't say." If I'd looked at her instead of snapping my suspenders, I could have seen her salivating. "I wonder, Fran and Bun, whether your handsome, courteous young friend could do me a teensy-weensy favor."

"What is it, what is it?" they clamored, adding in feminine sign language, "Honey, after that last drink, this mark is putty in your hands."

Well Mr. Protheroe it's too sweet my son's about to be married in New York and I bought him a bed at the Galeries Lafayette or Le Printemps I forget which but I have the receipt right here in my bag there look at it just forty dollars now to ship it would take months and months but since you're going over it won't be a bit of trouble to declare it just hand them this receipt I'll arrange everything with the store the bed'll be loaded on the ship Stanley will be waiting on the pier God bless you Mr. Proskauer for understanding a mother's heart full to overflowing with gratitude.

The old harpy never could have euchred me into it but for those two precious shipmates of mine wheedling and needling me to help her, and, who knows, they may have slipped something into my drink. At any rate, a week later the assistant purser on the *Berengaria* notified me they had a case in the hold, bearing my name. He thought it might be quite sizable, because the Cunarder's bow had been awash ever since we sailed. He thought there might be a bit of a delay unloading it on arrival, as the three winches were kept pretty busy.

"Not half so busy as the three winches—wenches—were kept who were loading it," I growled. I had to repeat it several times before he got it.

His sombre prediction was realized in spades. The *Berengaria's* fires were long since banked, my fellow-passengers had departed hours earlier, and still I sat in the customs shed, grinding my teeth and composing sulphurous limericks about Mrs. Fox. Finally, two inspectors materialized and signalled me to follow. In an area heaped with boxes and bales lay a wooden case large enough to accommodate an A.C.F. cruiser. The inspectors examined my customs declaration, her receipt, and the bill of lading the purser had given me.

"Here, hand me that pinch bar," said one. "I want a look at the contents of this box."

The *contents*—that was the word that demolished my house of cards. Who knew what was inside there? It could be opium, the Romanov jewels, half a dozen illegal Chinese. Oh, what a blithering idiot I had been! Wait, Officer, I wish to make a full-breasted disclosure—I mean I want to turn state's evidence. It's too late; he's torn away the board. Thank heaven—a mattress! Still, there could be dope inside. . . .

"Look, you claim you paid forty dollars for this bed," said the other inspector. "Are you aware they retail wholesale for a hundred and eighty?"

"I—I don't understand," I said, and tried to entrap him in semantics. "If it's retail, how can it be wholesale, too?"

"Oh, a wisenheimer, eh?" His voice rose an octave. "Let me see your passport, you."

"Hold it, Vic. Le me handle this," his colleague interposed. "Listen, bub, what are you—a dealer, an importer? Or is this article for your own use? No monkeyshines, now—remember, you're under oath."

With visions of myself striped like a zebra and stitching mailbags, I realized there was only one recourse: I would have to stoop to the level of Mrs. Fox. I assumed what I hoped was a syrupy, lovesick expression. "Well, gentlemen, to tell you the truth, I'm engaged to the dearest, sweetest girl in the whole wide world, and we're to be married next week." I paused and pulled out the vox-humana stop. "I brought this over for our little nest."

Averted though were my eyes in shame and self-loathing, I could tell nevertheless that I had struck pay dirt. I heard their commingled sighs of *Bruderschaft.*

"Well, that's different. . . . Sure, why'n't you say so before? . . . Good luck, my boy. . . . Here's your receipt. Run along, fella."

When I reached the barrier, it took no genius to distinguish the legitimate bridegroom-to-be. Tentacles outstretched, he was preparing to smother me with gratitude, buy me seven-course meals at Villepigue's in Sheepshead Bay, treat me to countless weekends at Grossinger's, but I threw him the receipt and split. Up those vertiginous stairs I went to my studio, and before long I was cartooning away as good as new. It was hardly an ideal occupation, but it was a damn sight easier than smuggling.

One Order of Blintzes, and Hold the Flimflam

A light rain was falling on the just and the unjust alike, and my cheeks glowed like twin pippins that February evening when I flung open the door of Cooper's Dairy Restaurant, on the lower East Side, and paused for breath. If my rosy flush suggested anticipation for the cuisine within, it was illusory; the operatic entrance and heaving bosom arose from overexertion. Dining at Cooper's demands a sprint along one of the most sinister crosstown blocks in New York—so fearsome, in fact, that it was chosen for a bloodcurling sequence in the film *Taxi Driver*, and he who would arrive with wallet and skin intact must be as fleet as the chamois. Except for the horns, knock wood, I was that chamois.

My quick survey of the interior was reassuring. A few somnolent patrons lingered at the Formica-topped tables, and, selecting the remotest—of the tables, that is; only a Rorschach could have evaluated the patrons—I spread my paperback against a hillock of seed rolls and prepared to consume my meal in peace. Everything boded well; the waiter's face wore its customary expression of gloomy martyrdom, the borscht had slopped over the bowl as tradition requires, and I settled down to the anthology of Simenon in the certitude that nothing on earth aids digestion like a velvety mixture of beets, sour cream, and murder.

Ten minutes into the mélange, the first streaks of dawn had silvered the windows of the Police Judiciaire on the Quai des Orfèvres, Maigret's brow was furrowed into corduroy over the strangulation of a prostitute in the Rue de Lappe, and naught but a telltale red smear remained where once was borscht. Then a deep, rather peremptory voice jerked me back into the present.

"Mind if I sit here, friend? They've closed the other section."

Had Maigret himself suddenly appeared in Cooper's and busted me for garrotting the *nymphe du pavé*, it would have surprised me less than the speaker. His corpulent figure was encased in a mink-collared overcoat set off by a midnight-blue homburg, and as he negligently drew off gray gloves and rested his malacca stick and alligator attaché case on a chair, I found my tongue with an effort.

"Er—no, of course not. I'm just boning up for my exam."

"Oh?" A hint of condescension tinged his paternal smile. "You're a student, are you?"

Too grizzled to masquerade as a rookie at the Police Academy, I opted for a safer identity. "Extension course at the New School," I said briefly, plucking a salt stengel from the bread basket. "Detective Fiction Since Edgar Allan Poe."

"Interesting," he commented. His smile broadened. "I suppose it's taught you a whole lot about the criminal mind?"

"I know plenty already," I said. "The business I'm in, Mac, you have to be a pretty shrewd judge of human nature."

"And what is that?" he asked, twinkling down from Parnassus.

"Yard goods," I said. "You know, mill ends and remnants— me and my brother run a store on Fourteenth Street. Boy, do we skin those Porto Ricans!"

It could have been my imagination, but from where I sat I heard a muffled click. In a flash, the grand-seigneurial manner switched to a wet shine in the eyes which was pure larceny. As he leaned forward intently, he came into focus—J. Rufus Wallingford, urging me to become expansive.

"I guess you two do all right there."

"You can say that again." I hooked thumbs into armpits. "Got a split-level rancher in Great Neck that cost three-fifty big ones, a Caddy Seville, and a paid-up annuity worth four hundred grand. I could quit tomorrow, except I still enjoy raking it in."

Our waiter, arms akimbo and stony-faced, had forborne to interrupt, but now his impatience, like the borscht, bubbled over. "Please, we're not running here a retirement village. Did you decide?"

"Ah, yes, yes, I must order." My tablemate caught up the menu and scanned it with obvious incomprehension. "Protose steak . . . eggplant cutlets . . . I don't recognize any of these dishes. Is this some kind of ethnic place?"

"Well, sort of—they get a good many Albanians. Bring me an order of cheese blintzes and a glass of tea."

"Cheese blintzes?" the stranger repeated doubtfully. "What are they?"

"Crêpes, dumplings. Little sachets of heartburn which lay on the stomach like lead. They come with blueberries and cherries if you prefer."

"Fine, fine. I'll have the same." His computer, plainly, was still calculating my net worth, which must have come up trumps, for he launched straightaway into the capework. "Sorry, I should have introduced myself. J. Willis Wainwright, vice-president of the Gripfast Mucilage Company, in Ashtabula."

"Jud Kluckhorn," I responded.

"A pleasure to meet you, sir. Say, I knew a Kluckhorn once— a fry cook at a lumber camp in Manitoba. Fritz Kluckhorn, a great fellow."

"No relation, but all us Kluckhorns are kooks. Ah-ha-ha."

"Ah-ha-ha. But to turn serious for a moment. You know, we do a lot of business in England, so I often see their newspapers. Are you familiar with the London *Times*? . . . Too bad. They run some marvellous crime stories—just the kind you're studying. However, that's beside the point." He withdrew a folded clipping. "Have a peek at this article they printed the other day."

Headlined "SAUDI PAYS £8.8M FOR WILDENSTEIN COLLEC-
TION," the account read:

The Wildenstein family collection of French furniture and works
of art, considered by the art world more distinguished than that of
Mentmore, has been acquired by a Saudi Arabian businessman, Mr.
Akram Ojjeh, for 75m francs (£9.8m) Last week it was announced
that he had bought The France, the transatlantic liner, for 80m
francs. He now plans to combine his two purchases, exhibiting the
202 superb Wildenstein items on board The France, according to
the Lebanese weekly, As Sayad. The liner will be anchored off the
coast of Florida and probably run as an hotel. According to Reuter
and Agence France-Presse, Mr. Ojjeh was born in Syria and became
a naturalized Saudi citizen in 1950. His fortune appears to be based
on his company, Technique d'Avant Garde Finance, hitherto noted
for high quality prefabricated buildings. The company has had
several very large contracts in Saudi Arabia and is believed to have
connexions with the Royal Family.

"Like, wow, man," I said, wide-eyed. "That's going to be
some hotel. Maybe I'll take Bernice and the kids there someday
instead of the Fountainblue."

"Yes siree, and you'll be able to afford it!" Wainwright declared. "Why do I say that? I'll tell you why I say that. Because
you're going to be one of the owners!"

I stared at him, incredulous. "I am?"

"Sure—right up there with the biggies." He cast a hurried
glance about. "Better lower our voices—that waiter's snooping
around. I can't go into the fine points right now, but here's the
action. Through a source I'm not at liberty to disclose, I've
learned that this Saudi, this Akram Ojjeh, is under-financed.
He's in a sticky position—the banks are holding a lot of his
paper."

"You don't say. Did they tell you?"

"Nobody has to. I'm in the mucilage business, man. Paper,
mucilage, accountancy—it's all related."

"You mean one accountant tells another," I murmured
craftily.

"I knew I couldn't keep anything from a sly fox like you. Now, you're a smart businessman, Kluckhorn. Given his situation, what would you do?"

I pondered. "Well, I'd take back the paper and print on it 'Fire Sale' in big letters. Then I'd hang up a bunch of schmottas outside our store on Fourteenth Street."

"God almighty, what's eating you?" Wainwright snapped. "This is a deal involving millions, not like that flytrap of yours." He quailed as my face darkened. "Er—excuse me, no disrespect intended. What I'm getting at is, several associates and I have formed a little syndicate to help Mr. Ojjeh out of his difficulties. Each of us is contributing a hundred and seventy-five thousand dollars to the pot, in return for which we receive fifty-one per cent of the hotel stock. You follow?"

"Yes, but talk slower, I'm afraid I'll miss something. Do you think— I mean, if an outsider—" I swallowed and plunged ahead. "Is there room for just one more investor in the syndicate?"

"Well, I'd have to consult my partners in the consortium, naturally, but I think we might be able to squeeze you in. Time, however, is of the essence, so if I could have a small check as evidence of your good faith . . ."

About how much, did you figure?"

He sponged the trickle of saliva from his necktie. "Oh, the amount is academic—we'd put it in escrow until the formal agreement's signed. Say about half—ninety thousand dollars."

"Hmm, that's not chopped liver— Oops, did you hear that? I mentioned chopped liver in a dairy restaurant!"

"I heard it," he said shortly. "Well, what's the answer? Are you coming in? I have to cable Lausanne."

"Wait, don't rush me. . . . Ninety thousand dollars. . . . No, I'd like to talk it over with my brother first."

"Is that all?" His sudden gaiety was almost infectious. "Why don't we pop over and see him together?"

"Oh, we can't do that." I drew back. "He's in intensive care at Beth Israel Hospital. He was freezing a bunion on his foot with dry ice. It burned a hole in the floor and he fell into the cellar."

Wainwright stared at me fixedly for a moment. "Would you mind just repeating that?"

"No, I couldn't bear to," I said decisively. "It's too painful. But I'll tell you what. You've been so generous that I'm going to squeeze you in on something. From time to time, I experience what are called reading reversals, and I had one a moment ago when you showed me that clipping."

"Look here, Kluckhorn," he began, inflating himself like a blowfish. "I fail to see what connection—"

"It'll dawn on you presently," I assured him. "Pray, examine the name of this Saudi gentleman you're befriending—Akram Ojjeh. If you reverse it, as I did, you will get 'hejjo marka.' Substituting two letters and eliding one, it becomes 'hello mark,' and since 'mark' is the usual synonym in your calling for a chump or a pigeon, we obtain the answer to your proposal. Do you remember Texas Guinan's renowned salutation to customers at her night club, 'Hello, sucker!'?"

His face slowly turned ruddier—a phenomenon almost impossible to credit. "Are you by any chance—" he sputtered, and then checked himself. "Are you alleging that my associates and I are a pack of swindlers?"

"Hardly," I replied. "To do so would usurp the function of a district attorney. Besides, I question the collective term 'pack' that you employ. While eminently proper for hounds or wolves, would it not be more accurate to describe yourselves as a goniff of swindlers?"

"Listen, wise guy," he burst forth threateningly. "Don't play games with me!"

"Wainwright, be reasonable," I chided him. "One minute you're courting me to join your caper, the next you flatly reject me. Vacillation like that can mean only one thing—our brief love affair is over. I must ask you to leave this table."

For years, despite the assurances of popular fiction, I always doubted whether overwrought individuals gave vent to their feelings with a frustrated "Bah!" and stormed out, but now it was confirmed. With a frustrated "Bah!," Wainwright snatched up his impedimenta and tore out of Cooper's like a shot off a shovel. Simultaneously, our waiter emerged from the kitchen juggling two plates and a glass of tea.

"Hoo ha!" he exclaimed, mystified. "Where's the other party? Did he lose his appetite?"

"No, his impetus, I'd say."

"Well, I'll look around under the tables," he promised. "Meantime, what about his blintzes? Could you eat them, too?"

I shook my head.

"Then maybe you'll take them with you?"

"O.K.," I agreed, "but don't wrap them. I'll need them as weapons on the run home."

That's the great thing about Cooper's. Between the food and the trip there and back, you may not survive. Still, you meet some very unusual people.

PART TWO

The Hindsight Saga
Fragments of an
Autobiography

The Marx Brothers
Nathanael West
Dorothy Parker
Three Little Photoplays
   and How They Grew

The Marx Brothers

One October evening in the fall of 1931, a few minutes after the curtain had risen on the second act of *Animal Crackers*, a musical comedy starring the Four Marx Brothers, the occupant of the seat adjoining mine, a comely person with a mink coat folded on her lap, suddenly reached through it and twitched my sleeve. I was then, and still fatuously conceive myself to be, a hot-blooded young man; and if I did not respond immediately, there were several cogent reasons. To begin with, the occupant of the *other* seat adjoining mine, whom I had espoused a couple of years before, was holding hands with me, so that I had none left over to twitch back. Furthermore, the custodian of the lady in mink, I had observed during the entr'acte, was a chap with an undershot jaw and a beefy neck, the kind of lout I knew would tolerate no poaching. More important than either consideration, however, was the fact that I was breathlessly and rapturously absorbed in Groucho's courtship onstage of the immortal Margaret Dumont, impersonating a dowager named Mrs. Rittenhouse. It was at least five seconds, accordingly, before I realized that my neighbor was extending a note and gesticulating toward an usher in the aisle to indicate its source. Straining to decipher the message in the half darkness, I grew almost dizzy with exultation. Mr. Marx acknowledged the card I had sent in during the break to express my admiration, and requested me to call on him backstage after the show.

While our meeting was in no sense epochal, it did have an

147

unpredictable consequence, and my forehead, to say nothing of my career, might have been far less wrinkled had I not paid this fortuitous homage. For the half-dozen years preceding, I had been a contributor, in the dual capacity of artist and writer, to *Judge* and *College Humor*. Both these magazines, during my undergraduate days at Brown University, had reprinted drawings I had done for the college periodical, and when faced with the choice of a livelihood, I turned naturally (if naïvely) to comic art. There were vicissitudes that seemed insurmountable at the time, but thanks to a stomach that shrank as they arose, I managed to weather them. About the end of 1928, my work was appearing in some profusion, and Horace Liveright, whose daring as a publisher verged on audacity, brought out a collection of it called *Dawn Ginsbergh's Revenge*. It was a curious little volume, bound in the horripilating green plush called "flock" used to upholster railroad chairs, and as far as one could tell, it had only two distinctive aspects. The title page omitted any mention whatever of an author—I presumably was so over-awed at the permanence I was achieving that I neglected to check this detail—and the dust jacket bore a blurb from, coincidentally, Groucho Marx. It read: "From the moment I picked up your book until I laid it down, I was convulsed with laughter. Some day I intend reading it."

To say, therefore, that I had set the Thames on fire by that fateful evening in 1931 would be hardly accurate. The brush and quill were yielding a pittance which I had persuaded the idealistic lady whose hand I held to share with me, and through some legerdemain we had managed to squeeze in two summers abroad on the cheap. But the magazines I worked for were feeling the Depression, and all of a sudden the barometer began to fall. I started receiving a trickle of letters from the bank that soon grew into a cascade. Perhaps, its officials hinted delicately, I would like to transfer to some bank that had facilities for handling smaller accounts. Maybe I didn't need a bank after all, they hazarded, but merely a mattress or a loose brick in the fire-place. A deep cleft, resembling the Rift Valley in East Africa, appeared between my eyebrows about the first of every month.

Beyond rending my clothes or dropping an occasional reference to the poorhouse, though, I was careful to conceal my anxieties from my helpmate. Whether she suspected anything from the newspaper recipes I left around the kitchen, cheap but hearty agglomerations of macaroni and tuna fish, I cannot say. If she did, she gave no hint of it.

This was our approximate situation, then, at the moment the summons from Groucho arrived, and it was without any portent that the encounter would be fateful that I hastened backstage after the performance. Once, however, we had exchanged cordialities—a bit awkward for my wife since Groucho was clad only in his shorts—he breezily confessed to an ulterior purpose in his invitation. One of the networks had latterly been entreating the Marxes to appear in a radio series, and he wondered if I could be cozened into writing it. Flattering as I found his esteem, I was frankly overwhelmed.

"I—I wouldn't know how to begin," I faltered. "I've never worked on a radio script."

"Neither has Will Johnstone," admitted Groucho. "He's the fellow we'd like you to collaborate with." He went on to explain; Johnstone, like myself a comic artist and a staff member of the *Evening World*, was the author of "I'll Say She Is," a boisterous vaudeville sketch which the Marxes had amplified into their first Broadway success. "Yes siree," he concluded somberly. "I can't imagine two people worse equipped for the job, but there's one thing in your favor. You're both such tyros you might just come up with something fresh."

It was a dubious basis for any undertaking, and yet, as events proved, his words had a certain perverse logic. Johnstone turned out to be a jovial, exuberant chap in his late fifties, a raconteur with a fund of newspaper stories. We put in a couple of enjoyable sessions that got nowhere, except for a misty notion that the Marxes might be characterized as stowaways aboard an ocean liner. On the day designated to report our progress, the two of us met outside the Astor, resolved to confess our inadequacy and throw in the towel. Luncheon with the troupe was as disorganized as my colleague predicted it would be. Groucho expatiated at length on his stock-market losses, Chico kept jumping up to place telephone bets, and Harpo table-hopped all over the dining room, discomposing any attractive lady who gave him a second glance. Finally, the issue could be postponed no longer, and Johnstone, courageously assuming the burden, divulged the sum total of our conferences. To our stupefaction, it evoked hosannas.

"Listen," said Groucho, after a whispered colloquy with his brothers. "You fellows have stumbled on something big. This isn't any fly-by-night radio serial—it's our next picture!"

Primed for a totally opposite reaction, Johnstone and I surveyed him speechless; we had expected to be pistol-whipped and summarily flung into Times Square, and in our humility, thought he was being ironical. Within the next half hour, the brothers dispelled any doubt of their enthusiasm. Pinioning our arms, they hustled us across the street into the office of Jesse Lasky, the head of Paramount Pictures. There was a short, confused interval brim-full of references to astronomical sums of money, contracts, and transportation to the Coast, inexplicably for our wives as well. We were to entrain for Hollywood within the week, it was tempestuously agreed, to write the screenplay. The Marxes, scheduled to terminate their Broadway run in a fortnight, were off to London for an engagement at the Palladium, after which they would return to California to shoot our film. When Johnstone and I reeled out into what was now truly the Gay White Way, our faces had the ecstatic, incredulous look of prospectors who had just blundered across the Lost Dutchman Mine.

The delirium of leavetaking for California was, of course, punctuated by the usual untoward incidents that complicate life at such moments. My wife—deliberately, I felt at the time—slipped on an icy sidewalk and fractured her arm, and Johnstone, an undisguised foe of Prohibition, was suddenly disheartened by rumors that applejack was unprocurable in Los Angeles. Solutions materialized for both dilemmas; at the eleventh hour, my consort was able to board the Twentieth Century encased in a cast, and influential friends of Johnstone's mercifully supplied him with three stone crocks of his life-giving ichor. To further restrict our mobility, we took with us our pet of the moment, a large and aggressive schnauzer whose antipathy to trainmen and porters kept the compartment in an uproar. He was eventually exiled to the baggage car, where he ululated for three thousand miles and spread neurasthenia among the postal clerks. Much more awesome than any scenery we saw on the trip, it developed, was Johnstone's creative drive. In less than sixty-five hours, he dashed off fifteen or twenty strip cartoons for his paper, not to mention innumerable water-colors of the sunsets, mesas, and hogans en route. How his hand remained sufficiently steady, considering the roadbed of the Santa Fe and the contents of the three stone crocks, was a mystery. I sometimes lay awake in my berth for as long as two minutes pondering it.

Of all the world's storied thoroughfares, it must be confessed that none produces quite the effect of Hollywood Boulevard. I have been downcast in Piccadilly, chopfallen on the Champs Elysées, and *doloroso* on the Via Veneto, but the avenues themselves were blameless. Hollywood Boulevard, on the contrary, creates an instant and malign impression in the breast of the beholder. Viewed in full sunlight, its tawdriness is unspeakable; in the torrential downpour of the rainy season, as we first saw it, it inspired an anguish similar to that produced by the engravings of Piranesi. Our melancholy deepened when the mem and I took an exploratory walk around the hotel. As we sat in a Moorish confectionery patterned after the Alcázar, toying with viscid malted milks and listening to a funereal organ rendition of "Moonlight in Kalua," the same thought occurred to each of us, but she phrased it first.

"Listen," she said. "Do we really need the money this much?"

"That's cowardice," I said, vainglorious because I had held my tongue. "Why, we just got here—you can't judge a place so fast. Besides, it's raining. It's probably beautiful when the sun comes out."

"It's no such thing," she retorted. "You're whistling in the dark, and you know it. It's the Atlantic City boardwalk—a hayseed's idea of the Big Apple. We've made a terrible mistake."

"Oh, we have, have we?" I shouted. Two or three cadavers near us startled out of their torpor turned to survey me, but I didn't care. "Well, you're certainly a comfort. Here we are in the mecca of show business, the paradise everyone dreams about, with one foot on the golden ladder—"

"Unscramble your metaphors," she interrupted coldly. "This town's already beginning to affect you."

"Well, you don't have to sprinkle weed killer over our hopes the first day," I said sulkily. "You could fake a little optimism."

"O.K.," she said, assuming an insincere metallic smile. "No more crabbing. Maybe it's that dismal hotel room of ours that got me down—let's go find a cheerful nest somewhere and start acting like forty-niners."

The bivouac we ultimately settled into, a modest duplex in a bungalow court, had only one advantage—it was new. Otherwise, it was an unalloyed horror, from its overstuffed suite to its painted bedsteads, from its portable gas heaters to its garish dinette. Seated there of an evening over our avocado salads while the radio tinkled out commercials for high-colonics, crematoriums, and sculptured broadlooms, one had the sense of living in a homemaker's magazine. After a few days, I could have sworn that our faces began to take on the hue of Kodachromes, and even the dog, an animal used to bizarre surroundings, developed a strange, off-register look, as if he were badly printed in overlapping colors. Our neighbors were the customary hodgepodge—studio technicians, old ladies studying Bahai, bit players, chippies, and all the mysterious lamisters who tenant the Los Angeles substratum. They rarely emerged from their burrows, but once in a while we could hear upraised voices extolling the virtues of various faith healers or laxatives. Country people in general display a preoccupation with their innards bordering on the religious, and in Los Angeles, a metropolis made up of innumerable Midwestern hamlets, it amounted to a fixation. Apart from dry cleaners, saddleries, and stores that eternalized baby shoes in bronze, almost every shop in the district was a health-food depot. I have no figures on the per-capita consumption, in Southern California during the early thirties, of soy bean, wheat germ, and blackstrap molasses, and I am thankful. It was frightening.

At the studio, where Johnstone and I were now daily applying ourselves to the script, another and equally fanciful atmosphere prevailed. The two of us were quartered in a ramshackle warren of tan stucco that housed thirty or forty other scribes. They were all in various stages of gestation, some spawning gangster epics and horse operas, others musical comedies, dramas, and farces. Few of them were writers in the traditional sense, but persuasive, voluble specialists adept in contriving trick plot situations. Many had worked before the advent of dialogue, in silent pictures; they viewed the playwrights, novelists, and newspapermen who were beginning to arrive from New York as usurpers, slick wordmongers threatening their livelihood, and rarely fraternized. My collaborator and I, however, had little time to promote social contacts, for a managerial eye was fixed on us to ensure that the script would be forthcoming on time. Herman Mankiewicz, our supervisor, was a large, Teutonic individual with an abrasive tongue, who had been a well-known journalist and *The New Yorker*'s first dramatic critic. Though he was married into the Hollywood hierarchy, his fondness for cards and good living kept him in a state of perpetual peonage and had made him a sort of Johnsonian figure in the industry. Luckily, his duties as our overseer lay lightly on him. He stressed the fact that we were to proceed as fancy dictated, cynically adding that in any case, the Marxes would keelhaul us.

"They're mercurial, devious, and ungrateful," he said. "I hate to depress you, but you'll rue the day you ever took the assignment. This is an ordeal by fire. Make sure you wear asbestos pants."

Johnstone, whose earlier association with the brothers had left no scars, was inclined to scoff at these sentiments, but several weeks later, an incident occurred that unnerved us both. One morning, we were called to Mr. Lasky's office and shown a cable from the Marxes in London. Stating their disenchantment with us in the most succinct terms, they recommended our instant dismissal and replacement by capable writers. Transfixed, we pointed out to Lasky that nobody thus far had seen a word we'd written. He nodded paternally.

"Don't be upset," he advised, smiling. "Actors, you know—they're all a little unstable. I've already replied. I told them to stick to their vaudeville and we'd worry about the movie end."

Evidently the vaudeville was providing its quota of headaches, because rumors of a very cool reception in England soon drifted back to us. Music-hall audiences were not yet attuned to anarchic comedy, and they saluted the Marxes' whirlwind antics by jeering and pitching pennies onto the stage. Insulated from their problems by a continent and an ocean, however, my collaborator and I continued to peg away at our script. We devised jokes and plot twists so hilarious that we could barely gasp them out to each other; we grovelled with laughter in our lazaret as we invented extravagant puns for Groucho, pantomimic flights and Italian malapropisms for his brothers. Zeppo, the youngest, was never a concern, since he was always cast as the juvenile love interest. His speeches were usually throwaways like "Yes, Father" or song cues on the order of "I think you have the loveliest blue eyes I've ever seen."

Six weeks from the day we had begun work, we were notified that the deadline was looming. The troupe was back in the country and about to converge on Hollywood, and we were to read the screenplay to them, *viva voce*, the following Friday night at the Roosevelt Hotel. We put in some intensive burnishing, though, truth to tell, our handiwork already seemed to us to outshine the Kohinoor. To make it still more acceptable, we decided to salt our pages with as many technical movie phrases as we could, many of which we only half understood. We therefore went over the action line by line, panning, irising down, and dissolving, painstakingly sandwiched in Jackman and Dunning shots, and even, at one point, specified that the camera should vorkapich around the faces of the ballroom guests. Neither of us, of course, had the remotest notion of what this last meant, and it was years before I discovered that it derived from a special-effects genius named Slavko Vorkapich. I still have no idea, between ourselves, whether his technique could be applied with impunity to the human face.

At eight-thirty on the appointed evening, I met Johnstone in the suite reserved for our audition. The onus of reading aloud a 126-page script weighed heavily on both of us, so we flipped a coin and I, to my despair, was elected. Half an hour passed without any sign of the quartet, during which I twice urged my colleague to abandon the whole enterprise and leave by the fire escape, but his dentures were chattering so loudly that he did not hear me. Fifteen minutes later, the first auditors arrived—Papa Marx, the progenitor of the band, accompanied by a fellow pinochle player. Our whiplash, Mankiewicz, turned up next, in company with his brother Joseph, then a rising screenwriter at Paramount. They were followed by Zeppo and his wife, who brought along a stately brace of Afghans they had purchased in England. The dogs had eaten the upholstery of a Packard convertible that afternoon and were somewhat subdued in consequence, but they looked intimidating, and they took up a position near my feet that boded ill. Harpo now strolled in with a couple of blond civilians he had dined with, and close on his heels the Chico Marxes, leading a scrappy wirehaired terrier which immediately tangled with the Afghans. In the midst of the tohu-bohu, Groucho and his wife entered; I supposed that thirteen constituted a quorum and made as if to start, but was told to desist—other guests were due. These, it proved, were three gagmen the Marxes had picked up in transit, each of whom was to furnish japes tailored to their respective personalities. (Zeppo, as indicated earlier, could expect only leavings.) Behind the gagmen came *their* wives, sweethearts, and an unidentifiable rabble I took to be relatives, and last of all several cold-eyed vultures obviously dispatched by the studio. When I counted noses and paws before ringing up the curtain, there were twenty-seven people and five dogs confronting me.

The very apogee of embarrassment, according to Madison Avenue, is to dream oneself in some stylish locale, say Carnegie

Hall, clad in a bra other than Maidenform or a supporter not manufactured by Haines. Had I been wearing either or both that night, I could not have experienced worse panic as I stammered forth the setting of our opus. Destiny, whatever its intentions, had never supplied me with forensic gifts, and my only thespian flight theretofore had been a minor role in a high-school pageant based on Pocahontas. The incredible folly of my position, the temerity of a virgin scenarist hoping to beguile a hardened professional audience, suddenly overtook me. I became faint, and the roar of a mighty cataract like the Zambesi Falls sounded in my ears. Stricken, I turned to Johnstone for succor, but cataleptic fear had seized him too; his face, the color of an eggplant, was contorted in a ghastly, fixed smile like Bartholomew Sholto's in *The Sign of the Four*, and I thought for one horrid moment he was defunct.

"Go ahead, man," said a voice I distantly recognized as Groucho's. "Get a move on. As the donkey said, we're all ears."

Short of committing hara-kiri on the spot, there was nothing to do but comply, so, clearing my throat with a force that loosened the sidelights, I continued. I had not proceeded very far before I began to sense a distinct change in the mood of my listeners. At first it was pliant—indulgent, so to speak—and there was an occasional polite ripple. This soon ceased and they became watchful—not hostile as yet, but wary. It was as if they were girding themselves, flexing for trouble they knew was inevitable. Then, by slow degrees, an attitude of sullen resentment stole into their faces. They had been betrayed, lured away from their klabiatsch and easy chairs by a will-o'-the-wisp promise of entertainment, and they grew vengeful. *Some* of them got vengeful, that is; the majority got sleepy, for by then I had stopped inflecting my voice to distinguish one character from another and had settled into a monotonous lilt like a Hindu chanting the Bhagavad Gita. I spared them nothing— the individual shots, the technical jargon, our colorful descriptions of sets and characters. At times my voice faded away altogether and I whispered endless pages of dialogue to the unheeding air. All the while, Johnstone sat with his eyes fixed alternately on his palms and the ceiling, patently trying to dissociate himself from me. Not once did he or anyone else bid me take respite or a glass of water. The whole room—exclusive of those who were asleep, naturally—was watching a man hang himself with a typewriter ribbon, and not a finger was lifted to save him. When I finally croaked "Fade Out" at the end of my ninety-minute unspectacular, there was no sound except the stertorous breathing of the dogs.

After an aeon, Chico stretched, revolved in his chair, and addressed Groucho. "What do you think?" he growled.

With the deliberation of a diamond cutter, Groucho bit the end off his cigar, and applying a match, exhaled a jet of smoke. "It stinks," he said, and arose. "Come on." As he stalked toward the door, he was engulfed in a wedge of sycophants hissing agreement and post-mortems. In another few seconds, the only occupants of the suite were a pair of forlorn sourdoughs numbed by the realization that the Lost Dutchman Mine was actually fool's gold.

Such was my baptism into the picture business, the glamorous and devil-may-care world of illusion I had envied from childhood. I crept away that night to lick my wounds, convinced that this was Waterloo, that contumely and public disgrace would be our portion forever. Happily, I was wrong; in the scalding light of day, our critics capriciously reversed themselves and decided that traces of our handiwork could be salvaged. It took five months of drudgery and Homeric quarrels, ambuscades, and intrigues that would have shamed the Borgias, but it finally reached the cameras, and the end product was *Monkey Business*, a muscular hit. I read the New York reviews in the most ideal surroundings imaginable—a café terrace at Bandol on the Côte d'Azur, midway between Marseilles and Toulon. A soft inshore breeze stirred my wife's hair, a Chambéry *fraise* waited at my elbow, and the schnauzer snored contentedly at our feet. Far more blissful, though, was the certainty that there wasn't a frosted papaya or a sneak preview within a thousand miles.

Even that prince of porcupines, Thoreau, couldn't have asked for more than that.

My own relationship with Groucho was, in a sense, a baffling one. I loved his lightning transitions of thought, his ability to detect pretentiousness and bombast, and his genius for disembowelling the spurious and hackneyed phrases that litter one's conversation. And I knew that he liked my work for the printed page, my preoccupation with clichés, baroque language, and the elegant variation. Nevertheless, I sensed as time went on that this aspect of my work disturbed him; he felt that some of the dialogue I wrote for him was "too literary." He feared that many of my allusions would be incomprehensible to the ordinary moviegoer, whom he regarded as a wholly cretinous specimen.

"What'll this mean to the barber in Peru?" he was wont to complain whenever he came across a particularly fanciful reference. The barber, in his mind, was a prototypical figure—not a South American, but a Midwestern square in Peru, Indiana, whose funny bone the Marxes sought to tickle. Groucho visualized him, exhausted from his day's work and attended by a wife and five children, staring vacuously at the screen and resenting japes he could not understand. I tried to convince Groucho that his comedy was unique, a kaleidoscope of parody, free association, and insult, but he brushed me aside. "That's O.K. for the Round Table at the Algonquin," he said impatiently. "Jokes—that's what I need. Give me jokes."

The producer charged with supervising *Horsefeathers*, as it happened, was the same awesome figure who had guided the destinies of *Monkey Business*, Herman Mankiewicz. The choice, I suspect, was a deliberate one on the part of Paramount's front office, for it needed a tough foreman to ride herd on our anarchical troupe. Mankiewicz, whose stormy Teutonic character and immoderate zest for the grape and gambling have since been well delineated in connection with the authorship of *Citizen Kane*, was a brilliant man, but if he had any lovable qualities, he did his best to conceal them. He had a tongue like a rasp, and his savage wit demolished anyone unlucky enough to incur his displeasure. I myself was the recipient on various occasions, but one, which Groucho delighted to recall many years later, deserves repetition.

On a very hot midday in July, it seemed, Mankiewicz betook himself to a celebrated restaurant in Hollywood named Eddie Brandstetter's, much frequented by gourmands, where he treated his palate to two whiskey sours and a Gargantuan lunch consisting of lentil soup with frankfurters, rinderbrust with spaetzle, red cabbage and roast potatoes, and noodle pudding, irrigating the mixture with three or four flagons of Pilsener. Then, eyeballs protruding, he lumbered painfully to his car and drove to his office at Paramount. Thrusting aside the handful of messages his secretary extended, he enjoined her not to admit any callers, however importunate, for the next couple of hours and retired into his private sanctum. With the Venetian blinds tightly drawn, he stretched out on a sofa, shielded his face with a copy of the *Hollywood Reporter*, and sank into a blissful snooze.

Barely ten minutes later, he was awakened by a timid, repeated knocking at the door. Mankiewicz's face, mottled with perspiration and mounting fury, swelled like a sunfish as he sat up, prepared to decapitate whoever had flouted his express orders.

"Who the hell is it?" he shouted. "Come in, damn you!"

Two pale-faced young men, twitching with fright, entered haltingly. They were Arthur Sheekman, a gagman Groucho had imported to assist with his material, and myself, and luckless as always, I had been nominated to voice our petition.

"I—I'm sorry to intrude," I began, "but the fact is—the truth of the matter—"

"What the devil do you want?" Mankiewicz barked. "Get the marbles out of your mouth!"

"Well, it's like this," I squeaked, moistening my lips. "In this sequence we're working on, we're kind of perplexed about the identity of the Marx Brothers—the psychology of the characters they're supposed to represent, so to speak. I mean, who *are* they? We—we wondered if you could analyze or define them for us."

"Oh, you did, did you?" he grated. "O.K., I'll tell you in a word. One of them is a guinea, another a mute who picks up spit, and the third an old Hebe with a cigar. Is that all clear, Beaumont and Fletcher? Fine," he concluded, forcing a poisonous smile. "Now get back to your hutch, and at teatime I'll send over a lettuce leaf for the two of you to chew on. Beat it!"

Nathanael West

If, in the latter half of 1932, you were a Midwestern music student at Juilliard, a fledgling copywriter with a marginal salary, or a divorcée rubbing along on a small alimony, the chances are that you lived at one time or another at the Hotel Sutton on East Fifty-sixth Street. The Sutton was a fairly characteristic example of the residential, or soi-disant "club," hotel designed for respectable young folk pursuing a career in New York. There was nothing in the least clublike about it, and it was residential only in the sense that it was an abode, a roof over one's head. Otherwise, it was an impersonal sixteen-story barracks with a myriad of rooms so tiny that their walls almost impinged on each other, a honeycomb full of workers and drones in the minimum cubic footage required to avert strangulation. The décor of all the rooms was identical—fireproof Early American, impervious to the whim of guests who might succumb to euphoria, despair, or drunkenness. The furniture was rock maple, the rugs rock wool. In addition to a bureau, a stiff wing chair, a lamp with a false pewter base, and an end table, each chamber contained a bed narrow enough to discourage any thoughts of venery. As a further sop to respectability, the sexes had been segregated on alternate floors, but the elevator men did not regard themselves as housemothers, and for the frisky, a rear stairway offered ready access or flight. The waitresses in the coffee shop on the ground floor wore peach-colored uniforms and served a thrifty club breakfast costing sixty-five cents. You

161

had a choice of juice—orange or tomato—but not of the glass it came in, which was a heavy green goblet. The coffee, it goes without saying, was unspeakable.

By definition, the manager of the premises should have been a precise, thin-lipped martinet with a cold eye who slunk around counting towels and steaming open the clientele's mail. In point of fact, he was an amiable and well-spoken young man named Nathanael West, whose major interest was books rather than innkeeping. Since I was his friend and brother-in-law, it was only natural that my wife and I gravitated to his hostel when *Sherry Flip* slid into the vortex. A relative with a surplus of rooms was a mighty welcome spar, and we clung to him gratefully. He fixed up two cubbyholes into the semblance of a suite, for which, unsurprisingly, we paid skeletal rates, and he was quick to apply financial poultices when the wolf nipped at our heels. His nepotism, in a way, was an outgrowth of his of situation, for he had been appointed manager by some remote uncle who owned the building. Literary tastes and executive talent rarely go hand in hand, but West, curiously enough, was good at his job. He had charm and a quick sense of humor, as well as an innate sympathy with the problems of his guests. This did not blind him to their deficiencies, nevertheless, and he often confided accounts of eccentric, and indeed clinical, behavior that suggested Dostoyevsky and Krafft-Ebing. He also gave us an insight into the sordid mechanics of operating a metropolitan hotel—the furtive inspection of baggage and letters, the surveillance of guests in arrears, the complex technique of locking out deadheads or impounding their effects, and similar indignities. I presume all of these were perpetuated on us in principle, even though we were kinsmen of the boss, but so subtly that we never caught on.

Had West dreamt of becoming a Conrad Hilton, he would have devoted his spare time to studying cost accounting or new methods of adulterating the coffee. The status of Boniface, however, increasingly irked him. He had never given up the hope of writing professionally, and in such leisure as he could contrive, was working on a second novel. It had its origin in a series of letters shown him several years earlier by a friend of ours, a lady who ran an advice-to-the-lovelorn column on the *Brooklyn Eagle*. For all their naïveté and comic superficialities, the letters were profoundly moving. They dealt with the most painful dilemmas, moral and physical, and West saw in them and their recipient the focus of the story he called *Miss Lonelyhearts*. From its inception to the final version, the book occupied him almost four years. He worked slowly and laboriously; he had none of the facility of the hack writer, the logorrhea with which so many second-rate novelists cloak their shortcomings. He openly disliked the swollen dithyrambs and Whitmanesque fervors of orgiasts like Thomas Wolfe, and the clumsy, unselective naturalism of the proletarian school typified by James Farrell repelled him equally. His chief orientation, as is apparent, was European. Among the Russians, Turgenev, Chekhov, and especially Gogol, with his mixture of fantastic humor and melancholy, appealed to him. He idolized Joyce, considering him, as most of us did, the foremost comic writer in the language, and was strongly attracted to the French surrealists like Aragon, Soupault, and Breton, whose experiments were appearing in *transition*. Along with his avant-gardist flair, there was a deep strain of the conventional in West's nature. He loved custom-tailored clothes—his tailor bills were astronomical—first editions, and expensive restaurants. He fancied himself a Nimrod and fisherman, largely, I often suspected because of the colorful gear they entailed. His taste in women, with whom he tended to be shy, was catholic enough, but he preferred tall, rangy girls who had attended certain finishing schools and universities, the type our generation called snakes. For a brief interval, he even owned a red Stutz Bearcat, until it burst into flames and foundered in a West Virginia gorge. He liked to think of himself as an all-around man.

It is axiomatic that when a couple of bibliophiles meet over a remainder bin, a little magazine always results. During the spring of 1931, West, an inveterate browser, became acquainted with William Carlos Williams at a West Forty-seventh Street bookshop. In a short while their union was blessed by issue—

that is to say, the first one of a quarterly called *Contact*, which they coedited with Robert McAlmon. The title page bore the defiant epigraph "*Contact* will attempt to cut a trail through the American jungle without the aid of a European compass," but the undergrowth must have proved too thick, because the editors shortly switched their policy from geography to merit. They extracted essays from Diego Rivera and Marsden Hartley, as well as contributions from e. e. cummings, Erskine Caldwell, George Milburn, and Ben Hecht (and with due modesty, of course, from themselves). The magazine published four or five numbers, and then, stricken by the anaemia that dogs all such enterprises, a total lack of advertising, folded.

Though West was left with bales of unsolicited manuscripts which eventually stoked the furnace, he did get to know a horde of writers during his editorial tenure, and many of them, trading on his largesse, dossed down at the Sutton on their visits to New York. At teatime the lobby frequently took on the air of Yaddo or a book-and-author luncheon. Burly, pipe-smoking poets with thick orange cravats—nobody has yet ascertained why poets affect neckwear that has the texture of caterpillars—stood around swapping metres with feverish lady librarians from the Dakotas; the girl at the newsstand who sold you the sports final, unless you were quick on your feet, would try to read you a quatrain in the manner of Rimbaud. One evening, as I was descending alone in the elevator, the operator, a cretin I was certain I had never seen before, halted his car between floors and turned to me with a businesslike gleam in his eye. I thought he was about to glom my stickpin and leave through the escape hatch, but when he spoke, it was in the rich Stanislavskian cadence of a Group Theatre actor.

"Excuse me, sir," he said deferentially. "The housekeeper told me you had a big hit on Broadway. I'm scripting a play too, on a Biblican theme, but I got stuck in the second act, in the obligatory scene. Could you recommend a good book or construction, or would you advise me to go back to the Bible?"

I advised him, and thereafter used the stairs. Not all the aspiring writers at the Sutton, however, were slated for anonymity. Lillian Hellman, whom I had originally met when she was a reader for Horace Liveright and married to Arthur Kober, was holed up there, struggling with her first solo effort, *The Children's Hour*. A pallid youth on the third floor, named Norman Krasna, hitherto a flack in the Warner Brothers publicity department, was endlessly retyping Hecht and MacArthur's *The Front Page*, hoping to learn something of dramatic structure. His toil eventuated in a clamorous comedy on public relations that left Broadway unmoved but swept him on to Hollywood and affluence. The one writer of celebrity in the establishment was something of a recluse. This was Dashiell Hammett, who, in the pages of magazines like *Black Mask* and four novels, had revolutionized the whole concept of police fiction. Like most innovators, he had reaped small financial benefit from his work and was on a lee shore. He had been living, prior to his arrival in our midst, at an opulent Fifth Avenue hotel where he had run up a whopping bill. Unable to pay it, he was forced, in English parlance, to "shoot the moon" and abscond with as many of his belongings as he could conceal. His knowledge of the mentality of house detectives provided the key. A tall, emaciated man easily identifiable in a crowd, Hammett decided to use fat as a subterfuge. He pulled on four shirts, three suits, innumerable socks, two lightweight ulsters, and an overcoat, cramming his pockets with assorted toiletries. Then he puffed out his cheeks, strode past the desk without a glimmer of suspicion, and headed for the Sutton, whose manager was acquiring kudos among literary folk as a Good Samaritan. West, a clotheshorse himself, recognized in Hammett a sartorial genius. He put him on the cuff and staked him to a typewriter and a bottle of beer a day. The upshot, the best-seller called *The Thin Man*, clinched Hammett's reputation.

It was another pen pal of West's, in this same seedy epoch, who sweet-talked him into a venture that addled our brains for years to come. About mid-autumn of 1932, my wife and I began to detect glowing references in her brother's speech to Bucks County, Pennsylvania. He had latterly been weekending there with Josephine Herbst, the novelist, and his accounts of the flora, the architecture, and the natives verged on the rhapsodic. Owing to its remoteness and the paucity of highways, the district was still altogether rural; but the submarginal land and the inroads of the Depression had brought about a wave of farm foreclosures, and property was ridiculously cheap. Inevitably, West conceived a romantic dream of ourselves as country squires. He visualized us cantering on fat cobs through leafy lanes, gloating over our waving fields of alfalfa, the great stone barns decorated with hex signs, and the lowing kine. He saw himself as a mighty shikar stalking through pheasant cover, gun dogs at his heels, clad in all the corduroy vests and bush jackets he had lusted for endlessly at Abercrombie's. Since I was stony at the moment, eroded by debt and hostile to any prospect of becoming a mortgagee, West started a campaign of suasion that was a masterpiece of sophistry. The Revolution, he pointed out, was imminent; how sensible it would be for us, when "La Carmagnole" rang across the barricades, to own a patch of ground where we could raise the necessities of life. Fish and game were so abundant in the Delaware Valley that shad, rabbits, and quail had to be restrained from leaping into the cook pot. If Roosevelt closed the banks as predicted, we could grow our own tobacco, cobble our shoes with tough, fragrant birch bark. He painted a pastorial of the three of us in our bee-loud glade, my wife contentedly humming as she bottled raspberry jam, he and I churning out an unending stream of prose. Where the requisite paper would come from, since we were to dispense with cash, he did not specify. Doubtless he expected the forest to supply it.

I turned a deaf ear to all such blandishments, but his sister, who was easier to influence, succumbed. One Monday morning, the two of them returned from a reconnaissance of the section pale with excitement. They had stumbled across the ultimate, the *ne plus ultra*, in farmsteads—an eighty-seven-acre jewel in the rolling uplands bordering the river. Their voices shook as they described the stone house on a hillside circumscribed by a tumbling creek, the monumental barn above larger than the cathedral at Chartres. The place, it appeared, belonged to a left-wing journalist, one Mark Silver, who had tried to launch a ne'er-do-well brother in the chicken business there. The brother and other rodents had eaten the fowls, and Silver, to compound his troubles, was involved with a tigress in New York who was threatening a breach-of-promise suit. To enable him to flee to Mexico, which seemed to him an ideal solution for his woes, he was willing to accept a token payment for the farm plus easy installments. In West's view, it was the biggest steal since the theft of the *Mona Lisa* from the Louvre.

I grudgingly went out with them to see the place, and in a trice also fell for it. The autumn foliage was at its height, and the woods and fields blazed with color. In contrast to the bedlam of New York, the only sound that disturbed the sylvan hush was the distant chatter of crows in the north forty. There was an air of permanence, of solidity, about the house and outbuildings that captivated and reassured. My glasses steamed over as a series of colored lantern slides flashed before me—sleigh rides, Hallowe'en parties, sugaring off, sugaring on, and bringing in the Yule log. We hastened through the dwelling, exclaiming over virtues like its massive fireplaces and deep window reveals and conveniently ignoring its drawbacks. Bathrooms, engineered kitchens, and oil furnaces bloomed in our overheated imagination; magically, we became a trio of Paul Bunyans, shearing off porches, cementing cellars, and relocating stone partitions. Sound as the house was, we had to admit that the previous tenants had left it in parlous condition. The living-room closet was heaped with empty walnut husks, and judging from the pots and dishes on the stove, the residents had departed as precipitately as the crew of the *Marie Celeste*. A tour of the farm buildings disclosed that Silver's brother, following the poultry debacle, had turned his hand to cabinetmaking. The sheds were piled with dozens of modernistic plywood bookcases, striped in bronze radiator paint and hot tropical colors. The monstrous things harassed me for years afterward; whenever I tried to chop them up for fireplace use, the fibrous, springy wood repelled the axe and perforated me with splinters. I eventually made an apocalyptic bonfire of them, nearly burning down the barn in the process.

Several years later, incidentally, I learned that a celebrated colleague had seen the property and its owners, just before we did, under peculiarly harrowing circumstances. George S. Kaufman was being shown some of the real estate available in the neighborhood, Kaufman strenuously protesting the while to his wife that he detested the out-of-doors, that country living was full of pitfalls, and that nobody had ever incurred a hernia in Reuben's. Up at the Silver Farm, as they ascended its winding lane, a lesson in firearms was in progress: Mark Silver, who could not open an umbrella without puncturing someone's lung, was initiating his brother in the mysteries of handling a shotgun.

"They call this the breech," he explained, opening the mechanism. "We place the bullet, or shell, in there. Then we close it, like so, and raising it to the shoulder, aim along the barrel and squeeze here."

He pressed the trigger smartly, unaware that the weapon was still trained on his brother's foot. Simultaneously with the explosion, the Kaufmans materialized as though on cue, just in time to see the hapless brother bite the dust. Silver stared at the casualty, his face contorted in horror, and then bounded up to the arrivals.

"Cain and Abel!" he bellowed, and smote his forehead. "Woe is me—I have slain my own brother!"

Kaufman took off like an impala, and it was a decade before he would consent to enter even Central Park. Had West and I had any such therapeutic experience, we too might have been cured of our obsession; but the poison was circulating in our veins, and a fortnight afterward, in a simple ceremony at the county courthouse, two blushing innocents were married to four score and seven acres. Raising my half of the five-hundred-dollar deposit baffled us until my wife came up with a brilliant expedient. The one piano at the Sutton, she suggested, was quite inadequate for the Juilliard scholars, who required sustained practice. She and I had a baby grand in storage, an heirloom

from her family, which we might be willing to sacrifice for a
consideration in a worthy cultural cause. Her brother went into
some pretty complex double-talk with the owners of the hotel to
justify his expenditure of two hundred and fifty dollars, but
they ultimately held still for it. After all, as West fluently
pointed out, he had single-handedly transformed the joint from
a flophouse into an artistic mecca.

For the next couple of months, every ounce of energy the
three of us could summon—along with whatever paint, hard-
ware, tools, and furniture West could liberate from the hotel
short of downright larceny—went into making the farm
habitable. The self-deceit of landowners is proverbial, but we
reached new heights; we became artisans as well, installing
pumps and plumbing, wiring the house, and even, in a Hercu-
lean spurt that left us crippled for weeks, implanting a septic
tank. All these furbelows, being makeshift, constantly tended to
remind us of our inadequacy. Water pipes we had painstakingly
soldered would burst their seams in the middle of the night, with
a roar like Krakatoa, and drench us in our beds. Tongues of
blue fire licked at our homemade electrical conduits; half the
time we reeled about with catastrophic headaches, unaware that
the furnace needed escape vents to discharge its burden of coal
gas. Each weekend was a turmoil of displacement. Groaning like
navvies, we trundled barrows of shale to and fro, unrooted and
redistributed trees, realigned fences, and change the entire
topography of the place. The vogue for Pennsylvania Dutch
artifacts had not yet become general, and there were quantities
of dough trays, dry sinks, horsehair sofas, Victorian wig stands,
and similar rubbish available around the county to any fool who
confused himself with Chippendale. We invariably did, and
spent endless nights in a haze of shellac dust, scraping away at
some curlicued gumwood commode to bring out the beauty
of the grain.

Spring was upon us with a rush of seed catalogues, and we
were about to occupy our demesne and see if we could subsist
on tomatoes, when the wheel of fortune took an unexpected
spin. The Marx Brothers besought me to go West and fashion

another movie for them, *Horsefeathers,* this time in collaboration with Kalmar and Ruby, the songwriters. Somewhat less than radiant at the thought of being sucked into the millrace a second time, I hesitated, but the long financial drought had sapped my resistance. At almost the same time, West's novel *Miss Lonelyhearts* was published to considerable critical acclaim. Its early promise of sales, unhappily, was blasted by the publisher's bankruptcy, and though another firm soon reissued it, the delay was fatal. There was, however, a small silver lining. The film rights were acquired for a handful of lima beans by Darryl Zanuck (who, parenthetically, transmutted it into a tepid comedy), and it was on the proceeds that West decided to chuck his job and devote himself to full-time authorship.

Our farewell to him at the farm, where he was starting to woo his muse with a few Spartan adjuncts like an inkhorn, a 14-gauge shotgun, and a blooded pointer, took place in an atmosphere of mingled resignation and hope. It seemed a cruel irony to be cheated of the rustic joys we had labored to achieve, and yet, if we were ever to enjoy them, a spell in the Hollywood deep freeze was unavoidable. As for West, his mood was jubilant; he was through forever with the hotel business, with pettifogging bookkeepers and commission merchants, with the neurotics, drunks, and grifters he had been called on to comfort and wheedle. He had two tangible licenses to hunt and to fish, and one, invisible, to starve as a free-lance writer. We toasted his future and ours with a gulp of forty-rod, and bidding him Godspeed, turned our faces to the setting sun.

Dorothy Parker

Dorothy Parker was already a legend when I first met her in the autumn of 1932. Her bittersweet verses and dialogues, her *bon mots*, and her love affairs had made her a distinctive figure in the group of journalists and playwrights who congregated at the Algonquin for lunch and at Tony's, Jack & Charlie's, and the Stork Club for more extended liquefaction. The way in which we met was not one I would have chosen—in fact, it was a scarifying ordeal—but since we ultimately became friends and neighbors, it is worth narrating if only as indicative of manners and customs in the Prohibition era.

The occasion was a cocktail party given by Poultney Kerr, the bibulous producer of *Sherry Flip*, the revue I had written some sketches for and which was about to begin rehearsal. The show at that point lacked a title, and Kerr, seizing on any pretext for a bash, invited forty or fifty social and theatrical acquaintances to drinks at his office in the hope that someone would come up with a frisky and forceful name for the enterprise. Halfway through the proceedings Mrs. Parker arrived, visibly gassed but dressed to kill in a black confection by Lanvin, a feathered toque, and opera-length gloves. Thirty-nine years old and a very toothsome dish, she immediately made every other woman in the assemblage feel dowdy, and for a moment the sound of their teeth gnashing drowned out the buzz of chitchat. When Kerr introduced us, she straightaway fired off a barrage of compliments likening me to Congreve, Oscar Wilde, and Noël Coward.

Inasmuch as my total Broadway output was confined to one sketch in the *Third Little Show*, I thought the praise a mite excessive, but I blushingly accepted the tribute. Having fortified the company with several rounds of malt, Kerr called for silence, explained the purpose of the gathering, and bade everyone don his thinking cap. Needless to say, all heads turned toward Mrs. Parker, who accepted the challenge.

"Let me see," she pondered. "What about *Sing High, Sing Low*? No, that's defeatist. It needs something frothy, sparkling —wait, I know! *Pousse-Café*!"

There was an all but imperceptible ripple, and several willowy young men murmured, "Splendid . . . Yes, definitely . . . Oh, I love it." In the hush that followed, I suddenly became aware of Mrs. Parker's eyes fixed on me with catlike intentness. "What do *you* think of *Pousse-Café*, Mr. Perelman?"

"Great!" I said, striving to put conviction into my tone. "It's gay and—and sparkling, you're right. But it lacks—how shall I say?—punch. I mean, *poose*-café—it's too soft, somehow."

"Oh, really?" she asked, with a slow and deadly inflection. "Well, then, here's something punchier. How about *Aces Up*?"

"*Aces Up*," I mused. "That's marvellous, very good. I just wonder, though, if we can't find something a *tiny* bit sharper, less static . . ."

"Well, goodness me." Mrs. Parker's words dripped sweet poison. "What ever shall we do? Our wrist has just been slapped by the house genius there, who feels that we're a bit dull-witted. Of course, *he's* in a position to know, isn't he, leaning down from Parnassus—"

"Look, folks!" Kerr broke in nervously. "Have another drink. Don't go, it's still early—"

"How privileged we are to have the benefit of Mr. P.'s wide experience!" she overrode him. "How gracious of him to analyze our shortcomings! I wonder, though, if Mr. P. realizes that he's a great big etcetera. Because he is, you know. In fact, of all the etceteras I've ever known—"

Well, fortunately for me, the bystanders who had witnessed the carnage recovered their tongues at this juncture, and the rest of Mrs. Parker's diatribe was lost in the babble. I made my escape, and when Kerr phoned me the next day to apologize for her conduct, I swore that if I ever met the woman again, I'd skewer her with one of her own hatpins. That evening I received a dozen magnificent roses from her accompanied by a note steeped in remorse. It was the beginning of a friendship that survived the next thirty-five years, with intermittent lapses. When my wife and I saw her again on the Coast, she was married to Alan Campbell and from all outward appearances was prosperous. The two worked successfully as screenwriters (and in fact I collaborated with them on a film at M-G-M several years later) and might have continued except that Dottie detested Hollywood. Laura and I, who shared her feeling, spoke often of our place in Bucks County; we tended to become lyrical about the countryside, the farmhouses, and the relative simplicity of life there, and evidently our encomiums had an effect. In time we began to notice the recurrence in Dottie's speech of the word "roots."

"We haven't any roots, Alan," she would admonish him after the fourth Martini. "You can't put down any roots in Beverly Hills. But look at Laura and Sid—they've got *roots*, a place to come home to. Roots, roots."

It was practically foreordained, hence, that a month or two after we settled down at our place, the Campbells suddenly materialized on the doorstep with shining faces. They were surfeited with the artificiality and tinsel of Hollywood, they declared; they wanted a farm near ours and they wanted us to help them find it. Property was still cheap in our area, though farther down the Delaware around New Hope, George S. Kaufman, Moss Hart, and several other playwrights had acquired houses and Bucks County was becoming known as a haunt of writers and artists. Dottie and Alan, however, were imbued with what might be called the creative spirit. Not for them a manor house equipped with creature comforts like bathrooms, stainless steel kitchens, and laundries. They wanted a place that had "possibilities", something they would have fun remodeling. It was clearly an assignment for Jack Boyle.

Jack Boyle was a stage Irishman, straight out of George McManus's comic strip, one of the cronies Jiggs was forever hobnobbing with at Dinty Moore's and incurring Maggie's wrath. He was by way of being a real-estate agent, though he spent a good deal of his time seated on the steps of our local post office telling yarns. In a sense, Jack was one of the most celebrated personages in the district, even if nobody there knew it, for his exploits were immortalized in a book called *The Professional Thief* published by the University of Chicago. He had specialized in stealing furs from department stores, employing a technique that baffled the New York police authorities for years. It was his practice to enter a store, just prior to closing, attired in a balmacaan or similar loose topcoat, and to secrete himself in one of the pay toilets. After the store's watchman had made his rounds, Boyle would hasten to the ladies' fur coat section, select a particularly valuable mink or broadtail garment, and return to his cubicle. Soon after the establishment opened the next morning, he would emerge wearing the loot under his coat and stroll off. The truly extraordinary feature of his caper, though, was that he always turned over the money given him by the fence to a cause he believed in: he was a philosophical anarchist. Eventually betrayed by an informer, he so confused the police with an explanation of his motives that they sent him to Matteawan, but he managed to escape and ultimately, after extended litigation, to beat the rap. Thereafter, he had changed his venue to our township, where he trucked an occasional load of wood to Greenwich Village or negotiated the sale of a farm.

It was a lead-pipe cinch that anyone with so colorful a background would appeal to Dottie, and the two instantly hit it off. A couple of days thereafter, Laura and I accompanied the Campbells on an inspection tour of several farms that Boyle listed. The second one we saw was such a plum that had our friends hesitated, we ourselves would have snapped it up. The central portion of the house, its two lateral wings, and the summer kitchen extending from it were all built of field stone. Three enormous Norway maples shaded the residence on its north side; on the south was an apple orchard in full bloom.

About fifty yards distant stood a stone barn slightly smaller than Aeolian Hall. The dwelling and its outbuildings, reached by a long lane that guaranteed privacy, lay on a gently rolling southern slope of one hundred twenty acres, and the asking price was four thousand five hundred dollars. As Boyle quoted the figure and all our jaws dropped in unison, he raised his hand.

"A word of advice before you grab it, friends," he told the Campbells. "I think you ought to see the inside first. It needs — well, it needs a little attention."

Even with his warning, none of us was prepared for the actuality. The interior of the house was in an appalling state; floors had rotted out in places, revealing the cellar below, fragments of plaster hung from the ceilings, woodwork gave way at the touch. A disused incubator for baby chicks was balanced crazily in the largest room, and a thick film of poultry feathers and cobwebs shrouded everything. It seemed incredible that the ruin was inhabited, yet, said Boyle, an old Ukrainian couple had been living there several years and cultivating a few fields, thanks to the generosity of the owners.

There is a specially insidious form of self-deception afflicting house hunters wherein they confuse themselves with Hercules, equal to any Augean stable they encounter, and the Campbells promptly succumbed to it. They ran around envisioning the rooms a clever architect could fabricate out of the shell, the baths and bedchambers and butler's pantries necessary for country living, and in all conscience we did nothing to disillusion them, for the prospect of having Dottie as a neighbor was a stimulating one. It did not occur to us that we had taken on the role of midwives, that the Campbells expected us to accouche the birth of their dream house, and that we would be called upon to provide sympathy and counsel—to say nothing of anodynes like Martinis—for the manifold problems plaguing them.

The next few months were a caution. The pair installed themselves at an inn near Doylestown were they groaned through all the legal complexities of acquiring their place, choosing an architect, and approving his plans. Infatuated with him at first, they fell out of love with him in short order; he was stodgy, un-imaginative, old-fashioned. The Ukrainians, who had been given notice to vacate, turned obstinate; they refused to adapt themselves to the new owners' timetable and hung on, maddening Alan beyond measure. He turned in desperation to Jack Boyle, who pointed out, reasonably enough, that the old people had chickens they were preparing to market, standing crops not yet ready for harvest.

"That's *their* problem," Alan retorted passionately. "Don't they realize it's costing Dottie and me seven hundred and fifty dollars a week to stay away from Hollywood?"

Three Little Photoplays and How They Grew

I

Bestowing the award for the most odious person you ever knew in Hollywood isn't the sort of thing you rush into; you're faced, so to speak, with an embarrassment of riches. I guess on reflection that I'd choose a comedian at Universal I'll call Eddie Buzzard, who perched on my desk all the time I worked there importuning me to make with the yocks. He finally surpassed himself—whipped out a lady's hair comb that he wedged between his lips in a version of the *risus sardonicus*, which terminated my two days at Universal. The choice of the second most odious person, on the other hand, is a cinch: a screenwriter named Jack McGovern. McGovern and I collaborated, in a manner of non-speaking, on the script of *Sittin' Pretty*, a Paramount musical I've miraculously escaped seeing to this day. All I remember is that it starred Jack Oakie and Jack Haley, that it chronicled their backstage rise *per aspera ad astra*, and that its hit song was "Jevva See a Dream Walking?" Don't let any purist tell you the initial words in that title were "Did You." It was "Jevva"—I was right there when its creator, fat, genial wordsmith Mack Gordon of the team of Gordon and Revel, first mumbled it.

The producer of *Sittin' Pretty*, Anatol Crown, was a bouncy hyperthyroid with an explosive laugh, a backslapper who generated an aura of noisy excitement that passed for good-

177

fellowship. At his bungalow office on the Paramount lot, I voiced the ritual falsehood required of all scenarists—namely, that the story verged on genius, that the opportunity to work on it was equivalent to knighthood—and was presented to Mc-Govern, a beefier forerunner of Archie Bunker, all rampant pugnacity and no neck. Consecrating our match under the authority invested in him by the All-Highest, B. P. Schulberg, Crown pledged us not to measure out our talent in coffee spoons but to give of our hearts'-blood if necessary. Later that afternoon, as the two of us sat in the offices we shared rereading the treatment, I felt McGovern's eyes drilling into me. Though we hadn't exchanged a word since our introduction, the hostility he exuded was almost palpable. Unable to think how I'd offended him, I decided at last that Anatol Crown was the heavy. During his locker-room talk, he had enjoined me to pepper the script with plenty of good brittle dialogue. Brittle dialogue, as typified in the comedies of Philip Barry and George Kelly, was much in vogue in 1933, but not with McGovern, who prided himself on being a plot expert, a master constructionist. Indirectly, I had been classified as an aesthete, a bookworm, and probably, in McGovern's fierce tribal code, as a pouf.

Most of the next day, McGovern lurked in his own cubicle, emerging only to stare balefully at me or to dispatch Marie, our secretary, for coffee. Ridiculous and absurd as it was, the fact was inescapable: McGovern was trying to freeze me out, to make me crack under pressure, and I determined to force a showdown. When I came into the office the following morning, though, he was absorbed in dictation to Marie.

"Why, here's Mr. Brittle," he said with sweet venom. "Just get a load of this, Brittle—it's a letter to one of my mother-in-laws."

"I'm not interested in your private affairs," I said with more hauteur than Lord Curzon reviewing a durbar. "What I want is an understanding—"

"And you shall have it, Algernon, the moment I'm through with his," he promised. "Read back, Marie—where was I?"

The body of the letter was short and unencumbered by affec-

tion for the addressee. It merely set forth that on emigrating to
the Coast he had left in her attic a trunk containing several
unproduced plays that he now wished her to forward. They
were, admittedly, sophomoric, but he was confident they would
fetch big bucks as screen material. He hoped she was well,
etc., etc.

"How do I sign off, Mr. McGovern?" Marie asked him.
" 'Yours sincerely'? 'Cordially yours'? or what?"

"A good question," he commented. "Sign it 'Your ex-son-in-
law' "—he paused in thought—" 'who might still be your son-in-
law if a certain party hadn't sat around the Clover Club and
Ciro's night after night with every faker and gigolo on the
Pacific Slope while the poor simp married to her was slaving
away at the studio and then, to top it off, one week after he
bought her an Auburn convertible for her birthday she had the
gall to file for divorce naming a very lovely person on South
Palm Drive that just because the two of them were in pajamas
when the dicks broke in . . .' "

The subordinate clause, a page and a half long, rambled into
other fragrant episodes of a union as joyless as any I ever heard
of in the City of Joyless Unions. Formulating it, though, seemed
to have exerted a therapeutic effect on McGovern similar to
phlebotomy, cupping him of some of his spleen. Not all, but
enough for us to arrange a modus vivendi; to reduce contact
with each other to a minimum, we agreed to write alternate
sequences of *Sittin' Pretty*. It worked out surprisingly well—
even if the combined first draft made no sense at times—because
of an unforeseen bit of luck. Anatol Crown's mind, at that
juncture, was elsewhere than on the script. He was planning to
elope with a starlet named Toby Wing.

We received a clear intimation that drama was brewing at a
conference he summoned us to on the fourth of August. I recall
the date because it was, of course, the anniversary of the Borden
murders in Fall River, an event sempiternal in the memory of
Rhode Islanders, and it was the same kind of weather—stifling,
humid, unendurable. As McGovern and I, still unspeaking,
approached the producer's bungalow, we beheld a striking sight.

Eight long-stemmed American beauties, seated in as many rowing machines on the concrete walkway, were being filmed for
a trailer plugging a picture called *Eight Girls in a Boat*. The
ladies had been rowing strenuously for three hours in the savage
heat and were beat, but the unit director, a perfectionist, was
mercilessly demanding fresh takes. It was one of those pastiches
of life behind the silver screen that used to cause Sidney Skolsky
to choke up and that still evoke Rona Barrett's noblest dithyrambs.

Bright-eyed as a teddy bear, Crown sat at the desk in his
knotty-pine office excitedly jabbering into a phone. Gordon and
Revel, the songwriting team, or more accurately, teamsters,
occupied twin chairs along one wall, and ranged on a davenport
along the other were three gagmen named Felsey, Greslow, and
Profundo.

"Hi, fellas, be with you in a minute!" Crown called out.
"Hello? . . . Who? . . . I was talking to the Thieves' Market in
Glendale. . . . Oh, you are—good! Listen, it's about that seventy-
six-piece dinner service I bought. You made a mistake—you
sent me two extra gravy boats instead of the creamers I ordered.
. . . *Creamers!* . . . How should I know how to spell it? . . . No,
I haven't got the slip—they never sent me a slip! . . . Well, then
look it up, look it up!"

He slammed down the receiver, circled around the desk to
shake hands with us warmly, and after a general commendation,
brought forth a criticism. We had lost one vital ingredient in
the original story, he said—credibility.

"Boys, the central premise in this picture can't miss, and why
do I say that?" he asked the room. "I say that because it's pure
gold. Oakie and Haley, two talented hoofers stranded in New
York, find jobs in a wholesale meat concern trimming sides of
beef, unpacking the frozen turkeys, and grading sow bellies.
The boss has a beautiful daughter that they flip over, so to win
her hand they organize a musical show to celebrate the old
man's birthday which builds up into the biggest hit on Broadway. That to me is a dynamite springboard for laughs and
entertainment, but somehow you failed to make it believable."

He looked around uncertainly. "Did anyone else have that reaction?"

The gagmen, who through an oversight or because their status was too lowly had not been provided with copies of the script, were handicapped for an answer, but all three felt the story wholly plausible and fraught with paroxysms of mirth. The songsmiths began a long Talmudic analysis of various Broadway hits to demonstrate that logic would have been an impediment, if not downright fatal, to their success. Halfway through it, Lucille, Crown's secretary, appeared in the doorway, signalling urgently.

"Mr. Crown—excuse me! I'm having trouble with those reservations up at you-know-where."

"Sh-h-h!" Aghast at the possibility that she might have disclosed some vital detail of his romance, he bounded over to whisper in her ear. Simultaneously, the phone on his desk rang. "Pick it up, someone!" he appealed. "Can't you see I'm busy?"

I did so. The caller was Irving Hoffman, a columnist on the *Hollywood Reporter* I knew slightly. "What are you doing in Crown's office?" he asked. "Oh, I remember now—we ran an item you were on his musical with that swine, McGovern." I signified that the individual in question was within earshot. "Then pour in some henbane—the whole world will applaud you. Listen, an informant of ours at a store in Glendale says that Anatol's bought a hundred-piece dinner service from them, which could mean he's nesting. What's the score?"

Ere I could confirm or deny, Crown commandeered the phone and shouldered the burden of his own public relations. He was chirruping away to Hoffman, pretending elaborate surprise at the elopement rumors, when a sudden tumult became audible at the bungalow's entrance. Amid a babble of voices, half a dozen people crowded in around a studio grip carrying a recumbent figure: one of the lassies on the rowing machines had fainted. Immediately, everyone in the place became a combination of Sir William Osler and the Mayo Brothers, shouting "Get some water—no, ammonia!," "Put her head lower than her feet!," and similar Aesculapian precepts. The fair oarswoman was placed on the davenport, her forehead was laved and her wrists chafed, and in short order, her coral lips were wreathed in a weak smile. It was at that moment that Anatol Crown, his interview with Hoffman concluded, forced his way through the crush. He stared at the girl dazedly a moment, then knelt down beside her.

"How are you feeling, honey?"

"I—I guess I'll be all right."

"That's good," he said. "Tell me, what do you think of the script so far?"

II

The first time my wife and I worked on the M-G-M lot, we did a four-month stint for the fabled Irving Thalberg, in the fabled Irving Thalberg unit, on a yarn called *Greenwich Village*. A soi-disant original, *Greenwich Village* was possibly the most towering pyramid of clichés ever piled up by the human head, second only to *Bouvard et Pécuchet*, and it cried out for Flaubert to do the screenplay, but Gus was busy dialoguing *Salaambô* over at Twentieth and we drew the assignment. Unfortunately, we never got a clear reading from Mr. Thalberg about whether he wanted *La Vie de Bohème* or another *Rip Tide: The Story of a Woman's Conflicting Emotions* or a singing disaster film like *San Francisco,* so in the end, as the Tarot pack accurately predicted, we went back to Bucks County and he to Elysium. And now, two years later, we were again in Culver City, prepared to weave a tapestry or incise a scrimshaw for Thalberg's acknowledged equal and fellow-Titan, the fabled Hunt Stromberg.

Our first encounter, in the opulent office of his two-story villa, was heartening; the man was incontestably a satrap, as all of them were, but he differed from Thalberg as chalk from cheese. He was a large blond Oklahoman, rather earnest, a bit bland, not at all imperious—he had none of the other's knifelike, tiger-of-the-deep menace. In fact, the candor of his approach did much to establish a rapport between us.

"You know, I've got a confession to make," he said. "I did something that would scandalize most Hollywood producers—I brought you folks out here without a definite property in mind. I said to myself, I said, for once let's find out what ignites people to write—let *them* choose the material that stirs their creative juices, that primes their creative pump—and then give them complete freedom and unlimited time to develop it. How does that strike you?"

The clang of the hammer ridding us of our creative shackles stunned us temporarily, but we managed to stammer out our gratification.

"Fine," he said. "Now, I'm badly in need of a vehicle for two of my stars, William Powell and Luise Rainer. Have you seen anything at all in the theatre, have you read a novel or a short story or whatever that might fit their talents?"

Well, there flashed before me a montage of all the marvelous fictional characters they could play, like Willie Baxter and Lola Pratt in *Seventeen*, Dido and Aeneas, and Tom Sawyer and Becky Thatcher. Still, I speculated, didn't Powell have a bit too much mileage on him to whitewash fences and hide in organ lofts? Luckily, before I had a chance to blurt out any of these ideas, which would have entailed countless technical problems, my wife had a brain wave.

"Do you remember that comedy of the Theatre Guild's that Lunt and Fontanne were in called *At Mrs. Beam's?*" she reminded me. Its locale, she explained to Stromberg, was a London boardinghouse, and the Lunts had played a Brazilian couple, a volatile, jealous pair of adventurers who pummeled each other senseless and disrupted the entire place with their intrigues. Was that the sort of thing he envisioned?

Stromberg glowed. "Sounds like a terrific romp—just what I was hoping for. I'll get hold of it toot sweet and we'll huddle in a day or two."

Thirteen days dragged by, and when he surfaced it was to request that we tell him the plot, he had been too busy to read the play. The detailed recital by two people of a comedy, even if their name be Feydeau, is about as zestful as a dish of cold farina, and Stromberg's reaction was predictable. In a setting devoid of glamour, he said, two Brazilians beating up on each other did not necessarily spell box-office. The transition to his next remark, however, was lightning-fast. Had we perchance ever heard of a play by George Bernard Shaw called *Arms and the Man?* We said we had. What about an operetta called *The Chocolate Soldier?* Yes, that was Oscar Straus' musical version of the Shaw play. Lord love you, Mr. Stromberg, I thought, what in the world can you be getting at? He cut short our suspense in the next breath. Arising with the air of triumph Cagliostro displayed when performing his illusions, he laid his finger slyly alongside his nose.

"I," he announced, "am going to combine the two—*Arms and the Man* and *The Chocolate Soldier.* The wit of Bernard Shaw and the musical genius of Oscar Straus."

When the roaring in her head subsided, my mate found her voice. "This is for William Powell and Luise Rainer?"

"No, no, of course not." He paused theatrically before unveiling his surprise. "For Jeanette MacDonald and Nelson Eddy!"

The two of us sat there, stomachs gripped by the sickening contraction one feels when the elevator plunges twenty stories into the basement. So the honeymoon was over; all that marmalade about the perfect wedding of talent and subject matter was really anaesthesia. What babes in the wood we had been. We should have foreseen that the pastry chef for meringues like *The Firefly, Maytime,* and *Rose Marie* would inevitably spring the Iron Butterfly and the Singing Capon on us. And now, as if things weren't dire enough, Stromberg gave the vise another turn. Dismissing the Shavian mélange, he fastened on Victor Herbert's most emetic operetta, *Sweethearts,* as his final choice— meetings to be held forthwith at which we would savor the music and thresh out the story line.

In reality, what took place was no conference but the most extraordinary solo performance. For the next three days, Stromberg manfully wrestled our common language until he pinned its shoulders to the mat. Pacing up and down and with occasional musical interludes, he dictated to a pair of secretaries a long, Baudelairean prose poem—his conception of the project—for our guidance in forging the screenplay.

"I visualize Nelson in this production as a man's man," it ran in part. "Athletic, a bon vivant, and independently wealthy, he is always to be found where the sporting fancy congregates, such as the Madison Square Garden, the Kentucky Derby, Hialeah, etc. Is there a big track meet, six-day bike race, golf classic, or heavyweight championship fight? Why, there you will find Nelson cheering on the contestants, posting wagers, deeply absorbed in the fray. He knows but little of love and romance, having been raised in Hell's Kitchen where he hewed his way with his fists in sharp contrast to Jeanette's patrician background. She has sprung from an unbroken line stretching back to the *Mayflower*, the crème de la crème bulwarked by money and social position. Dainty, headstrong, impetuous, she is like some gorgeous orchid; she recks not of the morrow, avid to indulge that instant whim which will not be denied. Collide they must, these two strong personalities, producing musical sparks that pour from their throats in Victor Herbert's deathless score."

In affliction of this sort, as Edmond Dantès discovered, one falls back on minutiae for consolation. We found ours in two phenomena—the first the behavior of Stromberg's shoelaces, which, as he strode back and forth, used to untie and drag like an Indian brave's travois. The second was the ballet he engaged in daily with his pipes. Not long before, in trying to break the cigarette habit, he had assembled a rack of the costliest pipes the tobacconists of two continents could furnish. There were stubby little briars covered in pigskin, meerschaums pre-colored by generations of Black Forest woodsmen, churchwardens that had belonged to the Stuarts, pipes with metal covers to be smoked in the rain while wearing veldtschoen shoes. Whenever a sudden craving for the weed halted his discourse, Stromberg would snatch up one of the pipes, ignite half a dozen wooden matches and fling them aside in a spectacular display of pyrotechnics, and puff till his cheeks empurpled. "I don't know—

I can't make these Goddam things work!" he would exclaim fretfully. None of our po-faced quartet felt it politic to suggest that a pinch of tobacco from his rosewood and mahogany humidors might help.

Our gauleiter's larynx having finally seized up from hyperactivity, we were released and wrote a treatment whose bromides made his seem paltry. Before we could begin the screenplay, though, real life obtruded on the world of make-believe: my wife's obstetrician learned that M-G-M had no lying-in facilities for an impending event and withdrew her from the combo. There was a fortnight's quest for a suitable collaborator, who, to our mutual astonishment, turned out to be another domestic team, Dorothy Parker and Alan Campbell. Since they were country neighbors, I moved swiftly to brief them on the taffy pull they were joining, but Stromberg was not to be denied the pleasure of bombinating to fresh faces, and a second three-day parley began.

While I narrowly escaped migraine from the repetition of all the platitudes, there was one compensation: it was piquant to observe how one's friends behaved in an industrial setting as contrasted with the drawing room. Mrs. Parker discharged no immortal epigrams or salty apothegms; she sat in a deep armchair, Churchillian glasses athwart her nose, knitting a gray artifact seven feet long that looked like a staircase runner and keeping her lip buttoned. Campbell was the drive train of the duo, toothy, voluble, bubbling with suggestions, charming the birds out of the trees. Stromberg roved to and fro, declaiming his guidelines and prose poems. Every so often, he would veer toward Mrs. Parker and address her with timid respect.

"I'd say we were making pretty good progress on the story, eh, Dorothy?"

Mrs. Parker would look up, plainly retrieving her attention from very far away, and reply with a hint of breathlessness, "Oh, I *do* think it's altogether marvelous, don't you?"

By the afternoon of the third day, I was plumb tuckered out, so I really wasn't wide-awake when it happened. I remember Stromberg's laces trailing across the carpet; I saw him fussing

with his pipes and complaining; and I do recall kind of a mysti-
fying nimbus swirling around Mrs. Parker's head that was not
quite a halo. It was Campbell's piercing scream that wrenched
me upward.

"Dottie!" he shrieked. "You're on fire!"

Well, she wasn't, actually—it was just kapok, the stuffing
in her chair that was touched off by one of Stromberg's matches,
and it smoked and smoldered a bit after we yanked her out and
rolled her on the floor. People ran in, throwing Lily Cups of
water on the cushions, but the damage was piffling. The damage
to the chair, that is—the damage wrought by *Sweethearts* is still
being dealt with by therapists, I presume. But they can hardly
hold my wife and me responsible. God knows we had little
enough to do with it.

III

One burning July afternoon in the late fifties, a violet-and-
peach-colored object that was neither a flying saucer nor a
sizzling platter but a twin-propellered Cessna materialized in
the desert sky above the Palm Springs airport. Simultaneously,
a violet-and-peach-colored Rolls-Royce piloted by a chauffeur in
matching livery drew up at the terminal's arrival gate. In two
shakes of a lamb's tail—the official signal for aircraft to land
in Palm Springs—the plane had landed and a flourish of
trumpets greeted its three passengers, two of whom were familiar
to any bystander. They were the renowned *vedette* Elizabeth
Taylor and her producer husband, Mike Todd. The third, who
bore more than a passing resemblance to the *Apollo Belvedere*
but could not be said, in all justice, to rank with him intellect-
ually, was the present writer. His chief distinction—if one may
borrow G. K. Chesterton's facility with paradox for a moment—
was that he possessed no distinction whatsoever. What startling
conjunction of the planets, therefore, what mysterious and inexplicable forces of the I Ching had mingled the destiny of this
utter cipher with that of these eminent face cards? For the

answer, the reader would have been obliged to wire-tap a trans-continental phone call between the celebrated showman and my literary agent, one Mark Hanna.

Mark Hanna was a rara avis, a saturnine, hyperbolic fashion plate who secretly believed that it took more talent to bushel a seam than to compose an ode to a skylark. With a rose tucked behind his ear, he could have had a fabulous career as Blazes Boylan in any production of *Ulysses in Nighttown* on earth, but he preferred to lounge in an out-at-elbows cardigan in his office and wrangle with his clients. His noontime call to me consisted of three simple declarative sentences.

"Mike Todd's just been on the blower from L.A.," he reported. "He says he can't eat, he can't sleep unless you sky out to discuss his next blockbuster, *Don Quixote*. In his book, you are the greatest writer since Danny Aligheri, the guy who wrote the *Inferno*."

"I once heard the same refrain played on a flute in Bombay," I said. "Someone was trying to lure a cobra out of a drain. What is all this leading up to?"

"A round trip economy-class to the Coast plus a tiny per diem. The man just wants to drop a few pebbles into your mind and see if it gives off the right kind of echo."

"In view of the man's affluence, to which I partially contributed in a previous blockbuster of his," I replied, "would you say that his offer is princely?"

"No, but coming from a former carnival hustler, it reminds one of the Medici. You know, son, you really should be more tolerant—we all of us have our deficiencies. You, for example—given a normal physique, you could be fulfilling your real talent today."

"And what is that?"

"Spading up potatoes on the North Fork of Long Island." There was an interval during which Hanna listened to the veins throbbing in my temples, and then he became truly avuncular. Why not treat Todd's proposal as a lark, a jamboree, a paid vacation in the sun? As my wrath ebbed, little beads of tolerance trickled in to fill the vacuum, and I yielded.

On reaching the Los Angeles airport, I was intercepted by a hireling of the impresario, bearing my name in a cleft stick, who marinated me for a couple of hours in a VIP lounge until the other occupants of the Cessna appeared. The mere rumor of Elizabeth Taylor, naturally, had produced crowds of idolaters like worshippers of Kali, moaning and twitching and scourging themselves with copies of *Confidential* and the works of Mrs. Aphra Behn. Todd, who fed on turbulence as on catnip, was in seventh heaven; he ordered batteries of phones plugged in, telexes to start clacking, outriders and emissaries to mill to and fro, and in the end a cuadrilla of police was required to escort us onto the airship. Somewhere in the course of the flight, I was apprised that we were bound for a desert hideaway sublet from Marion Davies, where Mike and I could rap undisturbed and Elizabeth could familiarize herself with Owen Johnson's Lawrenceville stories, in which she had been proposed for the twin roles of Doc MacNooder and the Tennessee Shad.

Our arrival at the *estancia* was almost as exciting as our take-off. Awaiting Elizabeth outside were her two sons by a prior marriage aged four and six respectively, in charge of a German nanny. While they were embracing, Mike rushed to the trunk of the car and burrowed inside. In a moment, he returned with an aluminum model of a naval destroyer or escort vessel about a yard long. A jewel of craftsmanship such as a retired admiral would treasure in his den, it must have cost at least nineteen thousand dollars at F. A. O. Schwarz.

"Look what Daddy's brought you!" Todd shouted at the boys. "Boom, boom! Come watch it work!"

The effect on the lads was hardly that intended: the younger fell to the ground howling in fright; the elder stared paralyzed at Mike, torn between curiosity and dread. Then, like a jump cut in film, the action switched abruptly to the swimming pool. The women and the smaller boy had vanished, and Mike, a cigar gripped in his teeth, stood tugging furiously on a string designed to operate the toy, his face contorted like a Japanese print. At length, whether it was his maledictions or the lighter fluid he kept spraying into it, labor, in accordance with the adage,

vanquished all; there was an explosion and a hissing out of all
relation to its size, and the craft shot away popping and snorting
like an old sea dog. It went on ricocheting off the gutters and
creating such hubbub that a gardener ultimately had to beat it
with sticks till it subsided.

That evening the three of us drove into Chez Aloof, a restaurant staffed by very aloof Armenians, to dine with an octo-
genarian couple—East Coast plutocrats, I gathered—who owned
a first edition of *Don Quixote* that Mike was angling to borrow
for an establishing shot in the film. Just what the aged bibliophiles stood to gain from the transaction was unclear and was
further diffused by wave after wave of Daiquiris that inundated
us before the meal. I felt the grog beginning to shiver my
timbers when I heard the old gentleman relating an occurrence
at Lindy's in the twenties.

"I was lunching there that particular day with a friend of
mine, a wide-wale-corduroy importer, when who should come in
but this gambler, a party named Wolfsheim. He always wore
cuff links made of human teeth."

"And hung around with the eponymous Jay Gatz," I added
automatically.

"What did you say, young man?"

I shrugged. "Oh, nothing. I guess you also collect first editions
of Scott Fitzgerald, don't you?"

"Listen, you," he said, grasping my necktie. "I'm eighty-nine
years old, but I got a good mind to knock your block off."

"Just go ahead and try, old-timer," I dared him, and fell into
a fighter's crouch like Battling Nelson's, which, inasmuch as I
was sitting down, was not very ominous. "I'm a wide wale too,
and I'm pretty handy with my flukes."

The dispute never reached the squared circle because everyone by then, the help included, was overcome by creeping aloof-
ness and our party dissolved. The next morning, I arose early
for a scheduled discussion of *Don Quixote*. The temperature
was already in the nineties and the rest of the household was
nowhere in evidence, but Todd was out by the pool, enmeshed
in phone calls. Through the tie line in his New York offices, he

was checking the foreign grosses of his blockbuster in Bulawayo, Dortmund, Nicosia, Juneau, and Stavanger, uttering mingled cries of jubilation and heartburn. Interthreaded with these were calls to his brokers, lawyers, press agents, backers, various casinos and racetracks, and stagefolk innumerable. At twelve forty-five he got up and stretched.

"That's all for now," he said. "Now, this aft I'm having some steam with Harry Conn at the Racquet Club. There's milk and cookies for your lunch in the kitchen, and I'll be back at four ready for work, so stand by—do you hear? Don't goof off anywhere."

As the hours dragged by and the heat rose into the low hundreds, I began to feel mutinous. How insupportable that those two panjandrums should luxuriate in the steam while I sat on this marble bench at poolside frying myself into a plateful of goose cracklings. And how self-centered of Mike, how inconsiderate of him not to suggest some pastime to beguile the time. A more kindly nature would have invited me to gather the grass clippings, or to botanize the many interesting genera of cacti baking away in the gneiss outside the estate. . . . Oh, well, the devil with these ungenerous reflections; I would do far better to immerse myself in the paperback copy of *Don Quixote* my host had laid out for our meeting. So I did so literally, draping its pages over my crown to buffer it against the pitiless rays of Old Sol, and slept like a baby until Todd's voice aroused me. He was on the phone again, this time checking the blockbuster grosses in Cayenne, Windhoek, Djibouti, Vaduz, and Binghamton. It was dusk when he finished.

"About time you woke up, for Crissake," he said. "O.K., got the cobwebs out of your brain? What's the verdict?"

"About what?"

"The story—what do you think I'm talking about, the World Series? Does it excite you?"

"No, I wouldn't say it does that . . ."

"Then what does it do?"

"Oh, Mike," I pleaded. "Don't ask me that, please. Everything's been so perfect up to now . . ."

Todd removed his cigar and stared at me in alarm. "Say, what the hell's wrong with you?"

"Look," I said earnestly. "I hope what I'm about to say isn't going to affect our friendship. You didn't write the story and I didn't write the story. Cervantes wrote it, and he's not here." I cast a hurried glance about. "That is, I *say* he's not here, but who knows?"

"Goddam it, will you get to the point?"

"All right. The truth is, Mike, no matter how many times I've tried to read *Don Quixote*, I've never been able to get beyond page six. Indeed, so soporific is its effect that I believe it should be withdrawn from libraries everywhere and dispensed only on prescription."

He looked at me as though he had just bitten into a quince. "So that's your considered opinion, is it, wise guy?"

"No, a much wiser guy's. Aldous Huxley once called it the world's most unread classic."

Todd eyed me vindictively. "And I thought you were the only one on earth to do the screenplay. Well, thank God I found out in time, and not from you."

"Oh?" I said. "From who else?"

"Harry Cohn," he said. "He warned me in the steam. He heard that Universal let you go after two days."

Which shows how life always catches up with you.

SECOND EDITION

What Color Is Your Parachute?

FOR RETIREMENT

Planning a Prosperous, Healthy, and Happy Future

JOHN E. NELSON and RICHARD N. BOLLES

TEN SPEED PRESS

Berkeley

Published in the United States by Ten Speed Press, an imprint of the Crown Publishing Group, a division of Random House, Inc., New York.
www.crownpublishing.com
www.tenspeed.com

Ten Speed Press and the Ten Speed Press colophon are registered trademarks of Random House, Inc.

A previous edition of this work was published in the United States by Ten Speed Press, Berkeley, CA, in 2007.

Library of Congress Cataloging-in-Publication Data

Nelson, John E.
  What color is your parachute? for retirement : planning a prosperous, healthy, and happy future / John E. Nelson and Richard N. Bolles. — 2nd ed.
    p. cm.
  Bolles's name appears first in the previous ed.
  Includes index.
  Summary: "A revised edition of the definitive retirement guide for people of all career stages"—Provided by publisher.
  1. Retirement income—Planning. 2. Retirement—Planning. I. Bolles, Richard Nelson. II. Bolles, Richard Nelson. What color is your parachute? for retirement. III. Title.
  HG179.B575 2010
  332.024'014—dc22

                            2010005578

ISBN 978-1-58008-205-1

Printed in the United States of America

Design by Betsy Stromberg

10 9 8 7 6 5 4 3 2 1

Second Edition

To my mother.
You were a better role model than I knew.

—JOHN E. NELSON

Contents

Preface

This book is part of what we call *The Parachute Library*. Like all books in that Library, it is not intended as a substitute or replacement for its best-selling centerpiece, *What Color Is Your Parachute? A Practical Guide for Job-Hunters and Career-Changers* (ten million copies in print), but as a supplement to it.

Why do we need a supplement? Well, each *time* of Life has special issues and special challenges, where we all could use a little extra guidance. The *time* of Life from age fifty, on, is one of those times. I have a friend named John Nelson, who is an expert on that *time* of Life, and therefore I have asked him to write this book.

My contribution to this book is twofold: (1) To frame some of the questions and challenges during this period, as I have done in my earlier work *The Three Boxes of Life, and How to Get Out of Them: An Introduction to Life/Work Planning* (1978). (2) To write this introduction and overview, to get us going.

The *time* of Life that we are talking about here is traditionally called "Retirement." Some people love that word. I'm not one of them. For me, it implies "being put out to pasture"—to borrow an image from a cow. It implies a kind of parole from a thing called *work*, which is assumed to be onerous, and tedious. It implies "disengagement" from both *work* and *Life*, as one patiently—or impatiently—waits to die. It thinks of Life in terms of work.

I prefer instead to think of Life in terms of music. My favorite metaphor is that of a symphony. A symphony, traditionally, has four parts to it—four movements, as they're called. So does Life. There is infancy, then the time of learning, then the time of working, and finally, this time that we are talking about, often called "retirement." But if we discourage the use of the word "retirement," then this might better be called the Fourth Movement.

The Fourth Movement, in the symphonic world, is a kind of blank slate. It was and is up to the composer to decide what to write upon it. Traditionally, the composer writes of triumph, victory, and joy—as in Beethoven's Symphony #3, the *Eroica*. But it may, alternatively, be a kind of anticlimactic, meandering piece of music—as in Tchaikovsky's Symphony #6, the *Pathetique*. There the Third Movement ends with a bombastic, stirring march. The Fourth Movement, immediately following, is subdued, meditative, meandering, and sounds almost like an afterthought.

Well, there are our choices about our own lives: Shall the Fourth Movement, the final movement, of our lives be *pathetique or eroica*—pathetic or heroic? Your call!

I like this defining of our lives in terms of music, rather than in terms of work.

To carry the metaphor onward, in this Fourth Movement of our lives, we have instruments, which we must treat with care. They are: our **body**, our **mind**, our **spirit**, and what we poetically speak of as our **heart**, which Chinese medicine calls "the Emperor."[1] Body, mind, spirit, heart. Some of these instruments are in shiny, splendid condition. Others are slightly dented. Or greatly dented. But these are the instruments that play the musical notes and themes of this time of our lives.

The traditional notes are: **sleep, water, eating, faith, love, loneliness, survival** (financial and spiritual), **health care, dreams** (fulfilled or unfulfilled), and **triumph**—over all adversities—and even **death**.

Traditionally, the themes for this period of our lives also include *planning*. But I believe the outstanding characteristic of the Fourth Movement in our lives is the increased number of things we call *unexpected*. And that can knock all our plans into a cocked hat. So I prefer to say that

---

1. www.itmonline.org/5organs/heart.htm

one of the notes we strike, is how to handle interruptions. Martin Luther King, Jr., perhaps put it best, just before his death:

> "The major problem of life is learning how to handle the costly interruptions—the door that slams shut, the plan that got sidetracked, the marriage that failed, or that lovely poem that didn't get written because someone knocked on the door."

Interruptions, in music, are the pauses between the notes; they are, in fact, what keep the notes from just becoming a jumble. Just listen to the first few bars of Beethoven's Fifth. Thank God for the interruptions, the spaces between the notes.

So, where have we come thus far? Well, I suggested that it is useful to think of Life after fifty as the Fourth Movement in the symphony of our lives—the movement that comes after the first three: Infancy, then The Time of Learning, and then The Time of Working. And it is useful to think that we have instruments, which play certain themes in this movement, as we have seen. That brings us to the $64,000 question: "Toward what end? What is the point of all these notes, all these themes, in the Fourth Movement? What are they intended to produce?"

Ahhh, when I think of the overall impression left with me after I hear the Fourth Movement of any great symphony, such as Schubert's Ninth, one impression sticks out, above all others. And that impression is one of *energy*. I am left with an impression of great energy. And the more the better, say I. Energy is lovely to behold, and even lovelier to possess. That energy belongs in the Fourth Movement because it brings the whole symphony to triumphant resolution.

This, it seems to me, is how people evaluate the Fourth Movement of our lives, as well. Not: Did we live triumphantly and die victoriously; but: Do we manifest *energy*? Do we manifest enthusiasm? Do we manifest excitement, still?

Ask any employer what they are looking for, when they interview a job candidate who is fifty years or older, and they will tell you: energy. They ask themselves, "Does the candidate (*that's us*) slouch in the chair? Does the candidate look like they're just marking time in Life? Or does the candidate lean slightly forward in the chair as we talk? Does the candidate seem excited about the prospect of working here?"

Energy in people past fifty is exciting to an employer. And to those around us. It suggests the candidate will come in early, and stay late. It suggests that whatever task is given, the task will be done thoroughly and completely, and not just barely or perfunctorily.

All right, then, *energy*. Where shall we find energy, after fifty? When we were young, energy resided in the physical side of our nature. We were "feeling our oats." We could go all day, and go all night. "My, where do you get all your energy," our grandmother would ask us. We were a dynamo of physical energy.

Can't say the same when we reach fifty, and beyond. Oh, some of us still have it. But as we get older the rest of us start to slow down. Physical energy is often harder to come by, despite workouts and exercise and marathons. Increasingly, our energy must more and more come from *within*. It must spring not from our muscles but from our excitement about Life and about what we are doing in this Fourth and final Movement of our Life.

That is why, past fifty, we need to spend more time on the homework of inventorying what in Life we are (still) passionate about. The questions of our youth—**what** *are your favorite skills?* **where** *do you most enjoy using them? and* **how** *do you find such a place and such a job or endeavor?*— become critical when we are past fifty.[2] The nicest compliment any of us can hear as we grow older, is: "What a passion for life she still has! Or, he has! It's thrilling to be around them."

And so, it is time to turn to the body of this book. All of the *frame* that John Nelson proposes, for our looking at this time of our Life, all the *questions* he suggests we must ask ourselves, and all of the *inventory* that he suggests we should do, are essential to finding our *energy* in this Fourth and final Movement of the symphony of our Life. Come with me, as we enter the main body of the book. And we shall make beautiful music, together.

—Richard N. Bolles

2. Detailed instructions for getting at these questions can be found in my book *What Color Is Your Parachute?*, updated annually, and available in any bookstore.

What to Expect from This New Edition

You may be wondering what's new in this edition of *What Color Is Your Parachute? for Retirement*.

First, you'll notice that this edition captures the continuing evolution of retirement as a life stage. Chapter by chapter, it shows how society is irrevocably remaking the *old* retirement into a *new* retirement. But because we're still in the process of creating it, no one knows yet, for sure, what that will mean. This book helps you prepare for that shift.

Second, you'll notice that this edition provides you with additional planning tools and techniques. Even with all the uncertainty, you'll still have more freedom in retirement than in any other stage of life. This book helps you design, and take concrete steps toward, the life of your dreams.

The universal dream is prosperity, health, and happiness—otherwise known as well-being. But many feel that economic uncertainty threatens their dreams. How do all these evolving forces affect you and your plans for retirement?

Financially, we've seen our retirement accounts and home values take the roller-coaster ride of a lifetime. Traditional pensions, which offer a guaranteed monthly benefit, have increasingly shown signs of inadequate employer funding. Social Security is facing a similar problem on a larger scale. The ballooning federal debt complicates long-term fixes for Social Security and Medicare funding problems. At all levels, governments will be forced to rethink the assistance they provide to a rapidly growing number of older citizens. Uncertainty has prompted many to keep working as long as possible. Have we now come to view continued employment as an expected part of retirement?

Geographically, we've begun to think more deeply about where we really want to live. Rather than speculating on future home values, we're viewing our home and community as environments that support the life we want to lead.

Medically, we know retirement is a life stage that brings increased interaction with the medical delivery system. But the system itself will be undergoing significant changes in the coming years—just when we'll personally need more care. One effect of economic stress is to drain our biological vitality, so it's even more important for each of us to build that vitality up.

Psychologically, the concept of retirement happiness as carefree decades of leisure is now out of date and out of step. It's being replaced by our desire for a deeper sense of fulfillment and engagement in life. From now on, we're more likely to recognize that our happiness is more connected to our sense of community than to our level of consumption.

You can use this book to gain insight and make plans for *all* these areas of your life, because it's unique. It's not a finance book (although it is about prosperity). It's not a medical book (although it is about health). And it's not a psychology book (although it is about happiness). It's a well-being book.

You might think of this as an *introductory course* on all the aspects of designing your retirement life. Or if you've already studied retirement, you might think of this as your *capstone* course, pulling all of your studies together. Either way, you'll find this book to be both a philosophical and a practical resource.

Finally, here's a bit of heartfelt advice for you. The best way to use this book is to actually do the exercises, fill in the blanks, and write all over the pages. I provide you with a *process* for designing your Ideal Retirement. But you, dear reader, must provide the *content*. That's how you make this *your* book, instead of *my* book.

After all, it's your retirement, isn't it?

—John E. Nelson

"I know that someday I will die, but I will never retire."

—MARGARET MEAD, renowned anthropologist

Chapter ONE

Retirement Is Dead— Long Live Retirement!

In centuries past, when a king lay dying, there would be great concern among the people. They were sad about losing a ruler they knew. And anxious, too, about getting a new ruler that they didn't know. The kingdom was changing. What would happen to them? As the old king took his final breath, and his successor became king, a cry would ring out among the people:

"The king is dead—long live the king!"

That is what's happening to the life stage we call "retirement." At all levels—individual, organizational, and societal—it's dying. And it's dying sooner than we thought. The successor is a new, unknown, and quite different life stage—which will also be called "retirement." The kingdom is changing. What will happen to you?

While all these changes are going on around you, you'll be making key decisions about your next stage of life. Because there are no rules for this new version of retirement, you'll need to design it for yourself. This book will help you make those decisions, and help you design the life you want to live.

Where do you stand now? If you've been working steadily toward the *old-fashioned version of retirement*, you can probably still get there, if you really want to. If you're anxious about the uncertainties of the *new retire-ment*, you can take concrete steps to protect yourself. If you're curious about the new possibilities that are opening up, you can explore those. And if you don't think you'll ever have a retirement (new or old), you can identify what might keep you going. Whatever your situation, you'll dis-cover something useful here.

You'll also discover that this book isn't about just one aspect of retirement. It's about you, and all the parts of your life. For example, most retirement books focus on finances, and come from the narrow perspective of money and managing the affairs of the world. Other books focus on health, and come from the narrow perspective of medi-cine and managing your physical body. Still others focus on happiness, and come from the narrow perspective of your relationship with your-self and others. *This book is unusual because it integrates all those aspects of your life.* So instead of coming from one of those narrow perspec-tives, this book takes your perspective. It's you-centered, rather than topic-centered!

Why You Won't Find Everything You Need within This Book

To design the life you want to live, you'll need to do some real research and make some important decisions. However, you won't find *all* the information you need within these humble pages. The world—and the world of retirement—is now simply too big and too complicated. It wasn't so long ago that there was a shortage of information out in the world, and the purpose of a book like this was to collect and preserve that scarce resource. To obtain in-depth information on a specific topic like retirement, you traveled to a repository in the physical world—a library or bookstore. There were only a few designated places where in-depth information was indexed, catalogued, and stored, so that you could obtain it when you needed it. The world was almost like a knowl-edge desert, and a book was like an oasis of knowledge. In that bygone era (just a few years ago), most people valued books mostly for the *con-tent* that they offered.

But now it's the opposite! There's a *surplus* of information in the world. There's more floating around than we know what to do with. From television to magazines to advertising to bloggers to Google searches, it's simply endless. It keeps pouring in, more and more of it, every day. We are awash in information. And it's not just of a general nature. Anyone with an internet connection can drill down to find and retrieve the most specific, technical, and obscure tidbits that you can imagine. Although some of what we access is simply data, much of it is actual knowledge. That is, it's well-considered advice from people who truly know what they're talking about, within their own area of expertise. The world isn't an information desert anymore.

If the World Is Full of Information, Then What's This Book For?

Due to the ever-present, immediate, and endless electronic delivery of in-depth information, there is now more of it available *outside* of books than *inside* them. If you can obtain knowledge through your broadband connection, then what's a book for? In this case, the book you're holding has a more important job than merely providing more information. Its job is to help you understand the sea of information in a new way. As it turns out, there are *three fundamental problems* with the way the sea of information operates.

The first problem with the sea of information is that it's actually incoherent. It just splashes around, with no sense of order. So this book provides a *coherent structure for organizing information*. That way, you'll be able to bring order to the chaos of the modern information world.

The second problem with the sea of information is that it's relentless. It's like a fire hose that's forever trying to fill you up, as though you were an empty barrel. So this book provides a way to *reflect upon, draw out, and crystallize* the wisdom you already have. It's at the confluence of the information stream and your own stream of consciousness, that you'll make your best decisions.

The third problem with the sea of information is that it's fickle—the current flows one way and then another. Because there's no direction, who knows where you might end up? So this book helps you *choose your own destination* and set a course to get there, no matter which way the winds are blowing.

Unlike the stream of information, this book is something secure that you can get a hold of. Unlike that anonymous information that flows by and is gone forever, when you use this book, you'll be organizing and clarifying your own information, thoughts, and dreams. (Try doing that with Google!)

Truth be told, there really is a lot of content in this book. Most of it can't be found anywhere else. But just as important, you'll find a unique *process* for designing the life of your dreams. A process that offers a coherent structure, recognizes what you already know, and provides a constancy of vision. When you read this book and do the exercises, you'll become better and better at navigating that ever-changing sea of information out there. You'll be the captain of your own ship, sailing toward your own destination.

Retirement As a Gradual Process

So—what *is* the destination, anyway? Where are we supposed to be heading? Why are we supposed to retire? After all, for 98 percent of human history, retirement didn't really exist!

For eons, most people worked for themselves, and with their families. They were hunters or farmers or fishers or craftspeople or traders. They pretty much kept working into their later years, because they weren't wealthy enough to stop working. (There have always been a few wealthy people who could stop working, of course. But most people couldn't.) As they aged, they worked at a slower pace, relying less and less on their physical strength and stamina and more and more on their acquired knowledge and skills. If they were clever and fortunate, they found ways to do more of the work that they liked (and less of the work that they didn't). But most people couldn't afford to stop working, and so they kept on, as best they could, as long as they needed to. Except in the case of sickness or accident, withdrawing from work was a gradual process. The human life course had a long and gradual arc, with gentle transitions from one life stage to the next. It was a natural way to live, and it was like that for thousands of years.

Before the industrial age, life transitions were more gradual.

The Life and Age of Man and *The Life and Age of Woman*, James Baillie, 1848.

So what happened? The Industrial Revolution! Many of the people who had worked the land or pursued their own cottage crafts went to work in factories for someone else, or for something else—a corporation. Most of them did it willingly, because they could earn more money and improve their material standard of living. The industrial laborer's life was very different, though. In factories, everything was standardized. All the machines were in rows. All the nuts and bolts were in standard sizes. And people's *activities* became standardized, too. Instead of using their unique skills, workers with the same jobs were supposed to do the same things in the same way. Also, people's working *time* became standardized. Everyone worked in shifts, with each shift's workers starting at the same time, taking a break at the same time, and quitting at the same time. At the end of the day, as one shift of workers left, another was waiting to take its place.

The work in factories was fast, demanding, and repetitive. People had always worked hard, but not in such a structured, mechanistic way. As workers aged, they couldn't gradually slow down. They couldn't focus more on using their knowledge and skills, as they had in preindustrial times. After all, factories were organized around efficient production, not around the natural life course of humans. Workers were seen almost as a part of the machines they operated. (Charlie Chaplin's movie *Modern Times* was a serious comedy on that topic.)

Factory owners decided to get the slower, older workers out of the factory by implementing a new practice: retirement. It was similar to replacing the worn-out part of a machine. After all, with an increasing population, there were plenty of younger, stronger, faster workers ready to fill those jobs. It was also pretty easy to sell the idea of retirement to workers—especially when it included a retirement pension! The jobs were physically demanding, dirty, and dangerous. Much of it was sheer drudgery, so the simple absence of this nasty work, in itself, was a reward. As general prosperity increased, more and more people were able to stop working as they got older. Given the nature of the work, who wouldn't want to retire?

THE ONE BEST WAY TO RETIRE?

In the early days of the twentieth century, the Industrial Revolution was getting up to full speed in the United States. The industrial workplace was so different from the old agrarian way of life that experts needed to develop completely new ways of thinking about work, workers, and the workplace.

A revolutionary thinker of the day was Frederick Winslow Taylor (1856–1915). He was essentially the very first management consultant. Taylor's seminal ideas were outlined in his book *The Principles of Scientific Management*. One seminal idea was to expand standardization from things (like nuts and bolts) to human behaviors. His goal was to discover the "One Best Way" to do each job and then make sure every worker did the job in that exact way. This thinking sparked a new profession—the efficiency expert—which ultimately transformed the industrial workplace. But it went way beyond industry. This way of thinking spread to construction, the military, offices, professions, and even schools. Peter Drucker, the famous management guru, suggested that "Taylorism" might have been the United States' most important contribution to new thought since the framing of the Constitution. The impact was International as well: *The Principles of Scientific Management* sold one and a half million copies in Japan.

We don't know what Taylor would have personally thought about a standardized approach to retirement. He only lived to the age of fifty-nine. However, the Taylorism movement wanted to standardize everything in its path, and that could have included retirement. Anyway, the idea of a standard approach to retirement is truly a relic of twentieth-century thinking. Isn't it time to move retirement into the twenty-first century?

A Standardized Approach to Retirement

Like everything else in the factory, though, retirement needed to be standardized. So employers selected standard ages for retirement. In fact, it was often called the "normal retirement age." It could vary, but let's take age sixty-five as an example. At that time, workers who made it to sixty-five were, in general, pretty worn-out. But not all of them. There was a huge variation in how worn-out people were at that age.

It didn't matter that at any given retirement age, one worker might be as fit as a fiddle and the next one had a foot in the grave. Or that one person loved the work he was doing and was productive, while the next one hated it and barely kept up. None of that was taken into consideration, and for the sake of standardization, retirement was based on age. After all, for employers and employees, age is easy to measure and to specify. How healthy a person is, or how much that person loves the job, is certainly more relevant to the timing of retirement—but that couldn't be easily measured.

So the die was cast. This standardized approach to retirement, based on age, meant that instead of the withdrawal from work happening gradually, as it had for most of human history, it became an all-or-nothing deal. When the idea of retirement was created, it was created as an event—a specific point in time. Before workers reached the retirement date, they went to work full time, every day. When they reached that date, they stopped working completely, all at once. Retirement was radically different than the more gradual transitions that humans had always known. But it made sense for the factory.

This standardize-everything mentality spread far beyond the factory and into offices and professions. The federal government took the same approach as the organizations that had implemented pensions. When Social Security was instituted in 1936 with a standardized age, that was the end of the story. Retirement became an all-or-nothing event. Retirement became the finish line of life.

In the old retirement, then, the idea of standardization stuck. It stuck with employees, with employers, and with the government. It has stuck around for well over half a century. But you're not stuck with it.

When you go about designing the new retirement, a good place to start is with the transition itself. Could you choose your own timing, and transition gradually, like humans did before retirement was created? Think how different that would be than an all-or-nothing event.

Is Retirement a Finish Line or Just a Marker along the Way?

Unfortunately, a retirement finish line can give us a countdown mentality: "Only five years, eight months, two weeks, and four days to go—hallelujah!" A countdown mentality can make us unintentionally put our life on hold. On a more subtle level, it can leave us feeling powerless, as if we were not in control of our lives. It can make us feel that we need to wait until the normal retirement age to become emancipated—when finally, at last, we'll be set free to do what we really want with our lives.

Or just as dangerously, a retirement finish line may induce us to retire on the standard schedule, even though we're not ready. What if we're not financially prepared to retire? What if we're as healthy as a horse with no signs of slowing down? What if we still find our work or coworkers engaging and energizing? The pressure of the standardized retirement age can make us disregard our own unique situation.

Rather than being driven by your "normal retirement age," perhaps there is another way that you can look at it. Is your work holding you up or holding you back? Sustaining you or squelching you? Is your job a leash or a lifeline? Those questions may be more relevant in deciding when and how to retire than the age on your driver's license.

Although your employer, your benefits provider, and the government all use standardized ages for retirement, that doesn't mean you have to. Instead of automatically accepting some arbitrary ages and dates, you can come up with your own. Then be sure to brainstorm with a knowledgeable expert (or two or three) on how to compromise between your own schedule and those all-important regulations. If you're short on money, you might need to customize for a later retirement age. If you're short on health, you might need to customize for more work flexibility. If you're short on happiness, you might need to customize for your sanity!

Depending on your job and your employer, you may have almost no flexibility in customizing your transition, or you may have a great deal. (If you're one of the ever-growing numbers of entrepreneurs or solopreneurs, you have carte blanche—so you can get really creative.) In some cases, employers are willing to bend over backward to accommodate workers, and in other cases they won't bend an inch. If your knowledge or skills are in high demand and low supply, your employer may be eager to entertain your creative ideas about a "flex retirement." But if your employer sees you as just one more cog in the machine and imagines that there are plenty more cogs where you came from, you don't have much bargaining power.

Your flexibility in your job, with your employer, in your industry is ruled by the particularities of your situation, rather than the generalities of the marketplace. You won't know how much you can customize your retirement transition unless you try. Also, you know best what the culture of your workplace is—and how close to the vest you need to keep your retirement cards. At some organizations, if an employee so much as admits that some day, in the far distant future, he or she might possibly want to retire, the employer will immediately suspect that the worker is starting to slack off and not taking the job seriously. If you know that to be the case at your organization, you don't need me to tell you to be discreet! If, however, your organization is one where you can be upfront about your long-term and short-term plans, that's much better for you and for your employer, too. Remember, you and your employer are both making up new ways of transitioning to retirement. You may need to be a trailblazer to customize your transition. Just be careful not to get burned!

TEN WAYS TO CUSTOMIZE YOUR RETIREMENT TRANSITION

Here's a list of ideas, just to spark your creativity. You might:

1. Change to a career you love, that you could do forever, more or less. (Probably less.)

2. Start a business on the side, and keep it going after you retire from your regular job.

3. Slash your living expenses, save like a crazy person, and take an early retirement offer. (But be ready to work again, if need be.)

4. Take early retirement like #3, but plan to try a new career. So what if it doesn't work out?

5. Refocus your job on what you do really, really well, then retire late because you're so valuable.

6. Get rid of the worst parts of your job, then work part-time to do only the best parts.

7. Negotiate a phased retirement, where your employer lets you taper off over months or years.

8. Open the door to a revolving retirement, where you come back periodically or for specific projects.

9. Take a standard retirement, then work for a customer, a supplier, or even a competitor.

10. Take a standard retirement, but become a consultant in your field. (Many people claim they're going to do this, but never follow through. Are you different?)

CAUTION: Finding a way to stretch your transition can be difficult, but it increases your financial security. Finding a way to cut short your transition can be easy, but it decreases your financial security. Always look before you leap.

Transitions and the Three Boxes of Life

Changing the way we transition to a stage of life is an important issue. There's an even more important one, though. What are the life stages themselves? Could you make up your own life stages, if you wanted to?

Let's start with the standard-issue life stages, and transitions, the way most of us were brought up to think of them. The retirement event has been the doorway from the life stage of work into the life stage of retirement. And much earlier, another event—graduation—was the doorway from the life stage of education into the life stage of work. These transitions divided life into three stages: education, work, and retirement. These have been so rigid, and so closed off from each other, that we could even think of them as *boxes*. (This idea was first put forth by Richard N. Bolles in his book *The Three Boxes of Life*.) They look like this:

For most of human history, these boxes didn't exist for most people. Children farmed and fished and crafted with their families from an early age. Then, when the Industrial Revolution happened, children went to work in factories instead. (It sounds appalling to you now, doesn't it?) When economic prosperity increased enough, society was able to create the education box. There was a cost to doing that, but it was an investment in the future. The education box directed the people in it toward the activities of learning and self-development. That meant that only adults would be in the box called work. They were the ones directed toward the activities of working and being productive. Finally, when prosperity had increased enough again, we created the box called retirement. There was a cost to society for creating that box, too.

The retirement box was unique in one way, though. Instead of being defined by what the people in it could and should do, it was defined by what they couldn't and shouldn't do! Specifically, they shouldn't be learning and developing. And they shouldn't be working and productive, either. You know the story of how the old retirement was born: It was created for older workers who were too worn-out to learn anything or produce anything new. There's a name for what they could do—it's called *leisure*.

So, across the life course, we were supposed to first focus on self-development (the first box), then on being productive (the second box), and then on leisure. So the *contents* of the three boxes look like this:

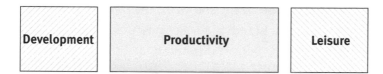

When young people are in the box of education, their parents, teachers, and peers create an environment that pretty much tells them what to do. They may think they're "doing their own thing." But if they get off course, others in the education box usually straighten them out—in a well-meaning way—and put them back on the standardized path. So when it comes down to it, the first box doesn't allow much freedom. Society in general, and families in particular, must provide support for that box, so they run the show.

Likewise, when people are in the box of work, the supervisors, coworkers, and their own professional expectations keep them in line. Although they're adults, the environment pretty much tells them what they should be doing. They definitely have more freedom and more choices. But society needs people in the second box to support the ones in the first and third boxes, so they pretty much keep their noses to the grindstone.

The Old Retirement Was the Final Box of Life

What about the retirement box? When the old retirement was created, the people in it were retiring from old-fashioned factories or other demanding work, and typically in declining health. Most of them were going to live only a few years in retirement. They were retiring to a life of leisure, because that's all they were capable of. And unlike the earlier boxes, there weren't many societal expectations. No parents, teachers, or supervisors to keep retirees in line. They were left alone, to do whatever they wanted, with the short time they had left. Society and employers provided significant economic support for this nonproductive life stage through Social Security and retirement pensions.

This was a major achievement of modern society. All three boxes were in place, and supported by societal institutions. Everyone knew what they were supposed to be doing, and when they were supposed to be doing it. The structure and funding for education was in place, and working pretty well. The structure and funding for retirement was in place, and working pretty well, too. After thousands of years of gradual life-stage transitions, the human life course had been changed forever. It was now neatly divided into three well-defined boxes. Society was great!

Breaking Down the Boxes

Then, as time went on, something amazing happened. The retirees didn't die. Well, they died, but not as soon as expected. For a variety of reasons, they kept living longer. Each group of retirees lived longer than the previous groups had. And they weren't just living longer, they were healthier and more active, too. The leisure box extended, and the Three Boxes of Life changed to look like this:

At the same time, workers were looking at the old retirement and deciding that they'd like to get there as early as possible. With personal savings, employer pensions, and Social Security, the average age for retirement became younger. The productivity box shortened a bit, and the leisure box was even longer. The three boxes looked like this:

Development	Productivity	Leisure

The retirement stage of life had been transformed. Instead of being worn-out and sick for much of their retirement, people were healthy and vital. Instead of lasting just a few years, retirement stretched out to a decade or more. And because no one was telling them what to do, retirees could do whatever they wanted. Some decided that an entire life stage based on leisure didn't make sense. They forgot (or never knew) that productivity and development were supposed to be off-limits. They took up formal and informal learning, new careers, significant volunteer work— you name it, they did it. They mixed up development, productivity, and leisure all in one box! They made the earlier, healthier part of retirement into a completely different stage of life than the old retirement was supposed to be. Only the later part of retirement looked like the original idea, as people became frailer and were winding down their lives. It looked like this:

Development	Productivity	Development Productivity Leisure	Leisure

From the Three Boxes to the Four Ages

In the 1980s, a historian at Cambridge University by the name of Peter Laslett had anticipated what would happen. He knew that the original idea of retirement—the old retirement—couldn't stretch enough to fit what was happening in the world. He saw that the healthy, active, early part of retirement wasn't very much like the frail, inactive, later part. They were altogether different ages of life. At the same time, the last years of the second box were becoming more and more varied. Some workers were retiring, or semi-retiring, in their fifties. They were still supposed to be in the second box but were living more like the healthy, active early part of the third box. Laslett realized that to understand what was going on, and to make plans for ourselves, we needed a fresh map of life. It looks like this:

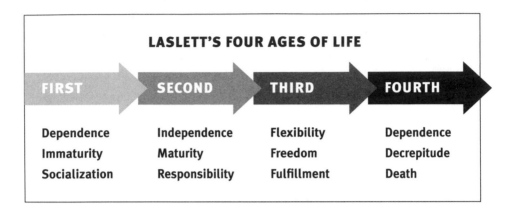

LASLETT'S FOUR AGES OF LIFE

FIRST	SECOND	THIRD	FOURTH
Dependence	Independence	Flexibility	Dependence
Immaturity	Maturity	Freedom	Decrepitude
Socialization	Responsibility	Fulfillment	Death

Laslett's description of the First and Second Ages are equivalent to the first and second boxes. His description of the Fourth Age has similarities to the original industrial-age retirement—sickly and short. But his concept for the Third Age is something else altogether. He recognized that for the first time in human history, we were creating a life stage that had significantly reduced responsibilities—but also continuing health and vitality. As people at midlife were gradually freed from child care and work, what would they do with that freedom? He suggested that this newfound opportunity could be the peak of human achievement. Rather than being *over the hill*, people could be *climbing the summit* of life. They could develop themselves to their full capacity and attain their greatest degree of life fulfillment. He even referred to it as the "crown" of life! Rather than defining it by specific ages, he suggested that the Third Age is defined by an orientation toward life. Laslett was a good role model, as his book on this subject was published when he was seventy-four. For many of us, the Third Age is most likely to occur between the ages of fifty and seventy-five. We may be working, retired, or somewhere in between. But that's less of a factor than our commitment to fully explore, develop, and express ourselves. The fact that you're reading this book right now is an indication that the idea of the Third Age probably appeals to you.

You Could Have a Third Age of Life— Whether or Not You're Retired

What interesting new combination of work, learning, and leisure would you like to create? The more creative you are, the less retirement income you may need. In our consumer culture, advertising tries to convince us that happiness can be found mostly with a credit card. It can take tons of money to fund a retirement that's based on all leisure all the time. You could be saving up forever to afford such a retirement.

In contrast, learning is pretty inexpensive. Public universities and community colleges often provide courses at nominal cost for retirees. Many faith communities sponsor programs for both self-exploration and socializing. Nonprofit entities such as Elderhostel sponsor low-cost opportunities to explore and learn about the world. Senior-level athletic events are also becoming more common. On a more individual level, you're free to explore hobbies or activities that are based on self-development rather than entertainment. Self-development can be a bargain.

Productivity can be even better than a bargain. It can cost as little or as much as you're willing and able to spend, and the result is often making money rather than spending money. One form of productivity is paid employment, which might help make ends meet. Or if you can afford to, you may choose to be productive as a volunteer, for no pay. And you may even find something in the middle—such as a job that pays less than you'd normally accept—so you can do something more important to you than just earn a paycheck.

For each of us, the right kinds of self-development and productivity can be just as satisfying as leisure—or even more satisfying. Add all this up and it's clear that a life stage based on three types of activities— leisure, self-development, and productivity—may allow you to live on less money than a leisure-based retirement would cost.

OK, You've Got the Job. When Can You Start?

If you're thinking this new Third Age approach to retirement might work for you, then the next question is, when can you start? If you're not going to be "over the hill" at any particular age, but will still be climbing the summit, then you don't need to retire based on some arbitrary calculation of how many years you've been on earth. After all, chronological age is only one way to think about where you are in your life's journey. (Biological age is another way—but we'll get to that in chapter six.) You may retire "early" for your age, or you may retire "late" for your age. So instead of thinking about chronological age, try thinking in terms of your life stage—what's actually going on in your life.

If you're still carrying the heavy burdens of raising children (or paying their expenses), pushing to keep going strong in your career, or paddling to keep your financial head above water, you're squarely in the Second Age, no matter how old you are. (Keep going—you'll get there!) On the other hand, if your children have flown the coop, if you have the choice at work of pushing hard or easing off, and if you've salted away enough money to make a paycheck optional, you may be ready for the Third Age, even though you're not ready to retire. Instead of the all-or-nothing old retirement approach, perhaps you can make a more gradual transition— as humans once did, naturally, for millennia. You can withdraw from work on your own schedule, and mix and match it with learning and leisure, however you want!

Just to get your Third Age imagination going, here are some questions to ask yourself about the three types of activities:

1. **Self-Development.** What do you really want to learn about, or how have you dreamed of investing in your ongoing development? Can you imagine exploring career options that would allow you to somehow get paid to learn or develop in this way?

2. **Productivity.** If you were determined to work at something that you absolutely love, what might that be? Could you afford to earn less money doing it—or even do it without pay—solely for fulfillment

and satisfaction? Can you imagine exploring career options that would allow you to get paid to work at something you love?

3. **Leisure.** What have you wanted to do, just for the sheer pleasure of it, but productivity and self-development seemed always to take precedence? As crazy as it may sound, can you imagine exploring career options that would allow you to somehow get paid to play?

If the Third Age sounds like crazy talk to you, and you just want to think about the old retirement and taking it easy, don't feel guilty. It's OK if you just want all leisure, all the time. You could be, like the original workers, just plain worn-out from all the work of the second box. You may really need to do absolutely nothing but enjoy yourself—without trying to be productive or self-developing—for a while after you retire. Farmers know that a field that's allowed to lie fallow for a year will yield a better crop the following year. That may be the case with your retirement; you may find you want to do something else later, after you're fully rested and recharged. In fact, you may surprise yourself.

What Should We Call This New Stage of Life?

This new way of thinking about the stages of life has folks in a lexical quandary. Because it's so different from the original idea of retirement, some people don't even want to call this new life stage *retirement*. They've come up with labels to try to articulate what a huge shift it represents. Here are some terms that you might see:

- The New Retirement

- Re-Firement

- Re-Wirement

- Rest-of-Life

- Second Half of Life

- Unretirement

- Renewment

- Re-Engagement

- Second Adolescence

- The Bonus Years

The change that's happening may ultimately be as profound as the creation of the original old retirement was. But we think that in terminology, a strange thing is likely to happen. As more and more people take this new approach—of greatest freedom, mixing it all up, development and productivity and leisure—it won't seem so unusual anymore. It will eventually become the normal thing to do. People will ask, "Wasn't retirement always about development and productivity and leisure?" The original idea of retirement of all leisure, all the time will have faded away, and this revolutionary new approach won't even need an alternative name. This radical new life stage will eventually come to be called, simply, *retirement*.

Retirement is dead—long live retirement!

Retirement is changing in many ways, and for many reasons. What was true in the past may not be true in the future. With so much uncertainty, how can you design the life you want to live?

Before making the big decisions about your retirement, think through these fundamental principles. Keep them in mind as you develop your specific strategies and tactics, and you'll be building on a firm foundation. Forgetting about them could lead to a shaky retirement!

1. **Retirement is a career transition.**

   Your transition may be away from work completely or from one career to another. The transition can be all at once or happen gradually over time.

2. **Retirement can be voluntary or involuntary.**

   You could choose the timing, or you might be terminated even though you want to keep working. You may think you're temporarily unemployed, but discover later that you're retired.

3. **Retirement is a stage of life.**

   Your retirement is not only an event, but a life change that occurs over a period of time. Your experience is unique, and yet it also has much in common with many other adults.

4. **Retirement includes biological aging.**

   Your body ages over the course of retirement, which results in decline and death at an unknown future time.

5. **Retirement requires economic support for an unknown time.**

   For you to remain retired, sources of material support must continue for as long as you live.

6. **Retirement changes your level of engagement.**

   Retirement increases or decreases your psychological engagement, and increases or decreases your social engagement with others. Both tend to decrease over the course of your retirement.

7. **Retirement is shaped by earlier life stages.**

   All the domains of your life prior to retirement will affect your life during retirement.

8. **Retirement well-being includes prosperity, health, and happiness.**

   Your well-being doesn't come from economic security, physical health, or life satisfaction, but from all three in combination.

"Without ignoring the importance of economic growth, we must look well beyond it."

—Amartya Sen, winner of the 1998 Nobel Prize in economics

Chapter TWO

The Retirement You've Always Wanted but Forgot About

Because the old retirement is dying, and no one is sure what this new life stage will be like—doesn't that mean we get to design it ourselves? Isn't this our chance to have what we've always wanted in life?

Yes! But designing a new stage of life is a big responsibility, and it doesn't come along very often. (Look how long the old retirement lasted.) So we're doing this not only for ourselves but also for those who will follow in our footsteps. We want to get it right.

Designing the old retirement was much simpler. The conceptual process went something like this: "I'll get retirement income and won't need to do that dirty, dangerous, boring, back-breaking work anymore!" That was enough. The organizing concept that guided the old retirement was simply *not working*.

According to Peter Laslett, we've now moved well beyond that simple original goal. For the new retirement, we've moved on to the idea that it should be the "crown" of our life. But to actually make that happen, we need a new organizing concept. What we choose is important, because it guides our thoughts and actions. It's what we use to imagine the future, set goals, and motivate ourselves. It drives how we gather information, make decisions, and take action. *The organizing concept we choose ultimately determines what we get.*

For the new retirement, we need a concept that's big enough to get the job done. A concept that describes what we really want in retirement. A concept based on human experience.

What We All Want in Life

We've always known what we wanted in retirement. But we learned it so long ago, we usually don't remember. To understand it, we need to go back to the beginning.

At the start of our human existence, we didn't know anything, really. We didn't even know we existed. And the way we learned anything was through our senses. That's how we made the fundamental distinction between our environment and ourselves. That distinction is embedded in our nervous system at such a deep level that we've forgotten how we even learned it!

Try this simple experiment right now, to remember how you did it. Tap your finger on this book, and then tap your finger on your cheek. How do you know which is you and which is the book? Here's how. When you tap the book, you feel it in only *one place*—on your finger. When you tap your cheek, you feel it in *two places at the same time*—on your finger and on your cheek, too. It's called the double touch. That, my friend, is how you learned that *you exist*, and that *the world exists*, too. (Had you forgotten how you learned this?)

To make sense of reality, we had to make a fundamental distinction: "Is it ME, or is it NOT ME?" We were a physical self, in a physical world.

We interacted with the world, and so the NOT ME expanded and differentiated. It was soft or smooth or rough or hard. (The one thing became ten thousand things.) At the same time, the self expanded and differentiated, too. It had physical sensations such as hunger, fullness, cold, warmth, pain, and pleasure. Then *a leap in consciousness* occurred. A new experience. It was definitely coming from the self. Except it wasn't like hunger or fullness. It wasn't *physical*—it was *nonphysical*.

So to make sense of reality, the first fundamental distinction had been: "Is it ME or NOT ME?" And now the second fundamental distinction became: "Is it *physical* or *nonphysical*?" We created a map with three dimensions:

Physical
(World)

Physical
(Self)

Nonphysical
(Self)

What Do You Want in Your Three Dimensions?

It was in our nature to need or want something for each of the three dimensions. You might say we're motivated to control them, or manage them, or be in balance with them. And it's not enough to just *survive*. We want to *thrive*. We don't just want each dimension to be OK; we want it to be positive.

This process didn't start with you and me, of course. We've been making these distinctions, and working to create this map, for eons. Since humans use language to think and communicate, we invented a word to describe what we want for each dimension:

- In our physical world, we want prosperity.

- In our physical self, we want health.

- In our nonphysical self, we want happiness.

The map looks like this:

Prosperity
(Physical World)

Health
(Physical Self)

Happiness
(Nonphysical Self)

We took thousands of years to split reality into these parts and invent words to describe what we want. Now, we're finally putting it all back together again! About four hundred years ago, we invented a single word—a unifying concept—that integrates all three experiences. The word is *well-being.*

Well-being is a state characterized by prosperity, health, and happiness. It's an ideal organizing structure for the new retirement, don't you think? After all, we've been working on it for a very, very long time. So we probably won't outgrow it. It describes what we want much better than *not working* ever did!

Conduct this thought experiment, to try it out:

1. Imagine, on the one hand, that you could choose *not working*. But if you did, you wouldn't get prosperity, health, and happiness. That is, you wouldn't be working—but you might be poor, sick, and sad.

2. Imagine, on the other hand, that you could choose prosperity, health, and happiness. But if you did, you wouldn't get *not working*. That is, you'd have well-being—but you might also be working.

Which option did you choose? (Or did you cheat, by imagining an option that had both? Good—you'll need that creativity for later in the book.) It's just a thought experiment, and you may never need to choose between them. But there is a possibility that you may need to keep working, in one form or another, to have the well-being that you want. Who knows what tough decisions you may need to make in the future? But if you ever need to make this one, at least now you've had some practice!

The New Retirement Is about Well-Being

Your goal, and the goal of this book, is to figure out how to have the *not working* of the old retirement and the *well-being* of the new retirement, too. You'll notice that most of this book is structured around well-being. Here's a quick description.

PART ONE. Prosperity is about creating a state of well-being for our physical environment. That includes the environment itself, and in the modern world, it includes the system we invented to support that environment—finance! (Prosperity existed as goats and cattle, long before there was anything called money.) It's the community where we're located, the house we live in, the furniture we sit on, the car we drive, the clothes we wear, and the trips we take. And it's also the paycheck, the 401(k), the IRA, and the Social Security benefits that give us control over the physical environment.

PART TWO. Health is about creating a state of well-being for our physical body. That includes our body itself, and in the modern world, it includes the system we created to support our body—medicine! (Health existed long before there were any doctors.) It's our vitality, energy, strength, flexibility, and endurance. And it's also the family physician, the cholesterol-lowering drug, the alternative medicine practitioner, and the insurance plan that provides access to treatment to support our physical health.

PART THREE. Happiness is about creating a state of well-being in our nonphysical self. That includes our inner happiness itself, and it includes the system we invented to support our happiness—our social system. (Happiness exists in two places: in our relationship with ourselves and in our relationship with others.) It's our fun and enjoyment, our blissful engagement, and our sense of meaning. It's also our family connections, our loving relationships, our true friendships, and our larger networks, which are the social side of our happiness.

These dimensions of life have been *philosophized* about for a long time. But now we're actually doing hard-nosed scientific research into them. We've learned a lot and have new insights into how they work. Knowing about each one individually, and how to make it a part of retirement, is a good idea. Each one stands alone just fine. But if we're going to base a new stage of life on them, there's something else you'll want to know. You'll want to know how they work together.

Here's an analogy for how the dimensions of well-being combine. If you want to bake a dessert, many recipes call for four basic ingredients: flour, sugar, eggs, and butter. It's amazing how many varied and delightful desserts you can create by using those four ingredients in different amounts and proportions. But no one of these ingredients can completely take the place of any of the others in the recipe. Not only does each contribute a different sensory pleasure to the eating experience, but each also plays an essential, irreplaceable chemical role in the transformation from dough or batter to baked dessert. If you don't have any eggs, you can't add more butter and expect the recipe to work. If you're out of sugar, no amount of flour can compensate. When you choose a recipe, you need to make sure you have enough of each ingredient on hand—no substitutions!

When you create your own recipe for Retirement Well-Being, you'll be doing the same thing. Think of prosperity, health, and happiness as your essential baking ingredients. Remember that you can compensate only so far! You can't add more money and expect it will turn into happiness. If you're short on health, you can't compensate with happiness. Sometimes you can't waffle, and you'll need to get more of the ingredient you're short on. Demand your just desserts.

Well-Being Has a Structure

Now that we've actually been studying prosperity, health, and happiness, it's possible to make a few observations about how they fit together in our lives.

It's obvious that all three dimensions affect each other. Positive effects in one dimension almost always have positive effects in the others. And negative effects in one can easily have negative effects in the others, too. But there's an important distinction between the dimensions. Prosperity and health are often seen as an *intermediate* goal, and happiness as an *ultimate* goal. That is, prosperity and health are the means, and happiness is the end. If you ask someone why they want to be prosperous or healthy, they often answer, "To be happy." But if you ask them why they want to be happy, they probably won't answer, "To be healthier" or "To be more prosperous." And yet, research shows that happy people are more likely to stay healthy and possibly be more prosperous, too.

Some amounts of prosperity and health are probably *necessary*, but *not sufficient*, to produce happiness. If you don't have much prosperity (you're poor), you probably won't be happy. If you don't have much health (you're sick), you probably won't be happy, either. But no amount of prosperity or health, either alone or in combination, can *produce* happiness. They make it more likely, but they can't create it. You need to create happiness directly. Also, remember that prosperity and health are physical states and happiness is a nonphysical state. For all these reasons and more, there's an actual structure to well-being. When you look at the diagram, you'll see that prosperity and health are the *foundation*, and happiness rests upon them.

RETIREMENT WELL-BEING

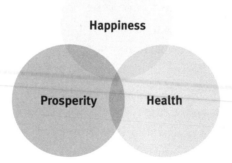

But it's also true that no dimension is more important than any other. Just like political parties and sports teams, each dimension has fans and opponents. There will always be people who argue that *their* dimension trumps the others (and they probably believe it). They have an emotional investment in the relative importance of that one dimension. They almost always know more about that one dimension than the others. So it's like the old saying, "If you're not up on it, you're down on it."

Four Truths about the Interaction of Prosperity, Health, and Happiness in Your Life

So we can see that the structure of well-being has implications for how we go about designing Retirement Well-Being. Beyond the basic structure, we've learned some important things about how the dimensions interact with each other and about how we interact with them, too.

Four basic truths about that interaction:

1. The Truth of Diminishing Returns. When we're low in a given dimension, an increase in that dimension will have a *big* effect on our total well-being. But when we're already high in a given dimension, an increase in that dimension will only have a *small* effect on our well-being.

Let's take prosperity as an example. You might remember a time when you were first living on your own and didn't have much in the way of material possessions or money. A small increase of $100 per month would have improved your well-being in all three dimensions. It would have raised your material standard of living. It would have made you instantly happier (ecstatic, possibly). And by decreasing your stress level or letting you eat better, it would have made you healthier. That increase in prosperity produced a big effect on your total well-being, because your prosperity was low. How about now? How much of an increase would you need to get the same impact on your total well-being?

The same is true for health, too. You might remember a time when you were really sick and couldn't even climb out of bed. Getting just a little increase in strength and energy could have improved your well-being in all three dimensions. It would have improved your health directly and allowed you to make yourself a good meal, perhaps. It would have improved your happiness directly, and also allowed you to rejoin the world of people. And it would have improved your prosperity by allowing you to go back to work. But what about when you're already healthy? You don't even notice taking those first few steps out of bed each morning.

The same is somewhat true for happiness. You may remember a time when you were working too hard and not taking time off. You hadn't done anything for ages! Then a friend or loved one forced you into an evening out or a social gathering. You were surprised how much fun you had. You realized your happiness had run a bit low, and that single event made a difference. We know that happiness has a measurable effect on physical health, too. It even has a demonstrated effect on productivity, which will help your prosperity. But what about when you're already happy? You hardly notice when one more day is added to a two-week vacation.

The truth of diminishing returns makes it very difficult to create retirement well-being by increasing only one dimension. But we tend not to notice that. We notice the times when increasing a low dimension had a big impact, and it sticks with us. When that dimension is high, we still think an increase will make a difference. Because it worked so well at one time, we think it will always be the key. However, just because prosperity— or health or happiness—was the solution *then*, doesn't mean it's the solution *now*. For designing your next stage of life, you need to take stock of where you really are in each dimension. Otherwise, it's like the old saying, "You can never get enough of what you don't need."

QUESTION: Across most of your life, which dimension has consistently been your highest? Your lowest?

2. The Truth of Specialization. For one reason or another, most of us specialize in one of the dimensions—*at the expense of the others*. One of the dimensions interests us more, so we learn about it, talk about it, hang out with others who are interested in it, and more or less become an expert in it. We might even end up with degrees or careers related to it. If we're more interested in prosperity, we might be drawn to finance or real estate or consumer goods. If we're more interested in health, we might be drawn to medicine or fitness or organic foods. If we're more interested in happiness, we might be drawn to psychology or education or social services.

Specialization is good, because we become experts in that dimension. But it also tends to make us view our well-being through that one perspective, rather than seeing all three dimensions clearly. For designing your next stage of life, you'll want to get the perspective of specialists from other dimensions, whether they are professionals or friends. Otherwise, you won't see your own blind spots. As the saying goes, "If your only tool is a hammer, everything looks like a nail."

QUESTION: For most of your life, which dimension have you specialized in?

3. The Truth of Compensation. We use the dimensions that are high, or that we're specialists in, to compensate for those dimensions that are low. Many things we want to accomplish, and many problems we need to solve, can be addressed from more than one dimension. Each dimension represents an *accumulation of resources*. For any given task, we get to choose which dimension—which resource—to use.

This applies to tasks large and small. Let's use a small task to illustrate. Three elderly people live in the same neighborhood, and each has a lawn to maintain. The task of lawn maintenance is exactly the same for all three. However, each person addresses it from a different dimension. They use a high dimension to compensate for a low dimension.

The first person has lived their life from the dimension of prosperity, and without hesitation, hires a lawn service to do the work. The second person has lived their life from the dimension of health, and without hesitation, does the work as a form of exercise. The third person has lived their life from the dimension of happiness, and without hesitation, asks one of their many friends for help. In this example, all three dimensions worked just fine! *However, there is usually one dimension that's easier, or more efficient, than the others.* But if you're low in the dimension, you can get creative. For designing your next stage of life, keep all your dimensions in mind when thinking about how to get what you want.

QUESTION: Across your life, what has been your most consistent pattern of compensation?

4. The Truth of Decline. Most of this book is about the Third Age of Life, rather than the Fourth. (There are already good books that focus on challenges of the Fourth Age.) Our focus here is on freedom and opportunity, which is why we're looking at Retirement Well-Being! But once we acknowledge the *trajectory* of decline, we can use the structure of well-being to anticipate and compensate. Might it be in our finances, or physical surroundings? In our body, or access to medical treatment? In our thoughts and feelings, or social connections? Decline often begins in a narrow part of life but then has a *cascading effect* into all the dimensions. Looking at specific trajectories in our lives helps us manage risks.

QUESTION: When you think about the trajectory of your life, which dimension holds a risk that you need to address in advance?

The Well-Being Model Organizes
the Sea of Information

Organizing the sea of information for the old retirement was much easier, for two reasons. First, the information we needed was just related to finding ways of *not working*, so that was a narrower topic. Second, the sea of information itself was much smaller and calmer in the era of the old retirement. The information we need for designing the new retirement is much broader, and fortunately, we can use the Retirement Well-Being Model to do it.

Also, the practical tools developed for planning the old retirement were almost completely related to prosperity—things like savings calculators, risk tolerance questionnaires, and asset allocation models. Those financial tools are still very important and easy to find. But now we need to develop practical tools for the other dimensions because they're not easy to find. The first edition of this book introduced some of the earliest tools for planning your health and happiness, too. This edition expands on those, but we're still just getting started!

We're fortunate, at least, that we've slowly been getting closer to retirement life planning. Researchers have been studying a variety of topics that, one way or another, relate to retirement. We can turn some of these scientific findings into tools and guidance that will help us plan for our well-being. That's what we call progress!

We know that the dimensions of Retirement Well-Being interact dynamically in real life. We couldn't separate them, even if we wanted to. But most researchers, journalists, and professional practitioners pretty much still look at them one at a time and separately. They need to split things into parts—and into further subparts—to be better able to learn about them, communicate them, and work on them. Science usually needs to break things down into smaller chunks to get a better look. After all, you can't fit an elephant under a microscope, can you? Remember the old riddle "How do you eat an elephant?" Answer: "One bite at a time."

So most of our sources of information—scientists, journalists, and practitioners—tend to focus on one dimension (and usually one aspect of that one dimension). Medicine, for example. Or psychology. Researchers in each field develop theories, conduct research, and create useful knowledge, but usually only within the boundaries of their own field. Journalists write articles about new discoveries, but usually from the perspective of one field. Practitioners work to keep up with new developments but only in their own field. Even when this system works well, it means that most knowledge is *field-centered* rather than *you-centered*. It's from the perspective of that field rather than from the perspective of your real life, in the real world. You're the only one who can pull these fields together to design your next stage of life.

So if we're going to organize information about all three dimensions of well-being, how can we do that? The good news is that organizing information is built into the concept for the Retirement Well-Being Model. Each of the three dimensions is directly connected to two fields of research and practice, as shown in the figure. Without the model, the sea of information would swamp us. But the organizing concept of well-being keeps us afloat!

THE RETIREMENT WELL-BEING MODEL

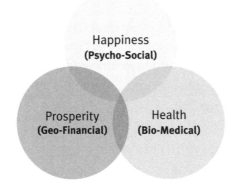

To design your retirement health, you'll benefit from Bio-Medical information; to design your retirement happiness, you'll benefit from Psycho-Social information. And for prosperity, there's a new term for information: Geo-Financial. These labels identify two fields you'll use for making key decisions in each dimension. They play essential roles and are full of good ideas for your retirement planning. That's why this entire book, chapter by chapter, is organized according to the Well-Being

Model and these fields of knowledge. Each chapter focuses on that one part of your life, and offers exercises that help you design your retirement. By the end of the book, you will have created a picture of your Ideal Retirement, chapter by chapter. In addition to envisioning what you want, the model is also valuable for evaluating how you're doing. It gives you a way to see all the parts of your life clearly, to see where you're on track and where you may be headed for trouble. The evaluation tool is the Retirement Well-Being Profile, and you'll find it in the Appendix section at the end of the book. You could even take that assessment right now if you'd like, although it will make more sense to you after you read the supporting chapters.

Geo-Financial

The Geo-Financial dimension—prosperity—is based on geography and finance. The original scope of retirement planning was finance, all finance, and nothing but finance, and of course that remains a key component. Now why, you may ask, is geography included? First, because the *relative* value of your money is greatly affected by where you happen to be on the face of the earth. (If you live in Manhattan, you couldn't afford to retire on a million dollars. But if you live in Manhattan, Kansas, you might live like royalty!) That is, your geography has an enormous impact on your cost of living. Second, your geography impacts your ability to earn an income, if you need to, or want to. Third, your home is traditionally one of your most important retirement assets. Figuring out how to use your home equity and still have a place to live is both an opportunity and a challenge for the prosperity dimension of retirement. To have the money you want for retirement, you need to be able to think both financially (see chapters four and five) and geographically (see chapter six).

Bio-Medical

The Bio-Medical dimension—health—is made up of biology and medicine. Medicine, of course, studies diseases and how to treat them. Where would you be in retirement without access to medicine? However, quite apart from the necessity of treating disease, it's helpful to understand the basic biological processes of your body. Health means not just the absence of disease but also *biological vitality*. You'll see it called other things, such as optimum health. To support that for yourself, you need to understand how your body works, how that changes as you age, and how you can support your body through those changes. Whether you're healthy or sick, knowledge from biology and medicine can help you achieve optimum health, which translates to greater well-being. The sooner you start acting on your Bio-Medical knowledge, the more health (strength, stamina, flexibility, good habits, you name it) you'll establish for your retirement. And the more health you build up, the longer it's likely to last. Remember, *health is an accumulated resource*, like prosperity. (You'll find more on this in chapters seven and eight.)

Psycho-Social

The Psycho-Social dimension—happiness—is made up of psychology and sociology. Psychology has often studied *un*happiness rather than happiness—similar to the way that medicine has studied disease rather than health. That means when most of us hear the word *psychology*, we think of mental illness and psychotherapy. But visionary psychologists are now doing research into how happiness actually works, and how we can build it into our lives. How's that for useful? On the social side, psychology has studied interpersonal relationships, and sociologists have studied retirement within society and among groups of people. We can use findings from these fields to come up with specific plans for our personal happiness and our happiness with other people. That's the kind of planning that can pay off now as well as later. After all, happiness is an *accumulated resource*, like prosperity and health. (More on this in chapters nine and ten.)

Well-Being Is Like an Elephant

Due to the specialization of the modern world, even the word *well-being* has a very different meaning depending on who is using it! Within each field, well-being has a specific, narrow meaning—not the overall, real-world, total life meaning that we want for the new retirement. Because these fields don't talk with each other very much, it doesn't matter that they have different definitions. But in the real world, seeing an article with the word *well-being* can be confusing, because it's usually just referring to one of the dimensions of well-being. You'll discover that medicine has one understanding of what it means, psychology has another, economics has yet another, and so on.

THE SIX FIELDS OF KNOWLEDGE FOR WELL-BEING

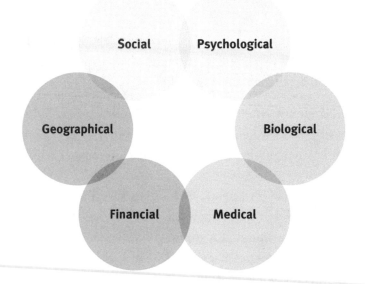

This means that there are medical researchers who spend their time studying "health and well-being." They've learned a lot about how to keep our bodies healthy as we approach retirement and progress through it. And there are research psychologists who spend their time studying "subjective well-being." They've learned a lot about how to conduct our lives in order to be happier as we travel along our journey. And, yes, there are economists who spend their time studying "economic well-being." They've learned a lot about how we can more easily accumulate money for retirement and how we can make it last as long as we need it to.

Earlier in this chapter, we looked at the structure and interactions of the three dimensions of well-being. To design the new retirement, that's the kind of information that we'll all need. But connecting one field's version of well-being with another field's version of well-being just isn't easy! It's a bit like the story of three blind wanderers who encounter an elephant. They don't know what an elephant is, but they want to learn about it. Because they can't see it, they have no way to know what the whole thing is like. So they split up, and each one takes a part to explore:

- The first one encounters the side of the elephant. He slides his hands back and forth across the elephant's hide. He stretches his arms out as far as possible but doesn't find anything else. He concludes that an elephant is like a wall.

- The second one encounters the elephant's leg. She puts her arms around it, but it won't budge. It seems to be planted in the ground. She concludes that an elephant is like a tree.

- The third one encounters the elephant's trunk. It coils around his arm, and he can feel how long and flexible it is. He reaches out but doesn't encounter anything else. He concludes that an elephant is like a snake.

That's the story of well-being. Economics sees it one way, medicine sees it another way, and psychology sees it a third way. Each field knows a lot about the dimension that it studies, but it doesn't have an easy way to connect with the others. That's true for your advisors, too. How often do financial planners, medical doctors, and counselors or coaches get together to help clients plan for retirement? (In a word, never.)

Using the Well-Being Model to Design Your Next Stage of Life

Now, because you know about the Well-Being Model, you have a new perspective. You have a conceptual structure for designing the new retirement. *Only you, dear reader, can see the whole elephant!*

The Well-Being Model isn't an esoteric theory or hypothesis. It's a practical, down-to-earth planning tool. You might think of it as a literature organizer, collecting information from different fields all in one place. Or as a puzzle, showing you where and how the different parts of your retirement can fit together. Or as a checklist, helping you make sure you've taken care of everything you were supposed to. Or even as a Swiss Army knife—you may not know which tool you'll need to use, or when, but you'll be glad it's in your pocket.

THE ELEMENTS OF YOUR IDEAL RETIREMENT

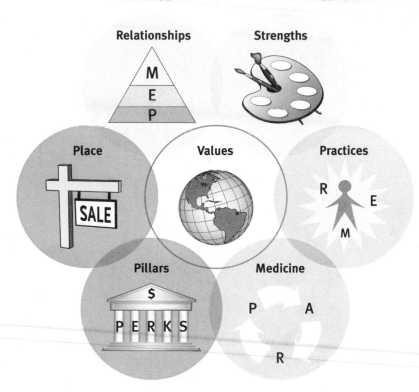

As an organizing concept, well-being is really a new way of seeing your life. The remainder of this book provides information about the different parts of retirement. Just as important, it provides you with a *process* for designing, and integrating, all those parts of your life. Your personal information and knowledge become the essential *content*. In each chapter, make sure to actually complete the exercise. That way, at the end of the book, you'll be able to assemble all those parts of your well-being into a picture of the life you want to live.

So keep going!

"Tell them I've had a wonderful life."

—LUDWIG WITTGENSTEIN, eminent philosopher

"I think I did a pretty good job."

—JULIA NELSON, John Nelson's mom

Chapter THREE

The Life You Can Live (Right Now)

How will you know you've had a wonderful life? How will you know you did a good job?

Midlife is a time when we're asking ourselves those questions. Asking whether we're getting what we really want from life—and whether we're making the contribution we want to make. We're evaluating, and reevaluating, what it is we're here for.

It's the perfect time to be asking those questions, too. That's because we're far enough along the journey to have experience and perspective. But, thankfully, there's plenty of the journey yet ahead. We're wrapping up the Second Age, or exploring the Third. We're making plans for what's next and can see the forks in the road. Or we may be at a crossroads and need to make some decisions right away. We may even have thought it was all figured out—and then things changed. But one way or another, we're facing *high-stakes decisions*. Some of those have good and bad choices, and a little research will help us choose. Need a mutual fund? We'll check out the stats from Morningstar. Deciding on a cholesterol-lowering drug? We'll read the articles on WebMD.

But there are plenty of things that can't be resolved through research and analysis alone. Questions that have no right or wrong answers. Decisions that would deadlock a jury or stump a blue-ribbon panel. These are choices that ultimately come down to what's most important to us.

For example, should someone keep their head down for a few more years at a job they hate, or take a pay cut to work at something they could love forever? Should someone stay in the family homestead where all their possessions (and memories) fit comfortably, or downsize to move closer to kids and grandkids? Although questions like these don't have clear-cut answers, they do have enormous consequences. At some point down the road, we'll look back and see that some choices would have served us better than others.

One of life's great truths is this: The questions that don't have right or wrong answers are the ones we use to evaluate our lives. The decisions we need to base on *internal values*—not *external data*—are the ones we judge ourselves by. When we look back, those are the ones that let us say, "I've lived a wonderful life" and "I've done a good job."

Or not.

The What, How, and Why of Making Decisions about the Life We Want to Live

This chapter won't provide answers to these values-based dilemmas. (How could it? After all, they're *your* values.) Instead, it will help you see the structure you use to make decisions, when you're at your decision-making best. You'll crystallize what motivates you at the deepest level, and clarify how you want to live the rest of your life. You may even decide to live a bit differently than you had thought. Heaven forbid!

What We Want

When we think about making choices among all the things we might want to do, it's often expressed in terms of interests, preferences, and attitudes. This is the WHAT of decision making. As in, "What interests you more: A or B?" Or, "Do you prefer X or Y?" We go through life having to pick things, one after the other, in the endless stream that comes our way. Likes and dislikes, one after the other. As though life were one long menu.

"Let's see . . . I'll choose this major . . . take that internship . . . go to work in that other industry . . . live in the city . . . vacation at the seashore . . . drive a Honda . . . because they're *interesting*. And, I'll marry that cute one with the brown hair and brown eyes . . . because, I *prefer* them." (Just kidding. True love is more than a preference. Isn't it?) And so on. Decisions, small and large, can all be made on preferences and interests. One thing to note, however. These may not be very deep parts of us, and they often shift as we go along. Who knows why? Yours have probably shifted many times as you've grown older and wiser. As you move from one life stage to the next, when you look back, you can see that they've shifted a lot. (Can you believe you actually wore that outfit?) Making decisions at the mall, or about a hobby, and sometimes even a job, based purely on interests is fine. But this level isn't sufficient for designing your next stage of life. You wouldn't want to use Second Age preferences for your Third Age. Who knows how unfashionable and out-of-date they might be? Instead, by connecting them to other deeper levels, you're more likely to find your *enduring* interests and preferences.

This is, admittedly, an oversimplification in order to shed some light on the subject. But it's useful to see that there are multiple levels of yourself that you can also bring into decision making. The next level is HOW, and it includes both how you approach the world and how you get things done.

How We Want to Do It

HOW we approach the world is our personality, or temperament. It's the pattern of how we *consistently* think, feel, and act. It's a set of traits that we express over and over (and over and over) in life. For example, one common personality trait is a dichotomy between extroversion and introversion. Extroversion means you tend toward being more outgoing and action oriented, with a focus on your outer world. Introversion means you tend toward being more reserved and thoughtful, with a focus on your inner world. It's not that you're exclusively one or the other, or that you are that way 100 percent of the time. Rather, it's that you consistently tend to think, feel, and act in that way. It's natural and automatic. You can exhibit the other behavior, of course, but it usually requires conscious effort to do so. (Stop right now to check whether you're more of an extrovert or more of an introvert. Got it? Good.)

Personality traits have been studied for decades now, so we know a lot about them. One thing we know is that unlike preferences, traits are quite stable over time. People pretty much keep the same underlying traits for an entire lifetime, regardless of circumstances. Walk into any kindergarten class and look for the strong extroverts. (They'll be easy to spot.) Now follow them for seventy years. They're likely to be extroverts in college, extroverts at work, extroverts in the retirement community, and even extroverts on their deathbed. The old adage "A leopard doesn't change its spots" was probably a reference to human personality traits. They shape our decisions without us even having to think about them. And as we get to know ourselves better and better, we actually *do* think about them. We may consciously make decisions that support and align with our traits. How about you? Do you know whether your tendency is to attend a big party or a small get-together? Book a lively holiday on a cruise ship or seek out a quiet vacation retreat? Do you make choices to consciously *reinforce* your traits or to *compensate* for them? Both approaches can be useful, depending on the situation.

The other HOW relates to our strengths and skills. These are HOW we accomplish things in the world. You might also think of these as abilities, gifts, or talents. (Did you already know that you are gifted and talented?) Strengths are a relatively new idea, with a focus on the deep underlying positive traits that we use to get things done. Persistence and creativity are good examples. Although strengths can be thought of as natural gifts or talents, we can also choose to develop them. They are the fundamental "HOW" behind our specific capabilities and competencies. We can use them across *all the contexts* of our lives—work, family, and leisure. Making decisions and designing our lives to align with our greatest strengths is probably a good idea. In fact, it's a great idea!

Skills are similar to strengths. Skills are HOW we accomplish things in the world, too. But although strengths are deep elements of our character, skills are learned behaviors. Skills are *specific abilities* that we might need to acquire to do a specific job, such as drive a fork-lift, design a website, or teach reading. When we learn a particular skill easily and well, it's probably because it's aligned with one of our more fundamental, underlying strengths. Because we acquire skills to do specific things, they're narrower than strengths are. They're often related to work. (Although we have specific nonjob skills, too, such as parenting or cooking.) Transferable skills relate to more than one job, though, and thus more than one context. That's why they're especially valuable when changing jobs or careers. We can certainly look for opportunities to put our skills to use in the Third Age. It's just that skills learned in our career may or may not be useful for other contexts. Our last day on a particular job may well be the last time we ever use a particular set of skills. (We may not miss using them, either.) Even though you've listed them on your resume for years, you may or may not be able to keep using your "skill set." On the other hand, your traits and strengths can always be put to use.

This level of HOW—your traits, strengths, and skills—doesn't tell the whole story, though. There's another level you can bring into designing your life: the WHY.

And Most Importantly, Why

Reflecting on WHY a person, place, or thing is important to us is fundamental to who we are. We can tell that something is important because it stirs up emotion. We feel good or bad about what happens or might happen. But we don't ask WHY very often, and truth be told, we don't need to. Most of the time we can just accept that our values and beliefs are doing their job. They're working just fine, and we let it go at that.

That is, until—and sooner or later this always happens—life changes. When internal or external forces bring us to a major crossroads, we want to be conscious of our values. When we transition to another stage of life, we want to be conscious. When we make those once-in-a-decade (or once-in-a-lifetime) decisions, we most definitely want to be conscious.

We want to be fully conscious at these key points, because if we aren't, we'll do things that we wish we hadn't. And we won't do the things that we wish we could have. (That is, we'll be sorry later.)

Remember the Retirement Well-Being Model?

Our values are at the center of our lives, and so they're at the center of the Well-Being Model, too. The three dimensions of well-being—prosperity, health, and happiness—are all tied to what's going on in the outer world. But our inner values drive our own personal definitions of prosperity, health, and happiness. We get to decide what our well-being is, regardless of what our friends or "the experts" might say.

The world and the media are filled with experts these days. There's not a shortage of information or advice—there's an overload. Remember, those three dimensions have six aspects: geographical, financial, biological, medical, psychological, and social. Those fields all have their own experts, with their own way of looking at you and at your life. To make decisions for our retirement well-being, we'll want to gather objective data, become informed, and get good advice from that external world of knowledge. But then, for the WHY, we need to look inward.

For example, what if you developed a serious disease? (Based on your family history or some other factor, you've already thought about some diseases you might get as you age. But for heaven's sake, don't imagine it too vividly! Also, make sure to de-imagine it, right after this example.) As you learn more, you realize that you might not pull through. You might not make it. There are multiple treatment options and no clear-cut, right, or wrong answer. There are simply options, trade-offs, and compromises. Which treatment you choose will not only affect whether you survive, it will affect your ongoing health, your finances, your future success, you opportunities for enjoyment, your independence, your ability to help others, and your place in your family and in society.

First, you'd gather *objective* data from the world. You need to get information from hospitals, insurance companies, drug makers, research studies, survivability rates, and so on. There is a lot of hard data and a lot of science out there. You also want the perspective of trusted advisors. What does your family doctor think you should do? What does the specialist think you should do?

But then you need the *subjective* part, too. You need to know your underlying motivations. You need to know what you most value in life.

After all, that's how you evaluate your options. Which option gets you closer to the life you want to live?

In the end, the WHY of the choice you make goes by many names. You might call it your:

Belief System	Perspective on Life
Definition of "The Good Life"	Philosophy of Life
Guiding Principles	Point of View
Life Goals	Value System
Life Purpose	Way to Live
Meaning in Life	Weltanschauung
Perceptual Filters	Worldview

For simplicity, going forward, let's use the term *core values*.

Core Values Are Subjective

Sometimes we think of them as our *deepest* values, because they provide us with a foundation and we are grounded by them. We're motivated to hold them tightly, and we find comfort in them. At other times we think of them as our *highest* values, because they are what we aspire to and are inspired by. We're motivated to rise toward them and are elevated in the process. Deepest and highest are both useful ways of thinking about our values, and they fit with the concept of core values. Your core values are somehow comforting and motivating at the same time. They are both grounding and inspiring, simultaneously. That's pretty amazing, isn't it? Your values are so powerful that it seems like a good idea to design your next life stage around them, don't you think?

Where do our values come from? You could say they develop organically, in the interplay between us and the world. The dynamic interaction of many factors—our genes, gender, upbringing, education, religion, ethnic group, income level, social roles, work environment, and political involvement would only be a partial list. As we encounter new circumstances, people, and ideas, our values change. Remember how the extroverted kindergartener is probably an extrovert for life? That's not true with values; they don't stay the same for one's whole life. It's ironic that while values are a deep part of us—like traits—our values are much more changeable. That's a good thing, though. Becoming a more fully developed adult often includes shifts in our values.

As you moved across the stages of life you assumed new roles, took on new responsibilities, and met with new opportunities and barriers. You held multiple roles at the same time, transitioning from child to young adult to citizen to worker to spouse to parent to whatever you're going to be next. In the same way that your interests and preferences shifted, so did your values. But your values are probably more important to you. That's why it's crucial to see that in addition to these *organic* sources of values, there are *synthetic* sources, too. In the modern world, we're bombarded with commercial messages from cradle to grave. They're synthesized in order to motivate us to consume something. After a lifetime of this, how do we know where our values really came from? Did they grow out of our own real-life experiences, or did we just absorb them from the commercial media? In order to really get down to our core values, first we need to take a good, hard look at what it means to live in a consumer society.

Bombarded with Consumer Values

As a consumer, you're a target. If you're a member of the baby boom generation, you're part of the most targeted market that has ever existed. Marketers came up with the term *target market* to describe a group of people they have determined have enough in common to need or want the same things. Businesses use those similarities to design new products and services, then sell them to that target market.

On the one hand, target marketing by businesses is good. It means they're thinking of us when they decide what to offer. And it's nice to be thought of. On the other hand, no one really enjoys being thought of as a target. It sounds too much like *warfare*. Maybe it really is a type of warfare. Marketers talk about *penetrating* a market and, they hope, *dominating* it. They think in terms of dividing and conquering—*segmenting* markets into smaller slices to more effectively target them.

Not that the products and services they are marketing to us aren't valuable; many of them are. Some of the stuff they're selling we truly want. Some of it we even truly need. It's just that we'd like to decide consciously, based on what's best for us. What's best for them is always more and more and more sales. They are, in a word, insatiable.

Marketers Know All about the Four Ages

While we think of the Four Ages as stages of life, marketers see them as target markets. When the baby boomers were kids, marketers realized how many of them there were and that it was a huge business opportunity. A gold mine. It's as though they asked themselves, "What can we pitch to kids and young people who are in the First Age?" The answer, of course, was kid cereals and toys and dolls and tennis shoes and fast food. They carefully researched how to package products and where to place them in retail stores to be more attractive to children.

Television arrived with the boomer generation, and marketers studied how to make TV commercials that would be most persuasive to kids, first during Saturday morning cartoons and much later on the cable channels oriented toward children and families. They figured out how to use the youngest members of the family to shake the money tree and generate sales. They mined the psychology of persuasion, the emotion in children, and the dynamics of power between children and their parents. They knew that kids—being the least skeptical members of any family—were the exposed flank in marketing warfare. They learned the importance of establishing the little consumers' brand loyalty at an impressionable age. In short, the marketers became experts at penetrating the child market. (How did they sleep at night?)

As the boomers became teenagers, marketers became experts at penetrating the teen market. Even though those in the First Age usually don't have a lot of their own money, they have high discretionary spending because they don't yet have financial obligations. And of course, young people in the First Age have influence, beyond their own small piggy banks, on the much larger family piggy bank.

We've been especially targeted in the Second Age because those are our peak earning and spending years. Marketers know what we're doing in that age—starting careers, getting married, buying cars, then buying homes, furnishing them, and taking vacations to get away from them. They know we need clothes, groceries, dinners out, and lots and lots of coffee.

Some very clever people have made a science and a billion-dollar industry out of studying how to get us to buy more stuff. They learned that educating us on the features and benefits of their product works, to a point. But getting us to associate an *experience* with their product is more effective. And when they can get us to connect the consumer experience with our *values*—bingo!

Consuming to Infinity

Where are these marketing geniuses turning their attention now? Just as they followed the baby boomers from the First Age to the Second, they've been making war plans and strategies for the Third. Millions of people and trillions of dollars are in *transition*. It's when our lives are changing and we're moving through life transitions that we particularly need new products and services.

It's also true that, in general, we may be at a financial high point when we're in the Third Age. We may still be pulling down a full-time salary and be at the peak of our earning power, but (ideally) finished with the financial obligations of raising children. We're cashing out of employer retirement plans and perhaps moving to a new house. Even if our investment accounts and home equity have taken a beating, if we're transitioning, we have a lot of money to deal with. Access to cash can even make us a bit impulsive. Marketers, of course, have been studying all this. And making battle plans.

Their plans *don't* have anything to do with optimizing our well-being. Or making our retirement engaging or meaningful. Or making sure we're socially connected or live in a vital community. Or keeping us truly healthy or physically active. Not that they don't want us to have these things—they just don't particularly care one way or the other. What they do care about is that we keep buying their products and services and experiences. And when we reflect back upon our lives, marketers won't care whether we lived a good life and did a good job. They'll just care whether we kept consuming—to infinity and beyond!

Their Secret Weapon Is Values-Based Marketing

Marketing has changed over the years. One thing you may have noticed is less use of the so-called hard sell—a pushy, obvious, obnoxious approach. Particularly in the branding of companies and products, you may have noticed more use of the so-called soft sell—a gentle, subtle, even witty approach. This didn't happen because the billion-dollar advertising industry decided to be nice and give consumers a break. It didn't happen because companies decided it was OK to sell fewer of their products and make a smaller profit. Just the opposite: Marketers figured out how to sell us just as much, or even more, with a breakthrough concept: *psychographics*.

We're all familiar with marketing *demographics*—the practice of profiling us by age, gender, income level, and other external characteristics. The idea is that those of us who are similar in those respects will be similar in the products and services that we need and buy. More to the point, the idea is that we'll also be susceptible to the same marketing approach. Marketing based on demographics works, of course, and is still widely used. However, researchers have discovered that beyond our external characteristics, our internal characteristics—based on psychological research—are the most effective way to profile us. We're actually more likely to fall for a given pitch based on our psychographics than our demographics. After all, we make decisions, including buying decisions, from the *inside*, not the outside. So they use psychographics to skim the surface of our preferences and to plumb the depths of our values.

Psychographics results in what most of us would call *lifestyle* marketing. We've all seen it, over and over. A company positions itself and its products (cars, coffee, clothes, condos, you name it) as a gateway to a certain lifestyle. The marketing message to consumers is that when we purchase that company's products, we automatically get the lifestyle that's implied. Research tells the companies about the values we aspire to live by (party animal, cultured connoisseur, loving caretaker), then they project those values onto their products. Instead of using a hard sell to push the features and benefits of specific products, they use the soft sell to get us to buy a lifestyle. It works because the lifestyles they invite us into are based on our deepest and highest values. Psychographics and lifestyle marketing may seem subtle, but don't be lulled by that subtlety—this is powerful stuff.

Buying a "Lifestyle" or Creating a Life?

Until recently, marketers have tended to use a simple attack to sell retirement-oriented products and services—a carefree, leisure-based lifestyle. The "Sun City"–inspired image that was appealing to your parents is an example. However, just as they knew about the Three Boxes of Life, they know all about the Four Ages, too. They've carefully researched the consumer values of boomers, which are different than those of earlier generations. Now they're creating products—and pitches—that appeal to those values. They're showcasing a variety of Third Age lifestyles (lifelong learner, youthful athlete, wise elder, and so on) to dangle in front of you, attached to their products, services, and experiences. The almost subliminal message is this: If these are your values, and this is the lifestyle you want, you can have it. Just get out your credit card.

The marketers want to define your retirement for you. Instead of building a life, they want you to buy a lifestyle. Instead of reflecting on your values, they want you to value consuming the right investments, the right insurance, the right real estate, the right travel, the right retail goods, and the right antiaging products. Instead of discovering your identity, they want you to simply identify yourself as a consumer. They want images of products and services dancing in your head so that you make acquiring them the goal and the purpose of your retirement. They want consuming to be your highest priority. They want you to believe that if you buy all the right stuff, you'll live the right lifestyle, have "the good life," and have their idea of a good retirement. And if you don't buy all the right stuff, you'll have a bad retirement—an impoverished retirement, an unsafe retirement, a nowhere retirement, a boring retirement, a nobody retirement, an old person's retirement! That's no one's idea of "the good life." In short, they want you to believe that you'll be in pain if you don't buy into *their* concept of what the new retirement should be. In fact, more ingeniously, they want you to believe you're in pain already if you haven't yet acquired all the stuff they want you to buy.

The businesses serving the "Third Age market" aren't bad or evil, any more than a predator like a wolf or a shark is bad or evil. Marketing and selling are just in their DNA. But that doesn't mean that you want to get gobbled up by them, either. Do you want to be *sold a lifestyle* dreamed up by an advertising agency? Or do you want to *design a life* based on your own core values? (With your own values, at least you know you're buying the right stuff!)

The reason these issues are so important right now is because we're designing a new stage of life for ourselves, and for others who will follow. We have the opportunity to define it as a life stage when people have freedom to live life according to their core values. But the challenge is that we're doing all this in an environment that promotes consumer values, instead of core values. *Caveat emptor.* (Or in English: Let the buyer beware.)

Activate Your Core Values Before You Design Your Next Stage of Life

Now that we've identified the consumer values that bombard us, let's move on to a process for identifying our own deepest core values. For each of the chapters that follow, you'll be looking at one aspect of well-being. An important part of each chapter is considering the objective information that plays a role in good and bad decisions. But it's also important to use your core values for all the subjective decisions you need to make. *Activating* your values means that you're conscious of them and motivated to use them in your everyday life.

When you activate your values, you're more likely to act according to them. Living in alignment with your core values allows you to say, "I lived a wonderful life" and "I did a good job!"

The Universe of Values

Many people—from prophets to philosophers to poets—have advanced the idea that a set of universal values exist. That some values are so important that they've been held by all people, at all times, in all places. There is certainly some truth to this idea. Most people would say they value a basic level of prosperity, health, and happiness, for example. Everyone wants well-being.

But there are probably other specific values that are more motivating to you. Values that you feel so strongly about, they guide your actions across most situations of your life. Even though those specific values may be very important to you, they may be only somewhat important to your spouse, and hardly important at all to your best friend. It's the *difference* in our values that we're most likely to notice. The difference in our values is what causes us to set different goals and choose different groups of people and situations. Our values often drive our actions. But as individuals we often hold many values and don't know which are most important until we're forced to choose between them. The following exercises will give you an opportunity to do exactly that. They're based on the Values Theory of Shalom Schwartz, of Hebrew University. More than twenty years ago he, too, wondered if there was a set of universal values and began searching for them. He discovered that while everyone doesn't *have* the same values, everyone *recognizes* the same values. That is, each person acknowledges the same range of values that may be held by others—whether they personally hold those same values, or not. Rather than universal values, you might think of them as a universe *of* values. A values universe!

After asking more than one hundred thousand people in sixty countries about their values, Schwartz has analyzed the data many different ways to confirm that human values actually have a structure. You'll be able to see that structure in the values universe on page 57. If you already know your three most important core values, enter them in the Life Circle on the following page. If you'd like to explore your values more deeply, continue to the Values Universe exercise that follows on page 56.

LIFE CIRCLES EXERCISE

What are your three most important core values, or guiding principles? Enter them in this Life Circle. If you'd like some help deciding what to enter, use the Values Universe exercise beginning on the next page. You'll also use them for your One Piece of Paper in chapter eleven.

My Ideal Retirement

includes living by these

core values:

_____,

_____,

and _____.

THE VALUES UNIVERSE

From the Values Theory of Shalom Schwartz

Our core values guide us on life's journey. We look to them for navigation and inspiration, as ancient travelers looked to the stars. We use them to orient our lives, decide if we're headed in the right direction, and determine if we're making progress. The Values Universe is a diagram (see opposite) that helps us find our way. It reveals the integrated structure of value systems, and the relationships between our values. The values in the center are a small sample drawn from the many specific values important to individuals and groups. The ten values around the edge are the comprehensive set of basic values that people in all cultures recognize. These ten basic value orientations are in conflict or congruence, as shown by their relative position around the circle. Closer together means they're more compatible; farther apart means more in opposition. The outer arrows show the broad underlying motivations that create the organizing structure.

Three Options for Activating Your Values

Depending upon how deeply you've explored your values and how much time you have, choose from the three options below.

1. The best option is to use the forty-item questionnaire (there are both female and male versions, beginning on pages 62 and 65, respectively). You identify what you value most, and also what you value *least*—which can be almost as important. See "Ten Steps to Your Values" on page 61 to get started. This option takes thirty to sixty minutes.

2. The second option is to use the diagram and descriptions on pages 57 to 60. Mark the values that most resonate with you, and personalize them with your own words. Then use the Core Values Activator on page 70 to see how active they are in your life. This option takes about fifteen minutes.

3. The third option—if you're convinced you already know your core values—is to use the Core Values Activator on page 70 as a reality check. This option takes less than ten minutes.

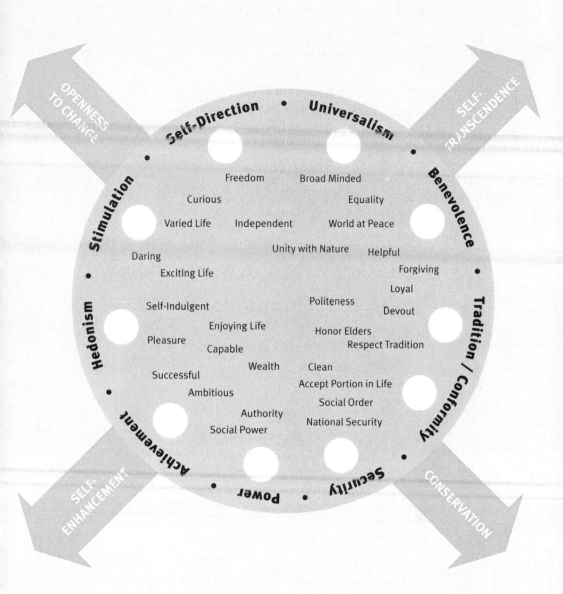

Freedom
Broad Minded
Curious
Equality
Varied Life   Independent
World at Peace
Unity with Nature   Helpful
Daring
Exciting Life
Forgiving
Loyal
Self-Indulgent
Politeness
Devout
Enjoying Life
Pleasure
Honor Elders
Capable
Respect Tradition
Wealth   Clean
Successful
Accept Portion in Life
Ambitious
Social Order
Authority
National Security
Social Power

Self-Direction • Universalism

OPENNESS TO CHANGE
SELF-TRANSCENDENCE
Stimulation
Benevolence
Hedonism
Tradition / Conformity
Achievement
Security
SELF-ENHANCEMENT
Power
CONSERVATION

Exercise based on the Values Theory of Shalom Schwartz, Hebrew University. Used with permission.

THE TEN BASIC VALUES ORIENTATIONS WITH A SAMPLE OF SPECIFIC VALUES

From the Values Theory of Shalom Schwartz

UNIVERSALISM: Understanding, appreciation, tolerance, and protection for the welfare of all people and for nature.

> **Broad-minded:** Tolerant of different ideas and beliefs.
> **Equality:** Equal opportunity for all.
> **Protecting the environment:** Preserving nature.
> **Social justice:** Correcting injustice, care for the weak.
> **Unity with nature:** Fitting into nature.
> **Wisdom:** A mature understanding of life.
> **World at peace:** Free of war and conflict.
> **World of beauty:** Beauty of nature and the arts.

Your own value words? _____

BENEVOLENCE: Preserving and enhancing the welfare of those with whom one is in frequent personal contact.

> **Forgiving:** Willing to pardon others.
> **Helpful:** Working for the welfare of others.
> **Honest:** Genuine, sincere.
> **Loyal:** Faithful to my friends, group.
> **Mature love:** Deep emotional and spiritual intimacy.
> **Responsible:** Dependable, reliable.
> **True friendship:** Close, supportive friends.

Your own value words? _____

TRADITION: Respect, commitment, and acceptance of the customs and ideas that one's culture or religion provides.

> **Accepting portion in life:** Submitting to life's circumstances.
> **Devout:** Holding to religious faith and belief.
> **Humble:** Modest, self-effacing.
> **Respect for tradition:** Preservation of time-honored customs.

Your own value words? _____

CONFORMITY: Restraint of actions, inclinations, and impulses likely to upset or harm others and violate social expectations or norms.

> **Honoring parents and elders:** Showing respect.
> **Obedient:** Dutiful, meeting obligations.
> **Politeness:** Courtesy, good manners.
> **Self-discipline:** Self-restraint, resistance to temptation.

Your own value words? _____

SECURITY: Safety, harmony, and stability of society, of relationships, and of self.

> **Clean:** Neat, tidy.
> **Family security:** Safety for loved ones.
> **National security:** Protection of my nation from enemies.
> **Reciprocation of favors:** Avoidance of indebtedness.
> **Social order:** Stability of society.

Your own value words? _____

POWER: Social status and prestige, control or dominance over people and resources.

> **Authority:** The right to lead or command.
> **Social power:** Control over others, dominance.
> **Wealth:** Material possessions, money.

Your own value words? _____

ACHIEVEMENT: Personal success through demonstrating competence according to social standards.

> **Ambitious:** Hard working, aspiring.
> **Capable:** Competent, effective, efficient.
> **Influential:** Having an impact on people and events.
> **Successful:** Achieving goals.

Your own value words? _____

HEDONISM: Pleasure or sensuous gratification for oneself.

 Enjoying life: Enjoying food, sex, leisure, etc.

 Pleasure: Gratification of desires.

 Self-Indulgent: Doing pleasant things.

Your own value words? _____

STIMULATION: Excitement, novelty, and challenge in life.

 Daring: Seeking adventure, risk.

 Exciting life: Stimulating experiences.

 Varied life: Filled with challenge, novelty, and change.

Your own value words? _____

SELF-DIRECTION: Independent thought and action—choosing, creating, exploring.

 Choosing own goals: Selecting own purposes.

 Creativity: Uniqueness, imagination.

 Curious: Interested in everything, exploring.

 Freedom: Freedom of action and thought.

 Independent: Self-reliant, self-sufficient.

Your own value words? _____

TEN STEPS TO YOUR VALUES

This looks more complicated than it really is. Just have a basic calculator handy, and take it one step at a time. You'll be glad you did!

1. Note whether you're female or male, and answer the forty-item questionnaire starting on page 62 or 65.

2. Copy all of your scores from the questionnaire into the appropriate value columns of the Values Universe Scoring Sheet on pages 68–69.

3. Add your scores within each of the value columns, to fill in all ten of the "Total" boxes.

4. Add your ten Totals together, and put that number in the single "PVQ TOT" box on the far right.

5. Divide your PVQ TOT box by 40, and put that number in the "PVQ AVG" box right below it.

6. Divide each of your ten Total boxes by the number printed below each one, to fill in your ten "Average" boxes.

7. Divide each of your ten Average boxes by the single PVQ AVG, to fill in your ten "Quotient" circles. Round to two decimal places (for example, 0.99).

8. Copy your ten Quotients into the ten corresponding circles of the Values Universe on page 57.

9. Identify which of your basic values are highest, and which are lowest. More importantly, what *pattern* do you see around your circle?

10. Read the descriptions on pages 58–60 to confirm which basic and specific values resonate most with you. Choose your own words to describe your own core values, and write them in your Life Circle on page 55.

To confirm how active they really are in your everyday life, use the Core Values Activator on page 70.

NOTE: This exercise prioritizes your values—but doesn't compare you with other people. A value that is not your highest could still be "higher than average." That's especially true for values on the Self-Enhancement and Openness to Change side of the universe. For example, if Hedonism is your second or third highest value, it's probably higher than for most people.

FEMALE QUESTIONNAIRE

Here are brief descriptions of some people. Please read each description and think about how much each person is or is not like you. Circle the number that shows how much the person in the description is like you.

How Much Like You Is This Person?	Not like me at all	Not like me	A little like me	Somewhat like me	Like me	Very much like me
1. Thinking up new ideas and being creative is important to her. She likes to do things in her own original way.	1	2	3	4	5	6
2. It is important to her to be rich. She wants to have a lot of money and expensive things.	1	2	3	4	5	6
3. She thinks it is important that every person in the world be treated equally. She believes everyone should have equal opportunities in life.	1	2	3	4	5	6
4. It's very important to her to show her abilities. She wants people to admire what she does.	1	2	3	4	5	6
5. It is important to her to live in secure surroundings. She avoids anything that might endanger her safety.	1	2	3	4	5	6
6. She thinks it is important to do lots of different things in life. She always looks for new things to try.	1	2	3	4	5	6
7. She believes that people should do what they're told. She thinks people should follow rules at all times, even when no-one is watching.	1	2	3	4	5	6
8. It is important to her to listen to people who are different from her. Even when she disagrees with them, she still wants to understand them.	1	2	3	4	5	6
9. She thinks it's important not to ask for more than what you have. She believes that people should be satisfied with what they have.	1	2	3	4	5	6
10. She seeks every chance she can to have fun. It is important to her to do things that give her pleasure.	1	2	3	4	5	6

11. It is important to her to make her own decisions about what she does. She likes to be free to plan and to choose her activities for herself.	1	2	3	4	5	6
12. It's very important to her to help the people around her. She wants to care for their well-being.	1	2	3	4	5	6
13. Being very successful is important to her. She likes to impress other people.	1	2	3	4	5	6
14. It is very important to her that her country be safe. She thinks the state must be on watch against threats from within and without.	1	2	3	4	5	6
15. She likes to take risks. She is always looking for adventures.	1	2	3	4	5	6
16. It is important to her always to behave properly. She wants to avoid doing anything people would say is wrong.	1	2	3	4	5	6
17. It is important to her to be in charge and tell others what to do. She wants people to do what she says.	1	2	3	4	5	6
18. It is important to her to be loyal to her friends. She wants to devote herself to people close to her.	1	2	3	4	5	6
19. She strongly believes that people should care for nature. Looking after the environment is important to her.	1	2	3	4	5	6
20. Religious belief is important to her. She tries hard to do what her religion requires.	1	2	3	4	5	6
21. It is important to her that things be organized and clean. She really does not like things to be a mess.	1	2	3	4	5	6
22. She thinks it's important to be interested in things. She likes to be curious and to try to understand all sorts of things.	1	2	3	4	5	6
23. She believes all the worlds' people should live in harmony. Promoting peace among all groups in the world is important to her.	1	2	3	4	5	6
24. She thinks it is important to be ambitious. She wants to show how capable she is.	1	2	3	4	5	6
25. She thinks it is best to do things in traditional ways. It is important to her to keep up the customs she has learned.	1	2	3	4	5	6
26. Enjoying life's pleasures is important to her. She likes to 'spoil' herself.	1	2	3	4	5	6
27. It is important to her to respond to the needs of others. She tries to support those she knows.	1	2	3	4	5	6

28. She believes she should always show respect to her parents and to older people. It is important to her to be obedient.	1	2	3	4	5	6
29. She wants everyone to be treated justly, even people she doesn't know. It is important to her to protect the weak in society.	1	2	3	4	5	6
30. She likes surprises. It is important to her to have an exciting life.	1	2	3	4	5	6
31. She tries hard to avoid getting sick. Staying healthy is very important to her.	1	2	3	4	5	6
32. Getting ahead in life is important to her. She strives to do better than others.	1	2	3	4	5	6
33. Forgiving people who have hurt her is important to her. She tries to see what is good in them and not to hold a grudge.	1	2	3	4	5	6
34. It is important to her to be independent. She likes to rely on herself.	1	2	3	4	5	6
35. Having a stable government is important to her. She is concerned that the social order be protected.	1	2	3	4	5	6
36. It is important to her to be polite to other people all the time. She tries never to disturb or irritate others.	1	2	3	4	5	6
37. She really wants to enjoy life. Having a good time is very important to her.	1	2	3	4	5	6
38. It is important to her to be humble and modest. She tries not to draw attention to herself.	1	2	3	4	5	6
39. She always wants to be the one who makes the decisions. She likes to be the leader.	1	2	3	4	5	6
40. It is important to her to adapt to nature and to fit into it. She believes that people should not change nature.	1	2	3	4	5	6

Now turn to the Values Universe Scoring Sheet on pages 68–69.

MALE QUESTIONNAIRE

Here are brief descriptions of some people. Please read each description and think about how much each person is or is not like you. Circle the number that shows how much the person in the description is like you.

How Much Like You Is This Person?	Not like me at all	Not like me	A little like me	Somewhat like me	Like me	Very much like me
1. Thinking up new ideas and being creative is important to him. He likes to do things in his own original way.	1	2	3	4	5	6
2. It Is important to him to be rich. He wants to have a lot of money and expensive things.	1	2	3	4	5	6
3. He thinks it is important that every person in the world be treated equally. He believes everyone should have equal opportunities in life.	1	2	3	4	5	6
4. It's very important to him to show his abilities. He wants people to admire what he does.	1	2	3	4	5	6
5. It is important to him to live in secure surroundings. He avoids anything that might endanger his safety.	1	2	3	4	5	6
6. He thinks it is important to do lots of different things in life. He always looks for new things to try.	1	2	3	4	5	6
7. He believes that people should do what they're told. He thinks people should follow rules at all times, even when no one is watching.	1	2	3	4	5	6
8. It is important to him to listen to people who are different from him. Even when he disagrees with them, he still wants to understand them.	1	2	3	4	5	6
9. He thinks it's important not to ask for more than what you have. He believes that people should be satisfied with what they have.	1	2	3	4	5	6
10. He seeks every chance he can to have fun. It is important to him to do things that give him pleasure.	1	2	3	4	5	6

11. It is important to him to make his own decisions about what he does. He likes to be free to plan and to choose his activities for himself.	1	2	3	4	5	6
12. It's very important to him to help the people around him. He wants to care for their well-being.	1	2	3	4	5	6
13. Being very successful is important to him. He likes to impress other people.	1	2	3	4	5	6
14. It is very important to him that his country be safe. He thinks the state must be on watch against threats from within and without.	1	2	3	4	5	6
15. He likes to take risks. He is always looking for adventures.	1	2	3	4	5	6
16. It is important to him always to behave properly. He wants to avoid doing anything people would say is wrong.	1	2	3	4	5	6
17. It is important to him to be in charge and tell others what to do. He wants people to do what he says.	1	2	3	4	5	6
18. It is important to him to be loyal to his friends. He wants to devote himself to people close to him.	1	2	3	4	5	6
19. He strongly believes that people should care for nature. Looking after the environment is important to him.	1	2	3	4	5	6
20. Religious belief is important to him. He tries hard to do what his religion requires.	1	2	3	4	5	6
21. It is important to him that things be organized and clean. He really does not like things to be a mess.	1	2	3	4	5	6
22. He thinks it's important to be interested in things. He likes to be curious and to try to understand all sorts of things.	1	2	3	4	5	6
23. He believes all the worlds' people should live in harmony. Promoting peace among all groups in the world is important to him.	1	2	3	4	5	6
24. He thinks it is important to be ambitious. He wants to show how capable he is.	1	2	3	4	5	6
25. He thinks it is best to do things in traditional ways. It is important to him to keep up the customs he has learned.	1	2	3	4	5	6
26. Enjoying life's pleasures is important to him. He likes to 'spoil' himself.	1	2	3	4	5	6

27. It is important to him to respond to the needs of others. He tries to support those he knows.	1	2	3	4	5	6
28. He believes he should always show respect to his parents and to older people. It is important to him to be obedient.	1	2	3	4	5	6
29. He wants everyone to be treated justly, even people he doesn't know. It is important to him to protect the weak in society.	1	2	3	4	5	6
30. He likes surprises. It is important to him to have an exciting life.	1	?	3	4	5	6
31. He tries hard to avoid getting sick. Staying healthy is very important to him.	1	2	3	4	5	6
32. Getting ahead in life is important to him. He strives to do better than others.	1	2	3	4	5	6
33. Forgiving people who have hurt him is important to him. He tries to see what is good in them and not to hold a grudge.	1	2	3	4	5	6
34. It is important to him to be independent. He likes to rely on himself.	1	2	3	4	5	6
35. Having a stable government is important to him. He is concerned that the social order be protected.	1	2	3	4	5	6
36. It is important to him to be polite to other people all the time. He tries never to disturb or irritate others.	1	2	3	4	5	6
37. He really wants to enjoy life. Having a good time is very important to him.	1	2	3	4	5	6
38. It is important to him to be humble and modest. He tries not to draw attention to himself.	1	2	3	4	5	6
39. He always wants to be the one who makes the decisions. He likes to be the leader.	1	2	3	4	5	6
40. It is important to him to adapt to nature and to fit into it. He believes that people should not change nature.	1	2	3	4	5	6

Now turn to the Values Universe Scoring Sheet on pages 68–69.

VALUES UNIVERSE SCORING SHEET

Universalism

3	
8	
19	
23	
29	
40	
UNI Total	
Divide by 6		= UNI Average
Divide by PVQ Average		= UNI Quotient

Benevolence

12	
18	
27	
33	
BEN Total	
Divide by 4		= BEN Average
Divide by PVQ Average		= BEN Quotient

Tradition

9	
20	
25	
38	
TRA Total	
Divide by 4		= TRA Average
Divide by PVQ Average		= TRA Quotient

Power

2	
17	
39	
POW Total	
Divide by 3		= POW Average
Divide by PVQ Average		= POW Quotient

Achievement

4	
13	
24	
32	
ACH Total	
Divide by 4		= ACH Average
Divide by PVQ Average		= ACH Quotient

Hedonism

10	
26	
37	
HED Total	
Divide by 3		= HED Average
Divide by PVQ Average		= HED Quotient

Conformity	
7	
16	
28	
36	
CON Total	
Divide by 4		= CON Average
Divide by PVQ Average		= CON Quotient

Security	
5	
14	
21	
31	
35	
SEC Total	
Divide by 5		= SEC Average
Divide by PVQ Average		= SEC Quotient

Stimulation	
6	
15	
30	
STI Total	
Divide by 3		= STI Average
Divide by PVQ Average		= STI Quotient

Self-Direction	
1	
11	
22	
34	
S-DIR Total	
Divide by 4		= S-DIR Average
Divide by PVQ Average		= S-DIR Quotient

Totals	
PVQ Total	
Divide by 40	
	= PVQ Average

CORE VALUES ACTIVATOR

Are your core values active in your daily life? If not—are they *really* your core values? Values are beliefs about what is desirable and undesirable, good and bad, or right and wrong. Some of the values we hold are situational, and apply to specific times, contexts, or people. Other values are much more core to who we are and transcend any specific situation. They guide us across all the domains of our lives. These core values determine the people and opportunities we seek out, and the ones we avoid. They shape the goals we set in life, and then motivate us to move toward those goals. Ultimately, they're the criteria we use to evaluate our own actions and the actions of others.

How can you tell if one of your values is really a core value? One good test is to see how *active* it is in your daily life. Do you hold it on a theoretical level—but it doesn't find its way into your daily life? Or is it active in only one domain of your life, but not in others? Or was it once a core value, but isn't anymore—and you didn't realize it? Or perhaps a new core value has emerged? Use this worksheet to see how active a value really is in your life. Or compare two or more values by completing a copy of the worksheet for each one.

The more active a value is in your life, the higher it's likely to score across the four areas below. You can remember the four areas with the acronym CORE, for Choose, Orient, Respond, and Express. As you ask yourself the following questions, and reflect on this value in your life, you'll come to a clearer understanding of what's really most important to you. Follow these steps:

Step One. Write the name of this value: _____.

Step Two. For this value, rate each statement on page 71 from strongly disagree (1) to strongly agree (5).

Step Three. Subtotal and total your scores to compare this value with your other values.

C	CHOOSE	Score	Subtotal
1	I choose this consciously.	1 2 3 4 5	
2	I know how this became important to me.	1 2 3 4 5	
3	This is more important than any particular situation.	1 2 3 4 5	
4	This is a central part of my identity.	1 2 3 4 5	
5	I would be a different person without this.	1 2 3 4 5	

O	ORIENT		
6	I orient my whole life toward this.	1 2 3 4 5	
7	I make plans for how to have this.	1 2 3 4 5	
8	This is like other values that are important to me.	1 2 3 4 5	
9	The opposite of this isn't important to me.	1 2 3 4 5	
10	I would trade almost anything else for this.	1 2 3 4 5	

R	RESPOND	Score	Subtotal
11	I respond emotionally to this.	1 2 3 4 5	
12	I automatically notice this in the world.	1 2 3 4 5	
13	I feel strongly motivated to have this.	1 2 3 4 5	
14	When this is threatened, I feel bad.	1 2 3 4 5	
15	When I pursue this, I feel good.	1 2 3 4 5	

E	EXPRESS		
16	I express this every day in some way.	1 2 3 4 5	
17	I have worked toward this over time.	1 2 3 4 5	
18	I have sacrificed other things to uphold this.	1 2 3 4 5	
19	I evaluate people and situations according to this.	1 2 3 4 5	
20	I'm drawn to people and situations that have this.	1 2 3 4 5	
		Total Score	

"Our nation's system of retirement security is imperiled, headed for a serious train wreck."

—JOHN BOGLE, founder of the Vanguard Funds

Chapter FOUR

Retirement Economics Is More Than Personal Finance

Does the topic of *personal finance* attract you or repel you?

No doubt you're attracted to all the wonderful things personal finance can do for you—having a nice place to live, going shopping, doing fun things with your friends and family. But the question here is about the nuts and bolts of personal finance, as a topic in itself. Are you interested in delving into money's inner secrets? How to get it, make it grow, protect it, and so on?

If your answer is yes, then the prosperity dimension of well-being may be an area of *specialization* for you. You may have a job working with money, or it might be your hobby. You read financial books, articles, and e-newsletters. You're curious about your retirement accounts and check on them. You enjoy swapping money stories with other financial specialists.

If that's not like you *at all*, then it's probably not an area of specialization. The subject may bore you, frustrate you, or even scare you a little. But it doesn't interest you one bit. You don't have a job working with money, and it isn't your hobby, either. You check your accounts from of a sense of obligation (or not at all). When the topic of finance comes up at a social gathering, you either change the subject or tune it out.

No matter which end of that specialization spectrum you're closer to, you'll discover this chapter isn't what you might have thought. Most retirement books are personal finance–oriented and offer variations of the same nuts and bolts information. If you expected an explanation of qualified plan types, advice on mutual funds, or tips on cutting your taxes, you won't find that here. You can get that stuff from the sea of information.

Instead of being stuck at the surface layer of personal finance, we'll take a deeper look at the economics that drive your retirement stage of life. In this chapter, you'll:

- See how the evolution of retirement relates to today's financial problems

- Identify practical strategies that your financial advisor doesn't know about

- Tap into resources that you probably wouldn't have thought of

The Retirement Crisis

You may be worried about your retirement finances or feeling pretty good about them. Regardless of your personal situation, you know from ongoing media coverage that many workers are concerned about being adequately financially prepared for retirement. Many are facing a similar set of challenges. The same themes keep coming up, over and over. They're less optimistic about their employer's retirement plan. They haven't been saving enough personally and are carrying too much debt. They weren't that confident about how to invest their savings, and now they have ridden the roller-coaster ride of a lifetime. They believed home equity was the foundation of financial security, but aren't so sure anymore. They know that Social Security and Medicare are underfunded, and are worried about what will happen to them.

There are so many theories about what has gone wrong that it's like a multiple-choice question. How did we all get into such a pickle?

a) Lack of personal responsibility

b) Greedy financial companies

c) Not enough government control

d) Too much government intervention

e) Globalization and outsourcing

f) All of the above

Even if we could pick the right answer, it wouldn't be relevant to your personal planning. The high visibility news stories seldom provide insight or ideas for how to approach your next stage of life. (They do get attention and sell advertising, though.)

Rather, we'll look at the most important stories that aren't in the news. These are more relevant because they're more likely to prompt your own creative ideas for designing a new stage of life. We'll start by reviewing approaches that people have used for support as they stopped working in later life. Our task isn't just to design the new retirement—we need to design a new way to pay for it, too. Due to a changing demographic and economic environment, we'll need to weave together elements from many approaches to make it work.

The Family Approach to Retirement Economics

Workers have had the old retirement available for a century or so, but people have always gotten old. What did they do for the fifty centuries before retirement was invented? There are some important clues here for us.

After all, the need to support older people has always existed. How did we meet that need? At the *family level*. But it wasn't called retirement, and it didn't require money. Even after money was invented, working people could live their whole lives with little need for coins or currency. People grew their own food, built their own houses, made their own clothes, and taught their own children. Parents had an economic relationship with their children, in addition to the social one. There was an understanding between them. A family contract of sorts. Here's a simplified version.

Parents raised their children by teaching them how to become productive in the world. Children learned by working alongside their parents to gain the skills for a particular way of life. It could have been farming or fishing or herding or a craft or trade. These multiple generations may have lived together as an extended family or as nuclear families that were geographically close to each other (probably right next door!). Siblings had an economic relationship, too. Children pooled their risks with their siblings, so that if one had a catastrophe such as a fire, the others helped rebuild. They pooled their opportunities too, such as building or buying new equipment. It wasn't just brotherly (and sisterly) love—it was a reciprocal economic arrangement. Insurance companies and banks weren't available, so they used the family contract instead.

The family contract addressed the aging of the older generation, too. We already know that aging and withdrawing from work had always been a gradual process, and that's what happened. The children took up the slack, but the parents didn't slack off! They contributed to the family's welfare in important ways. They helped maintain the household or cared for and taught their grandchildren. From their long experience, they provided practical knowledge on many topics. They offered connections to the community for the benefit of the family. Both genders made contributions, and both were valuable.

This original approach to retirement economics was based on a reciprocal relationship between the generations. It wasn't a one-way deal, with the children (and grandchildren) supporting the older parents. There was reciprocity between the generations, as they all contributed to the family's welfare. The reciprocation was also across an entire life span, with children paying parents back for teaching them a way of life. Property, in the form of land or tools of the trade, was part of the deal, too. Underneath the social relationship, there was this reciprocal economic exchange.

This is how "retirement" operated for thousands of years, and it still does in some places and situations. Even in modern times, it's the basic economic principle behind the *family business*! Although it phased out as societies became industrialized, it was still common just a few generations ago. Do you remember the television show that was famous for the closing line of every episode, "Good night, John Boy?" That was *The Waltons*—a multigenerational family operating on this principle. It was set in the 1930s.

As societies industrialized, people left traditional ways of working to become employees, because the hard cash increased their material standard of living. They could buy things they couldn't produce themselves. They migrated to cities and towns, where the jobs were. There, life wasn't about making the stuff they needed for daily life, but about making the money to buy the stuff they needed for daily life. It shifted from making their daily bread to "Another day, another dollar." Economics shifted from the multigenerational family contract to an individual and nuclear family cycle of earning and spending money.

For designing the new retirement, here's the sixty-four-thousand-dollar question: When the younger generation went to the factory, what happened to the older generation? The pattern of life they had planned on, and worked for, didn't happen. Forces beyond their control changed the way they had planned to retire. *They all needed to design their own solution to retirement.* (That's what you'll need to do.) Some of these parents probably worked themselves to death, without having another generation to reciprocate with. Some were able to sell their holdings and get money to retire in the modern sense. Others needed to live with their children and grandchildren in the city, even though they couldn't contribute to the family in the way they had anticipated. Societal transitions force changes in individual's plans, whether they anticipate them or not.

That's not to say the family approach isn't alive and well today, even in the era of personal finance. When folks sell the family farm or business to have money to retire, that's using the family approach. When someone receives an inheritance and it allows her to retire, that's the family approach. And when a single person who can't afford to retire somehow finds and marries his true love (who can afford to support two retirements), that's the family approach, too. You'll notice immigrants from developing nations using it, regardless of their educational or socioeconomic level.

There are (at least) three strategies you can take from the family approach that may be useful in making the new retirement work for you:

Practical Strategy #1: Reciprocal Exchange. The multigenerational family can be a powerful economic unit. How might you create a new form of *reciprocal exchange* (not a one-way street) that would harness your family's power?

A pyramid scheme is a financial arrangement in which a small number of early members receive payment from a larger number of later members. The schemes collapse, because they can't recruit enough new members at the bottom to make payments to the old members at the top. They're unsustainable.

Human societies were the original pyramid schemes—except they're actually population pyramids. A small number of old people were like the early members at the top, and a large number of workers were like the later members at the bottom. The younger ones helped the older ones with food, shelter, personal care, or money. It was positive, because honoring parents and elders is one element of a just society. It was also sustainable, because most people didn't live to be that old and they had plenty of children. The family approach to retirement economics worked this way.

The population pyramid still stacked up like that when retirement was invented. There were many more workers than retirees, so the societal approach to retirement economics (Social Security, Medicare, and employer pensions) was relatively inexpensive, per worker. But as people live longer and have fewer children, the top of the pyramid gets broader compared to the bottom. This isn't a onetime effect of the baby boom generation; it's a permanent shift. This has never happened before, and it will profoundly change society. One inescapable change is that the societal approach to retirement will become more expensive, per worker.

Personal investments for retirement may be affected, too. Will home values and stock prices become depressed as a relatively large number of retirees try to sell out to a relatively small number of workers? No one knows for sure, because this has never happened before. But one thing is certain—retirement is changing!

U.S. Census Bureau: U.S Population Trends, www.census.gov/mso/www/pres_lib/trends2050/textmostly/index.html

AGE DISTRIBUTION OF THE U.S. POPULATION, BY SEX: 1950

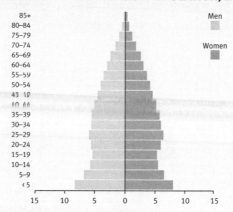

AGE DISTRIBUTION OF THE U.S. POPULATION, BY SEX: 2000

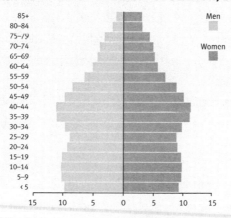

AGE DISTRIBUTION OF THE U.S. POPULATION, BY SEX: 2050

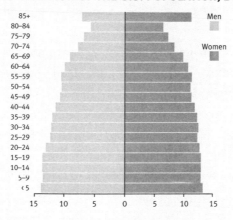

This is close to the spirit that animates a family business. It's about identifying the unique resources and abilities each could contribute and the unique needs each may have. It's about creating a synergy that benefits the entire family.

To scratch the surface, let's imagine some possibilities. Who needs elder care, and who could provide it? Who needs child care, and who could provide that? Who has unused land, or extra space in her home? Who could put that to use? Who might benefit from owning a two-family residence, with family living in both units? Who might benefit from sharing a vacation home? Who might be able to start a family business together? Who has money, time, or expertise? (Third Age entrepreneurship needs to be very tight with money, but it can be generous with time.)

This is a way of thinking that families have traditionally employed but that has disappeared from most Americans' thought patterns. It's still common in much of the world and among families that immigrate to the United States. There is much that Americans can relearn!

Practical Strategy #2: Adopt a "Family." The benefits of reciprocal exchange aren't reserved for biological families. Especially if you don't have access to a family of your own, how else could you become part of a supportive community?

Although families are multigenerational communities, that's not an easy relationship to find outside of your biological kin. The most common form is the old-fashioned neighborhood. (See chapter six.) Living in close proximity to First, Second, and Third Agers creates more opportunities for informal reciprocal benefits. In true neighborhoods, people look out for each other, remember?

It's relatively easy to find single-generation communities, where most people are in the Third Age. The most individual version is considering being a long-term roommate. This is easiest to do if you're single, of course! But remember that many people enter the Third Age as part of a couple and then, for a variety of reasons, become single. If that were to happen, rather than being a family of one, consider becoming a roommate. The next version is more formal and usually referred to as cohousing. This is a creative legal-financial arrangement that creates common ownership of property among people at the same life stage. The most common version is choosing to live in a "retirement community." However, most of the developments that go by that name are just places to live, and they don't create reciprocal exchange. (To look for a true community, see chapter six.)

Practical Strategy #3: Improvisation. In times of great transformation, when established practices break down, families need to improvise. How might you explore creative ways that your family can improvise together?

In modern society, most people are tight-lipped about their finances and personal affairs, even within their family. Not until someone needs help or leaves an inheritance do the others know what his or her situation was. Openly communicating about the subjects in family strategies #1 and #2 might seem a little . . . unconventional. But times of transformation mean that conventions are breaking down and not working as well. That's why you need to be *unconventional!* The place to start is by opening up communication with family, friends, and others you're in community with. Only then can you explore ways of improvising as an economic "family."

The Societal Approach to Retirement Economics

This is the original old retirement, and the approach we grew up under. It's been around our whole lives, so it's deeply embedded in the way we think. Just like the family approach, it will always exist, but will now need to change in order to accommodate the enormous shift in our demographics. It came about as the family contract was replaced by the employment contract, and a new way had to be found to economically support people as they aged.

Workers were being paid in money, of course. They knew they needed to save for a future time when they couldn't work anymore, and no doubt they did their best. But moving from tangible prosperity (land, animals, equipment) to intangible prosperity (savings accounts and investments) requires an enormous conceptual shift. People struggled with it. Many people still struggle with it today, don't they?

Personal savings wasn't enough to provide retirement security, and the need could no longer be addressed at the family level. So instead it was addressed at the societal level, through the government and organizations. In the words of President Franklin Roosevelt:

"Because it has become increasingly difficult for individuals to build their own security single-handed, government must now step in and help them lay the foundation stones."

In 1935, the Social Security Act created a system for providing old-age benefits for Americans. The goal wasn't to reward retiring workers with a lengthy period of leisure. Rather, the goal was to provide a safety net for a few years to those workers who managed to live past the age of sixty-five. A generation later, in 1965, the Social Security Act was expanded to provide medical benefits under Medicare. Both of these plans are funded by equal contributions from workers and their employers, out of everyone's paychecks.

Society also created the environment where it became common for employers to provide pensions for retiring workers. The number of plans increased steadily over the decades of the twentieth century. In 1940, about four million workers were covered by pension plans. By 1960, that number had grown to more than twenty-three million! The federal government created an incentive through the tax structure for organizations to create and maintain retirement plans for employees.

By the mid-twentieth century, these three separate approaches for providing retirement income—Social Security, employer pensions, and personal savings—had acquired a name. They were called the three-legged stool of retirement security. Although the origins of this metaphor aren't completely known, the concept of the three-legged stool has become very well known (at least among retirement geeks).

Taken as a whole, this three-part financial retirement system is a marvel of engineering. Or, more accurately, social engineering. Before it was developed, retirement as leisure was relatively uncommon. Afterward, retirement became taken for granted. Of course, each person didn't necessarily have all three sources, or the same income from all three. Rather, the three-legged stool created a system of retirement income that provided support and stability for society in general.

Society had succeeded in *institutionalizing* the Three Boxes of Life. Along with public education for the first box of life, the three-legged stool for the third box of life became one of the most profound achievements of the twentieth century.

But Now the Three-Legged Stool Is Wobbly

In general, this system worked well for our parents and grandparents. But now it's creaking and cracking and beginning to wobble. No one knows what will happen with Social Security, employer pensions, and personal savings, but here are a few reasons why we can't depend on the three legged stool like we could in the past.

The First Leg: Social Security

Social Security has been a popular favorite for more than seventy-five years now. The happiest day of the month, for many millions of people, has been the day the envelope from Social Security arrives in their mailbox. (A few even wait to greet the mailman.) For some, it has added to the total wealth that will be passed on to their heirs. For others, it has provided the extras in life that they couldn't afford otherwise. And, for millions, it has been their *largest source of income* and keeping them afloat. But all feel entitled to their monthly payment and look forward to it. Future recipients of that monthly payment feel just as *entitled!*

That's why Social Security's wobble is high profile; it has made head-lines for years and will continue to do so. Where do all those payments come from? It was designed primarily to be a pay-as-you-go plan, mean-ing that the current workers' contributions that are going in are used to pay the retired workers' benefits that are going out. But the ratio of workers paying into the system has fallen in comparison to the number of retirees collecting benefits. This is mostly due to a decreasing birth rate in the United States, because families don't need to have as many children as they did in the era of the family contract. A lower birth-rate means fewer workers paying in. (Workers emigrating to the United States bolster that number, though.) The other factor is an increasing life span, as people have taken longer and longer to kick the bucket. That increases how many years of payments each retiree receives and also how many are still living and receiving payments. Not surprisingly, this means that the total contributions coming in are shrinking in proportion to the total payments going out. On the current trajectory, there won't be enough money to pay all the benefits. Social Security will run short of money. Medicare is on an even more precarious trajectory.

We'll need to either increase the contributions coming from work-ers and employers or reduce the benefits, or some combination of the two. The sooner that course corrections are made, the less drastic they'll need to be. The *mathematical* resolution of this problem isn't that big of a deal. There are people endowed with very powerful, very warped minds—economists and actuaries—who actually love puzzles like this. Unfortunately, the *political* resolution is a very big deal. Lawmakers tried—and failed—to find a middle ground for fixing the problem when economic times were good and the federal deficit was in much better shape. Who knows whether they'll work together better in bad times? As with every political issue, there are those who claim that the prob-lem is nearly insurmountable, and others who claim that it's not really a problem at all.

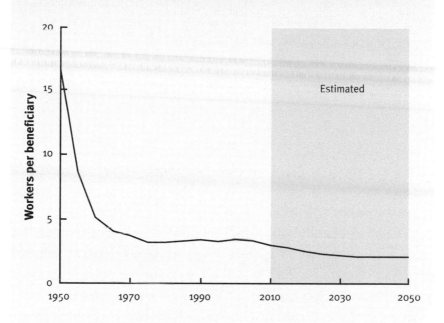

The Social Security funding crisis is like an accident in slow motion. Demographically, it's been unfolding for *decades*. The challenge is that the system operates on a fundamental premise; incoming payroll taxes from workers must be sufficient to pay outgoing benefits to retirees (and other beneficiaries). Because you understand the changes in the population pyramid, you already know we're headed for trouble.

The graph above shows how the number of workers per beneficiary has fallen over time. In 1955 there were more than eight workers for each beneficiary, although the ratio was dropping quickly. But since the 1970s, there have been more than *three* workers for each beneficiary. Now the ratio is dropping again and may end up at only *two* workers for each beneficiary. That may not sound like much, but it's a 33 percent reduction!

When incoming payroll taxes were greater than outgoing benefits, the system built up a surplus for the future. But starting in 2010, payroll taxes coming in fell below the benefits being paid out. The surplus will only cover the difference until 2037. Then benefits would need to be cut by about 25 percent! How do we fix it? We need to increase the payroll tax, carefully trim benefits, or delay the retirement age. *Maybe all three.* If we do it sooner, rather than later, the changes won't be as drastic. So even though this accident is unfolding in slow motion, it's urgent!

SOURCE: 2009 Annual Report of the Board of Trustees of the Federal Old-Age and Survivors Insurance and Disability Insurance Trust Funds, Table IV.B2.

There's another complication. Social Security built up a surplus for the future, in anticipation of when benefit payments would exceed contributions. But the broader federal government has actually *borrowed* against the Social Security surplus. There's no question that the government is good for it. It's just that, to pay Social Security back, they'll have to raise taxes or cut spending elsewhere. Only time and the prevailing political winds will determine how much, and how soon, we should be worried. Even if the first leg isn't wobbling yet, we can hear it creaking loudly. It's crying out for repair.

The Second Leg: Employer Pensions

Pensions have been a popular favorite, too. They haven't provided a monthly mailbox smile to as many people as Social Security has. But they have transformed retirement for many millions of Americans. The *monthly* aspect is important, because the term *pension* is used to refer to many different types of retirement plans these days. However, employer pension actually refers to a very specific type of plan. A pension was the original type of plan that an employer *promises to pay for* and accumulates a benefit for only one purpose: retirement. A profit-sharing plan that an employer may or may not contribute to isn't a pension plan. A salary savings plan that an employee may or may not contribute to, such as a 401(k), isn't a pension plan, either. It's only a pension plan if there's a requirement to provide a *defined benefit* at retirement or a *defined contribution each year*. It's only a pension if there's a *commitment*.

There's another feature that most pensions share. At retirement, pensions provide a *monthly income for life*. So no matter how long the employee lives, they can't outlive their money, as they might in the case of an investment account. This is the type of plan that formed the original leg of the three-legged stool. You can see why it provided a solid foundation for retirement—a pension was something you could count on. A happy mailbox every month, for as long as you lived!

However, a smaller and smaller proportion of workers will ever receive benefits from this type of plan because of two trends in the U.S. workplace. One trend is from the employee side. Because employees tend to move from company to company more than they used to, they are less likely to stick around long enough to earn this type of pension. It takes many years of service to build up a benefit. Unlike times past, few employees consider themselves to be lifers at a given job, and so they don't reap the benefits of this type of long-term benefit structure.

The other trend is from the employer side. The number of employers still willing to foot the bill for a traditional employer-funded pension is steadily decreasing. Government employers at all levels have generally stayed with this traditional approach, and they are still likely to maintain pension plans. (Although some of these plans are facing the same type of funding problems as Social Security is.) At the opposite end of the spectrum, smaller companies have rarely provided them. Large companies are somewhere in between, historically sponsoring pension plans, but many have now terminated or frozen them. The total number of traditional pension plans reached a peak of more than 114,000 in 1985, but well over two-thirds of those are now gone. In recent years, the news has been filled with stories of well-known employers reducing or eliminating these benefits.

Why are employers doing away with pensions? First, the regulatory compliance for these plans became so complex that some employers decided it wasn't worth the bother. Second, and probably more important, plans designed to reward long-term service were simply out of touch with the need to attract and retain new talent. Third, employees themselves seemed to have a better understanding of, and appreciation for, profit-sharing and 401(k)-type plans. Another reason—one that's less cited but pretty obvious—is that many employers who have eliminated their traditional defined-benefit pensions were simply looking to reduce costs. Employers who replaced pensions with profit-sharing and 401(k) plans almost always were able to cut their costs significantly. (This is echoed in the emerging trend of employers eliminating or reducing medical insurance coverage for retirees.) In any case, the combined result of these two broad trends (employee and employer) is that fewer people can look forward to getting a monthly pension for as long as they live. For U.S. workers, the second leg is definitely shorter.

You may ask, "Aren't 401(k) plans the 'modern' replacement for the second leg?" That's a good question. These hybrid employer-employee savings accounts go by a variety of names, often the section of the Internal Revenue Code that made them possible. Depending on where you work, it could instead be a 403(b), 457, SIMPLE, Thrift Plan, or some other type of payroll savings plan. Although the details vary, all of these plans, in all these environments, are essentially the same thing: Your employer provides an easy way for you (*you, you, you!*) to save for your own retirement. The cornerstone of these plans isn't an employer contribution, like in a traditional pension. No, the cornerstone is your own savings. Technically, these plans are salary-reduction plans. (Guess whose salary gets the reduction to fund them? You get only one guess.)

If you're fortunate, your employer may match part of your contribution or make other types of contributions. However, in general, there are no required employer contributions in these salary savings plans. If your employer is *generous*, you could be on the receiving end of some hefty contributions—every bit as valuable as anything you might get from a traditional pension. But if your employer is *stingy*, you could be carrying the ball all by yourself, with no contributions at all from your employer. (Do you know how generous or stingy your employer is?) A 401(k)-type plan simply provides a framework for you and your employer to make contributions into your retirement account, and each of you decides whether to put in a little or a lot. So if your employer only puts in a little, you'd better put in a lot!

To rephrase the question at hand: "Are these plans part of the second leg or part of the third leg?" The answer is . . . yes. They don't fully measure up to the original concept of the second leg, because they don't have the level of commitment of a traditional pension. But they are like an employer pension in that they're maintained by the employer, who does have significant responsibility to make sure everything is on the up-and-up and who may make some contribution. But they're like personal savings in that you're the one who needs to save the significant money (through payroll deductions) to create a retirement benefit. For an increasing number of workers, 401(k)-type plans are the only second leg they'll have. Any way we look at it, the second leg is wobbling.

The Third Leg: Personal Savings

One reason the first and second legs worked so well is that they were automatic. People didn't need to do anything in particular to build up benefits in those legs, other than work for a paycheck. The workers paid attention to the week-to-week, month-to-month money. And Social Security and the employer pension paid attention to the age-sixty-five-until-you-die money.

Workers do pretty well with month-to-month money. After all, most people don't spend their entire paycheck on the same day they get it. If they get paid on Fridays, they don't live like royalty on Friday night and like paupers by the next Thursday. No, they try to level things out so that they don't have such drastic peaks and valleys in spending. Most people, even if they're not financial specialists, get pretty good at leveling it out. Week-to-week, month-to-month, and over a whole year or longer, people more or less level out their spending. Through trial and error, they learn how much to spend right away and how much to save so that they have something left to spend later. It's a skill that people acquire over time, because they get many weeks, months, and years to practice.

But shifting modes to think about age-sixty-five-until-you-die money isn't natural for most people. It wasn't needed back in the era of family retirement economics. People had always saved, of course. They saved for a new piece of equipment. They saved for years to buy a piece of property. People were accustomed to doing that. But the third leg of the stool was a new idea. Saving, saving, saving for decades in order to then s-l-o-w-l-y spend over more decades. How would that work?

Franco Modigliani won a Nobel Prize in economics for coming up with an explanation for how people are thought to save, which he called the Life Cycle Hypothesis. (Milton Friedman advanced a similar concept

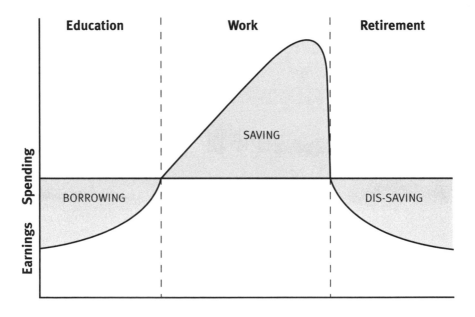

THE LIFE CYCLE HYPOTHESIS OF SAVING

called the Permanent Income Hypothesis.) Modigliani assumed that people are *rational agents*. That means they anticipate what's going to happen in the future, figure out the right course of action, and then use willpower to follow through. He said that people don't spend based on their *current* level of income but on the level they *expect to average over their lifetime*. When we expect to have a higher income in the future, we're more likely to dip into savings—or borrow money to spend more than our current income. That's because we expect to make plenty of money later, and we'll catch up to our spending over time. So in the *early* part of our lives, we tend to spend more than we earn, through *borrowing*.

On the other hand, when we expect to have a lower income in the future, we're more likely to put money into savings and spend less than our current income. Instead of continuing to borrow like when we were younger, we flip-flop over to saving. That's the kind of long-term retirement saving envisioned as the third leg of the three-legged stool. Modigliani suggested that even if we overspend in the early part of our life cycle, we make up for it by underspending in the middle part. Similar to leveling out our spending from paycheck to paycheck, the Life Cycle Hypothesis says we try to level out our spending over our entire lifetime. That's how the third leg of the stool—personal savings—would be able to work. Because we're rational agents!

In general, though, it hasn't worked out that way. Many (most?) workers apparently aren't rational. Over the past twenty-five years, the aggregate percentage of our income that we've set aside as personal savings has steadily declined. When you look at the graph on page 92 you might even say it has plummeted—from a peak of about 11 percent in the early 1980s to almost nothing by the year 2005. Saving was so low that it was initially calculated as negative! It would have been the first year since the Great Depression that we collectively spent more than we earned. For the rate to fall that low, some Americans had to spend from their savings; others had to borrow from credit cards, mortgages, car loans, college loans, or home equity loans. The true opposite of saving isn't spending—it's borrowing. In 2009, the savings rate rose sharply. But given the tough state of the economy and the high rate of unemployment, it's probably not that

PERSONAL SAVINGS RATE

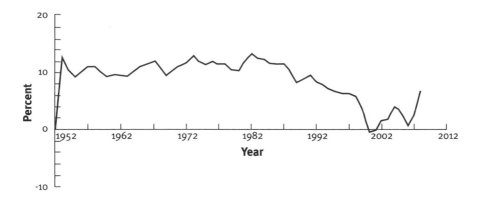

Americans suddenly decided to sock away tons of money. Maybe they just stopped borrowing so much. In any case, there is nothing to suggest that Americans are now committed—over the long term—to building a solid and secure third leg. (We can always hope.)

Maximizing the Societal Approach

The societal approach (like the family approach) is still very much alive. For some workers, it's the way that they'll be able to afford to retire, even if the three-legged stool is wobbling. Thanks to years of service under pensions and Social Security, millions will still have a happy mailbox (or e-deposit) every month, for as long as they live. However, if you missed out on getting a full employer pension, there are still (at least) two strategies you can use to maximize your retirement savings.

Practical Strategy #1: Maximize Social Security. Your Social Security benefits represent our collective society's commitment to help support you in retirement, and these benefits are more valuable than you realize. How might you *maximize* the benefits you receive?

This isn't about gaming the system, but about making smart decisions for accruing your benefits and for collecting them. We're willing to pay for professional services to maintain other valuable assets such as our home or investment accounts. But we don't think about getting advice for Social Security benefits. With boomers becoming eligible to apply for benefits, more advisors will turn their attention to strategies for maximizing benefits.

For example, gaining just a few more years of credited service may help those who were in and out of the workforce over their career. With today's blended families, couples that live together but haven't married should see how tying the knot could affect their benefits. And everyone—*everyone*—should double and triple think the age at which they apply for benefits. How much earned income you'll have and your biomedical prospects for living shorter, or longer, than the average retiree are both important factors. They should shape your decision about taking a smaller benefit at age sixty-two, or a larger benefit later. (See chapter eight regarding your personal life expectancy.) There are now strategies for beginning benefits at age sixty-two, and then *paying them back* to Social Security later, to trade up to a higher monthly benefit. Have you ever heard of such a thing?

Practical Strategy #2: Tap into a Pension. Benefits from a traditional employer pension can provide peace of mind for life, but they are becoming harder and harder to get. Can you tap into one of these plans for a partial benefit?

If you already work for an employer that provides a traditional pension, you know you want to accrue the maximum benefit you can. But be savvy when choosing your payout option, too. (By the way, the joint-and-survivor monthly benefit for your spouse may have a lower payment but probably a larger total payout over your lifetimes.) If you worked for one of these employers years ago, you may have the opportunity to accrue more benefits by working there again, or you may even be able to buy back benefits from the first time around. These plans are so complicated that they can make a CPA's eyes glaze over. Get expert advice.

If you have never been in a traditional pension, you should know that older workers typically accrue benefits faster than younger workers do. So if you're looking for a job, strongly consider finding one of these hidden gems. Look at government employers, schools, large corporations, and smaller companies that have been around for a long time. Even five years of plan participation at the end of your career can produce a significant benefit. In some cases, you can even earn pension benefits for part-time work after you retire from your primary career. But you'll need to do your detective work to find these diamonds in the rough.

The Rational Agent Approach to Retirement Economics

This approach sprang up as the societal approach passed its high point. It's based on the belief that people are *rational agents*. That means, given enough information and choices, workers will automatically save however much they need in order to retire.

When the three-legged stool was created, saving was pretty simple. It was downright boring, to be more accurate. People were content to save in plain old bank accounts and earn interest. One reason is because a decade earlier, many Americans had begun investing in stocks, and they rode a market bubble all the way up to the stock market crash. (The one in 1929, not 2009.) Having been burned, they resolved to stick with guaranteed, low-yielding investments in the solid banks that had weathered the crash and the Great Depression. Only a few rich or courageous (or foolish) souls invested in individual stocks and bonds.

But decades later, when 401(k) plans were supplementing and then replacing traditional pensions, personal saving became much more exciting. Within 401(k) plans, participants could choose different investment strategies, which they couldn't do inside employer pensions. And outside the 401(k), new types of accounts such as IRAs were passed into law. Financial instruments such as mutual funds and variable annuities proliferated and multiplied. In a few decades, personal saving for retirement went from boring to bewildering! And it was being marketed to the max. There were armies of stockbrokers and mutual fund salespeople marching out every day, loaded with investment products, reminding workers of their need to save for retirement. There were also the more recent "no-load" providers, offering products wholesale, via mail and telephone (and eventually the Internet). In addition to the products themselves, more and more investment *information* began pouring in, too. Although it was only a river of information in those days, and not yet a sea.

This environment was no problem for the rational agents of the Life Cycle Hypothesis. These workers would recognize that employer pensions were weakening and would embrace the 401(k) plan as a worthy successor. They would sign up for their employer salary savings plans, learn about the investment options, carefully determine which were appropriate for them, and follow through with ever-increasing plan contributions, as they monitored and managed their investments. They would carefully shore up the second leg, as traditional pensions disappeared.

But they wouldn't stop with the second leg; these rational agents would shore up the third leg, too. They would also invest in IRA accounts, Roth IRA accounts, tax-deferred annuities, variable life insurance policies, and just for good measure, section 529 college savings plans for the kids. (And of course, they would remember to read the prospectus before investing money.) That would take care of the third leg!

All the retirement geeks—employee benefit managers, 401(k) providers, mutual fund companies, insurance companies, investment representatives, and even the government—shared a set of common beliefs. They all believed that people *really were rational agents*, just as Franco Modigliani and other economists had theorized. They all believed that if people simply had *access to financial information*, they would come to the right conclusions. They all believed that if people simply had *enough choices*, they would choose good ones. And most important, they all believed that if people simply understood the need for *personal responsibility*, they would become responsible and save enough for retirement.

We already know how all that turned out. If you've forgotten, peek back at the personal savings graph on page 92. However, in retrospect, it makes complete sense. Under the rational agent approach, the workers who actually *are* rational agents did just fine. They anticipated the future, made good decisions, and used willpower to follow through. They compensated for the wobbly stool just fine. (That is, until the stock market and real estate crash of 2009. But that's related to a different concept in economics, about *rational markets*. Hmmmm.)

Nonrational Agents in the Rational Agent Approach

What about all the other workers—the ones who weren't rational agents? The *nonrational* agents? What could they possibly have been thinking? (You'll want to know what they were thinking, so you can avoid it!) Let's examine the fundamental decision of how much to consume. Should they spend all their income, or should they save a bunch of it?

Because economists are fond of the idea that things are in equilibrium, or in balance, we'll use an example called the *Spending-Saving Seesaw*. You can see that spending is on the left side of the seesaw, and saving on the right. First we'll look at the consumption economics of a rational agent and then at three nonrational agents. For the rational agents, the seesaw is in balance. They adjust their spending and saving according to the Life Cycle Hypothesis, of course.

RATIONAL ECONOMICS

Spend   Save

Spending-
Saving Seesaw

However, for most people—the nonrational agents—it isn't easy to balance the seesaw. The first reason has to do with temptation. If they're going to save their income, they only get one chance to save it, and then it's gone forever. That's because the only income they can save is today's income.

But spending doesn't work that way. If they're going to spend their income, they get *three chances* to spend it. That's because they can spend *today's* income, obviously. They can also spend *yesterday's* income, by taking money from savings. And they can also spend *tomorrow's* income, by borrowing. (It's paid back from tomorrow's income.) You can see what that does to the seesaw. It's a lot of temptation!

TEMPTATION ECONOMICS

The second reason has to do with how people perceive today's money versus tomorrow's money. When people save, they give up spending the money today in order to spend it (plus interest) tomorrow. We know from behavioral economics that people perceive spending today's money as *much more* valuable that it really is. And they perceive spending tomorrow's money as *much less* valuable than it really is. It's like they're looking through the wrong end of a telescope. You can see what that does to the seesaw. It makes tomorrow seem too small and dim compared to today.

BEHAVIORAL ECONOMICS

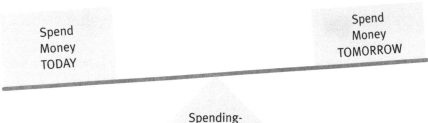

The third reason has to do with the market economy. We know that businesses are driven to earn a profit through satisfying the needs and desires of consumers. So to understand market forces, we need to ask two questions: "How much profit can businesses earn by getting people to save?" as opposed to "How much profit can businesses earn by getting people to spend?" The answers determine how much outside pressure will be applied to consumers.

It turns out that a good profit can be made by businesses that get people to save via their CDs, mutual funds, and other products. But there's more profit to be made in getting people to spend, for two reasons. The first is the profit to be made on the goods and services consumers spend money on. The second is the profit to be made in loaning consumers money to spend. The saving end of the seesaw loses again.

MARKET ECONOMICS

Profit on getting people to SPEND

Profit on getting people to SAVE

Profit on getting people to BORROW

Spending-Saving Seesaw

Here are two practical examples.

Which do you see more of in the newspaper: colorful ads for consumer goods or colorful ads for investment accounts?

Which do you receive more of in your mailbox: offers for snazzy new savings plans or offers for snazzy new credit cards?

To estimate how profitable an activity is, see how much the business spends on trying to influence you. It's obvious that much more is spent on getting us to spend and borrow than in getting us to save. So workers have to contend not only with their *inner* forces but also with *outer* forces. It's enough to tempt a rational agent!

However, that's not to say the rational agent approach doesn't work. In the most general sense, it works better for workers with more formal education than those with less. It works better for workers with higher incomes than those with lower incomes. It works better for workers who receive a lot of financial education than those who receive little or none. (And if you're a financial specialist, it's probably been working for you.) But we're looking for a new approach that will work for as many people as possible. What's the answer? If the rational agent approach is where our society is headed, how can we make it work for as many workers as possible? The answer, dear reader, is in the next chapter.

"I would rather spend my time enjoying my income than bothering about my investments."

—CLIVE GRANGER, winner of the
2003 Nobel Prize in economics

Chapter FIVE

A New Approach to Retirement Security

In the last chapter, we reviewed a variety of approaches to retirement economics, and gathered clues for how to approach the new retirement. Now, it's time to draw on the best elements of each!

We saw that the family approach was a very strong life cycle system, because it worked for millennia. It was so strong that it stifled personal initiative. When a young person aspired to be a farmer but was from a family of fishermen, leaving the family occupation was a huge gamble. But an older farmer or fisherman who had a family didn't need to worry about how to get along in later life. It had been natural for them to have children, and it didn't matter whether they were consciously planning their own "retirement." Instead, the system was *automatically* oriented toward that goal. They still had to exercise personal responsibility by working from dawn till dusk. But their work focused on the months and years, while the family economic *system* took care of their life cycle.

We saw that the societal approach was a strong life cycle system too, because it worked for generations. It allowed for more personal initiative in choosing an occupation. And after workers did choose, it was natural for them to focus on their occupation over the months and years ahead, not on a retirement decades in the future. Yet, the system was automatically building their retirement benefits *even before they realized how important it was.* They still had to exercise personal responsibility by staying with an employer long enough to earn a pension. But they were working with a system *oriented toward their life cycle goal.* A worker didn't need to worry about how to get along in later life.

We saw that the rational agent approach worked well for the few rational agents, but not for the rest of us. Instead of an external system, it assumes there's an *internal* life cycle system within each person. If we provide information and choice, the internal system will supposedly do the rest. It's clear that our internal system attends to the months and years of earning, spending, and saving, of course. But the rational agent approach also assumes our internal system correctly anticipates financial needs *decades in the future,* properly calculates savings needed *to the end of life,* and exercises sufficient discipline to follow through, *both before and after we retire.* The Life Cycle Hypothesis is an elegant theory, but we can't count on it. Humans have never lived like that before, and we only get one chance at the life cycle. The stakes are just too high! But this approach offers an important breakthrough: *Information and choices are good.* Educating people on personal finance is absolutely essential as daily life becomes ever more financial.

The New Retirement Economics: Autopilot

For designing the new approach, we've learned (at least) two things that are essential. First, when we have *automatic external systems* oriented toward our goal, we're more likely to get there. Second, when we have *freedom and knowledge* (or access to knowledge), we're more likely to get there, too. This new approach is called retirement autopilot, because we need to take control but also use intelligent external systems.

Retirement has been like traveling by airplane. In the family approach, we knew we'd get there but couldn't even choose the destination. In the societal approach, we could choose a destination but were mostly like a passenger. In the rational agent approach, we were put in the pilot's seat and could choose any destination we wanted. Except some of us actually were pilots, while many of us crashed and burned. The retirement autopilot approach is the next stage. We must choose a destination and course. But instead of needing to do everything manually, we turn the myriad details over to automatic external systems that keep us on course. We can still take the controls, of course. But if we become distracted, forget the destination, or even fall asleep, we're still making progress toward our goal. The autopilot frees us up to do something else. If we truly are a pilot (a financial specialist), the autopilot allows us to consider other destinations, plot alternate courses, check the weather report, and chat with other pilots about flying. It takes over the mundane tasks of flying and frees pilots up for *higher level* pilot activities. But if we're like most people and we're *not* good pilots (or financial specialists), we have peace of mind knowing the systems keep us on course.

The key elements of the retirement autopilot approach look like this:

1. **Sources of Income.** Five pillars, or PERKS, provide more stability than the old three-legged stool.

2. **Financial Education.** Both rational agents and nonrational agents make better decisions when they know more.

3. **Automatic Systems.** Automatic systems for saving, investing, and distributing money are more reliable and efficient than humans are.

4. **Fiduciary Advice.** Experts free from conflict of interest can improve decisions at key points in time.

Let's take a peek at each of the four elements.

The First Element of Retirement Autopilot: PERKS

It turns out the three-legged stool wasn't a good reflection of what people have been doing in the *real world*. When we look at the sources of retirement income that you're most likely to actually use, we can see there are five of them. Five pillars of retirement income. It's time to recognize what they are, be more conscious of them, and make specific plans. You'll want to take really good care of your *largest* pillars. At the same time, building up *additional* pillars would give you more stability, wouldn't it? Later, you'll learn about making the pillars more *automatic*, too.

The acronym for the five sources is PERKS. Perks used to be perquisites, or special privileges that go to bigwigs. But retirement security isn't just for bigwigs—we all need PERKS.

P Is for Personal Savings

This pillar is just like the personal savings leg from the old retirement. It's the pillar that offers us the most freedom and choice, which also means it *demands* the most of us. It doesn't even exist unless you take the initiative. You can take the initiative to set up automatic savings programs, however.

E Is for Employer Plans

For most of us, this pillar will *not* be like the employer pension from the old retirement. It will refer to 401(k)-type employee savings plans, with some employers kicking in a little, others a lot. Although sponsored by employers, they require much more of us than the original employer pension did. As with personal savings, this pillar may not even exist unless you take the initiative. Employers will increasingly offer automatic features for you to take advantage of.

R Is for Real Estate

This wasn't recognized as part of the three-legged stool, even though it's been around for a long time. For most of us, real estate is simply the American dream of owning our own home. (Unless you're a real estate investor, too.) Workers have always used homes for retirement security; they paid off the mortgage and had a free place to live. But in the new retirement, many people imagine using home equity as a source of income, too. That's asking for double duty; a place to live and a stream of income at the same time. If that's your goal, you'd better plan extra carefully. The good news is that all by itself, paying down your mortgage is the essence of an autopilot program.

K Is for Keep Working

Continuing to work in some form was once the *only pillar* of retirement income! During the societal era, it was supposed to disappear. Doesn't the metaphor of a three-legged stool suggest sitting on our duff? But in the new retirement, many of us can't afford to do that. We'll need to work, at least a little. All the other pillars are your *financial capital*, because they're measured in accumulated dollars. This pillar is your *human capital*, because it's measured in your future value as a worker. In the old retirement, your human capital dropped to *zero* when you reached retirement. You were worthless! But in the new retirement, you may not be worthless. If you have biological health, psychological strengths, and social connections, you still have human capital. But we haven't figured out automatic ways to make sure you can keep working. Because of these unknowns, this pillar is the *least dependable*. Take good care of your human capital, but don't depend on it!

THE FIVE PILLARS

S Is for Social Security

In the old retirement, Social Security was intended as a safety net for people who lived long enough to become too old to work. Then, as people lived longer and longer, it became a key source of retirement income for nearly everyone. It's the most automatic of the pillars. At the same time, it's the pillar you have the *least control* over. Your strategy is to maximize the benefits you're entitled to, and then hope that society keeps its promise.

So there you have them: the five pillars of retirement income. Even if you're not a bigwig, you can still have PERKS!

The Second Element of Retirement Autopilot: Financial Education

As it became obvious the rational agent approach wasn't working, a new term emerged: *financial literacy*. (You'll be hearing about it, a lot.) Coined by well-intentioned thinkers in education, government, and nonprofit organizations, the idea is to finally get serious about increasing peoples' *knowledge* to make good decisions. It's about using education to turn nonrational agents into rational agents. It's a great idea. In the coming years, you'll see more efforts and programs from many entities on a variety of financial topics, including preparing for retirement.

However, you know it's only *part* of the solution. If financial literacy is just knowledge on financial topics, it isn't enough. Financial literacy needs to include knowledge on how to use autopilot systems and how to get good advice. Instead of just trying to make people into rational agents, we need to connect them with systems that support them over time.

So even you, dear reader, should polish up on the nuts and bolts of finance after you finish this book. It's painful, I know. But you're going to be bombarded with programs designed to increase your financial knowledge anyway. They emerge from three basic philosophies. Which is most likely to resonate with you?

"Facts of Life" Financial Education

The philosophy here is to provide us with the financial "facts of life." Like teaching us about the birds and the bees, the assumption is that we're naturally curious about the subject and eager to know all the intimate details. Sort of like a variation on a best-selling book of the 1970s: *Everything You Always Wanted to Know About Money (But Were Afraid to Ask)*.

Because the people creating these programs *actually do* find money that interesting, they imagine others will, too. It doesn't occur to them that we're already living in a sea of financial information. It doesn't occur to them that if the curiosity is there, people will seek out the information. But if people aren't curious, the existence of another fact-filled website, publication, or curriculum won't attract much interest.

Financial education like this can work in a mandatory or compulsory setting, though, like an employer-sponsored retirement plan or a school. But just because they make us learn this financial stuff doesn't mean we're interested. Or that we'll remember to practice "safe spending" in the moment of passion.

"Scare and Scold" Financial Education

The philosophy here is that the "facts of life" aren't sufficient, because people are naturally complacent. Probably even lazy. At the very least, they're somewhat clueless. Anyway, the well-intentioned folks behind this approach tend to believe that people are motivated only by doom and gloom. That only a potential catastrophe will awaken them from their stupor. So the core theme of the "scare and scold" scenario warns people that they're probably doing something wrong and urges them to take action to avoid disaster.

The "scare and scold" approach makes surface statements like these (*which have these underlying messages*):

- "Most people aren't saving enough for retirement." (*Translation: You aren't saving enough for retirement.*)

- "You need to plan ahead." (*Translation: You haven't planned ahead, have you?*)

- "Building retirement security takes time." (*Translation: It may be too late for you, anyway.*)

- "Saving is easier than you think." (*Translation: Can't you at least try?*)

- "Start today!" (*Translation: Or you'll be living in a tar-paper shack and eating dog food.*)

If this motivates you to learn, it's not because you suddenly love finance. No, it's probably because dire warnings tend to grab your attention and get you to *imagine nasty outcomes that you don't want.* If you're the type of person who imagines what could go wrong, and then takes steps to safeguard against it, this could be exactly what you need. (It's called defensive pessimism.) Although not an especially enjoyable way to get motivated, it can sometimes be just the ticket. It may be good to scare the dickens out of ourselves now and then.

"Motivational" Financial Education

One underlying assumption here is the same as "scare and scold": that information by itself isn't sufficient. It knows that people tune out when information seems irrelevant to them (like high school algebra). It works best when offered in the context of people's lives. The educators behind this approach think humans are good at accomplishing things. But they need a motivating positive vision of what they want. The "scare and scold" will startle people initially, but then they grow accustomed to it and it ceases to motivate them. On the other hand, a positive goal can keep us motivated forever. That's why this book helps you create a vision of the life you want to live. If you get the vision right, you'll learn what you need to know and take the actions you need to take to get there. Aren't humans great?

The Third Element of Retirement Autopilot: Automatic Systems

Autopilot systems are available to help us accomplish the three essential tasks of financial retirement: saving, investing, and distributing our retirement money. We'll look at these tasks and how the automatic systems might work. However, the systems are in the form of products, services, and arrangements that will vary and even go by different names. Autopilot systems are catching on, though, and multiplying in type and number. The details will change, but once you start thinking this way, you'll be able to spot them.

Autopilot Saving

Autopilot saving is about getting around the spending-saving seesaw. It's about replacing willpower with systems power. It's about saving the money before you even get it, or turning it into that phone bill you need to pay. But your goal is to make it not only automatic but also as *painless* as possible.

Your Social Security pillar is the epitome of autopilot, because your FICA is deducted from your pay, whether you ask for it or not. But your employer plan pillar may be a problem. In the world of 401(k)-type plans, doing the wrong thing (not saving) has been automatic. And doing the right thing (saving) has required a manual override of the system.

When you change to a new job, the *default* contribution for your retirement savings is *zero*, which is definitely the wrong amount. It's not taking you in the direction of your retirement destination. Doing the right thing requires a manual override. You need to overcome your own internal inertia (the tendency to keep things as they are) and also the external inertia of your new employer's payroll and benefits department. You must complete the enrollment forms, choose a contribution percentage, and select a beneficiary. Later, when you're able to afford a higher contribution percentage, you have to overcome the same inertia to increase your contribution. For you and your employer, *it's easier to do nothing*. And yet that keeps you headed in the wrong direction!

What if we made all the *right things* into defaults? That way, even if we did nothing, we'd be headed in the right direction!

Some employers are catching on and implementing an arrangement called auto-enrollment. When you start a new job, a moderate percentage of your pay is automatically withheld and contributed to your retirement. There's no inertia to overcome. Your employer needs to tell you, and you typically have ninety days to opt out (if you're determined to do the wrong thing). An even cooler arrangement is called auto-escalation. You agree to allow your contribution percentage to increase at specific dates in the future. (It's painless today, right?) Those future increases are when you get raises, so the increases aren't even painful when they happen! You can always manually decrease, but you probably won't, because of your inertia. However, your inertia now keeps you on the right course instead of the wrong course. By doing nothing, you're doing the right thing. Doesn't that make life easier?

If you're not starting a new job, march into your payroll and benefits department and demand these savings arrangements. If they're implemented, it's usually only for new hires, not for existing employees.

For your personal savings, are you getting some creative ideas? It will take a little more legwork to find options. The beauty is that it takes initiative only *one time*—when you put it into place. It doesn't require ongoing initiative and willpower to keep saving. Explore what new options may be available from your investment providers. At the very least, they should offer an *automatic monthly transfer* from your bank account into a longer-term retirement account.

If you have debt, paying that down is as good as personal savings. Especially for credit cards, not paying those high interest rates are an excellent return on your money. So don't make a manual payment each month, especially one for just the minimum amount. Instead, set up an automatic payment for a larger amount. You'll need to get up your gumption only once, instead of over and over.

That's like your real estate pillar. You have an automatic saving arrangement called a mortgage payment. Instead of coming out of your pay before you see it, like a 401(k), it *turns saving into a bill* that you must pay. You can improve it, though, by setting up partial mortgage payments based on your paycheck cycle, instead of monthly. It will be less painful, and you'll actually build up equity faster, too.

Autopilot Investing

Unless you specialize in financial well-being, you probably dislike making investment decisions. Most people don't like saving because it's simple and boring. But they don't like investing because it's complicated and volatile. Some people have so much trepidation that they allocate their portfolio just *one time*, and then don't change it for years or even decades. That's inertia at work again. Unfortunately, portfolio management means not just selecting appropriate investments initially but also *rebalancing* them as they fluctuate in value. Over the long term, it means *reallocating* them to be more conservative as you approach retirement. If your trepidation and inertia keep you from making these changes, you're in deep trouble.

Autopilot investing is now probably available for your employer plan and your personal savings, too. It turns your inertia from a vice into a virtue. Avoiding your investments becomes a good thing instead of a bad thing. An autopilot retirement account does those portfolio tasks you're *supposed* to be doing, but it does it automatically. It also reduces your temptation to make hasty changes when the markets have a big drop.

Until the advent of autopilot investing, it wasn't easy—or cheap—to manage retirement portfolios. It took a lot of investing knowledge and skill to set up an account with the right allocation in the first place. And then it took a lot of boring operational follow-through to keep up with it, rebalance it, and then shift it to become more conservative as you approach retirement.

Before, the choices were either paying significantly higher fees to have this done or taking it on yourself. Understandably, many people opted to have it all done for them, but they paid a huge price, often 1 percent of their account balance every year. (That may not sound like much, but it really cuts into the value of your portfolio.) And workers who *didn't* pay to have it done but opted to do it themselves usually wound up not doing it. They had good intentions, but it was just too complicated. Then they devoted a lot of time and energy worrying about what was happening to their investments because they *weren't* managing them!

But with the autopilot breakthrough, the cost is falling. Instead of an expensive service, it may be available as an automated account or fund, without the extra charges. The terminology for these accounts isn't standardized, and not all providers offer all types. However, for both your employer plan and your personal savings, these are five common types that you'll see:

1. **Balanced Fund.** The most old-fashioned type of automatic investing, this fund generally maintains the account at the same split between stocks and bonds (often sixty-forty). This is more automatic than having to manually split your money between two funds, but it's a one-size-fits-all approach.

2. **Auto Rebalancing.** This automated service periodically shifts your investment allocation back to whatever split you had originally selected. Therefore, if you did a poor job of allocating your investment split in the first place, it keeps replicating that error. It also doesn't get more conservative as you approach retirement.

3. **Lifestyle Funds.** This is like having a range of balanced funds to choose from, instead of just one. There are more aggressive and more conservative versions. Unlike the one-size-fits-all balanced fund, you're more likely to find something off this rack that fits you well. However, it stays the same over time. You might choose an aggressive one early on, but then need to overcome your inertia and trepidation to change to a more conservative one later. It's up to you to remember.

4. **Life Cycle Fund.** This is like a lifestyle fund, except it automatically shifts from aggressive to conservative as you progress through your life cycle toward retirement. This is the most fully automated type of account. Some are called *target* funds, because you choose based on your target date for retirement. As your target retirement date

approaches, the fund automatically shifts into a more conservative split. However, if you don't plan to draw on your investments beginning at your target date, you may actually want a later target date. You might choose based on when you plan to start *accessing* your retirement account.

5. **Managed Account.** This uses technology to create a more personalized service than a lifestyle or life cycle fund. Instead of a fund whose assets are all managed in the same way, this can be more closely matched to your situation. However, as with a custom-tailored suit rather than one off the rack, you're likely to pay much more. Most people are better off choosing something from the life cycle fund and saving their money.

Whatever your provider offers, consider the most automatic approach that you can. Then you can concentrate on making a really careful decision, knowing you're relieving yourself of the burden of many decisions in the future.

Autopilot Real Estate: Saving and Investing

Real estate, especially your residence, is a unique combination of saving and investing. Home equity results from two distinctly different processes, and most of the time from both. The first process is amortization; the second is appreciation.

Amortization works this way: For an extremely simple example, let's assume you purchase a home for $100,000 with a 10 percent down payment, and you borrow the remaining $90,000. Over the term of the mortgage, let's say fifteen years, you make monthly mortgage payments. As you do, the mortgage balance decreases to $89,000, then $88,000, and so on. Your home equity is building up, slowly and steadily. At the end of fifteen years, even if the house is still only worth $100,000, you now have $100,000 of home equity. Amortization operates a lot like saving does.

But appreciation is more like investing, because you need to ride out market fluctuations. We'll use the same example but ignore the slow, steady amortization process for a moment. Let's say that in the first year, the market value of your home increases from $100,000 to $110,000. Even though that's only a 10 percent appreciation in market value, it *doubled your equity* from $10,000 to $20,000! Appreciation is more exciting than amortization, wouldn't you say? It's actually appreciation combined with *leverage*, but always remember that a lever can move both ways. Instead of increasing, let's say the market value of your home decreased from $100,000 to $90,000 in the first year. Even though that's only a 10 percent depreciation in market value, it *reduced your equity to zero!* Still exciting, but in a different way.

Homes in most real estate markets increase in value over the term of a fifteen-year mortgage. It's the synergy of both factors—the steady saving of amortization and the investing volatility of appreciation—that work together to create home equity. Trying to ride appreciation over shorter periods, without amortization, makes it easy to get burned. Taking home equity loans short-circuits amortization and puts people at the mercy of volatility. Remember, the American dream of home ownership is based on amortization and appreciation over long periods of time.

Autopilot Income Needs to Last As Long As You Do

Finally, the pot of gold at the end of the rainbow—retirement income! But wait a minute. Your transition to retirement income isn't the *end*, it's just a marker along the way, remember? When you finally do retire, you probably have *decades* of retirement life ahead of you. After all, there's no way to know when you're going to kick the bucket. (Check out your retirement biology in chapter eight.) How much income should you take to keep from running out of money?

This wasn't even a question in the family approach. In the societal approach, this only relates to personal savings, because Social Security and traditional employer pensions both pay monthly benefits *for life*. But under the rational agent approach, this is a very important, high-stakes issue. That's because most retirement assets end up as *account balances*, rather than monthly benefits. There's nothing automatic about taking account distributions; it's completely manual. It's a tough question for everyone. Not even a rational agent knows how long they're going to live.

When retirees fly off into the sunset, they typically manage their own account withdrawals. Unfortunately, they often goof it up! They may think they can afford to retire, but they really can't. Retirees are likely to withdraw too much, rather than too little. They tend to generally underestimate what their cost of living will be. They tend to be too optimistic about how well their portfolio has performed and will perform in the future. They tend to find "special circumstances" that justify extra withdrawals, above and beyond what they planned. They use a year-by-year method and can only see a few years into the future. Retirees are trying to do it all by themselves, manually.

Just like autopilot saving or investing, the goal of autopilot income is to combine good decision making with automatic processes that keep you on track. There are two kinds of autopilot, and you might use them in combination: autopilot *products* and autopilot *services*.

Autopilot Income Products

The prototype for automatic income products is the traditional employer pension. Plan participants don't receive an account balance but a monthly payment called a *life annuity*. This isn't a product but a type of plan benefit. Plan actuaries know statistically how long the *average* retiree is likely to live, but half will die later and half will die sooner. You might think the ones who die *later* than average get a better deal, and you'd be right. They collect more payments. But even the ones who die *sooner* get a good deal. That's because the value to them isn't only in the number of payments they receive. There is also value in being able to *plan on living forever*, knowing you'll never run out of payments. After all, when participants retire, there is no way for any of them to know *which group* they will end up in! They can all afford to be optimists. There is real value in security and in peace of mind.

What about people who don't have an employer pension? They can have access to the same kind of security through an insurance product. Insurance companies have actuaries who know how long people are likely to live, too. So they offer a type of insurance policy called an *immediate annuity* that works like the life annuity benefit of the traditional pension plan. The person who buys the annuity knows that half the policyholders will die later than average, and half will die sooner. Part of the value is that personally they can afford to be an optimist.

What about you? Should you consider an immediate annuity? There are two factors to consider. First, how good of a pilot are you? If you're *not a good pilot* and know it, then you're a candidate, and you should research immediate annuities. There's less chance of crashing and burning. But if you manage your financial affairs well, you might easily do better on your own. Second, how long are you likely to live? Health assessments now provide hints about whether you might be in the later or sooner group. If you're in the *later* group, you're also a candidate, and you should research immediate annuities. They can be on just a single life, or a joint and survivor annuity for a couple. But at least with immediate annuities, once you know what you want, you can compare apples to apples from multiple insurance companies. That allows you to shop for a good price and for a highly rated company that's likely to be in business long enough to pay you. Whatever conclusions arise from your research, please remember that an annuity should be only *one part* of your solution.

Be aware that insurance companies, insurance agents, and investment representatives want to sell you a gazillion different products that all go under the broad label of "annuity." Deferred annuities, variable annuities, equity-indexed annuities, and so on. These all have many more moving parts, and are *much more profitable to sell you,* than the simple immediate annuity we've been talking about. If you even breathe the word *annuity* to any of these marketers, visions of BIG commissions will dance in their heads, they'll get dollar signs in their eyes, and you'll hear the sales pitch of a lifetime. On the other hand, the demand for autopilot income products will actually prompt the creation of worthwhile new types of annuities. We'll need to watch for them. Be careful out there!

In addition to immediate annuities, there's a new category of autopilot product emerging. Instead of creating income from your employer plan or personal savings, it taps into a different pillar—your real estate, in the form of your personal residence. It's called a reverse mortgage and creates a monthly stream of income for life. It allows you to access your home equity while still living in your home, without needing to make payments on a home mortgage or home equity line of credit. However, all autopilot income products decrease your flexibility in order to create a lifetime stream of income. So do some serious planning about where you want to live in retirement before investigating a reverse mortgage. At the very least, make sure you do the retirement geography exercises in this book! Also, be as careful about researching a reverse mortgage as you would an immediate annuity. As they become more common, they'll be marketed heavily and subject to some of the same abuses as annuities. That's why, aside from autopilot income products, you should consider autopilot income services.

Autopilot Income Services

The prototype for autopilot income services is the traditional income portfolio. It holds some combination of dividend-paying stocks, corporate or government bonds, and interest-bearing certificates. These instruments all generate income *automatically*, without having to liquidate any principal. This time-honored income philosophy can generate payments for as long as you live, while leaving the principal intact for your heirs.

Unfortunately, most people can't live on just the income from their portfolio and need to liquidate their principal, too. That's where things get complicated. The income portfolio is like cruising along at a level altitude and never needing to worry about hitting the ground. But once you start liquidating principal, you start losing altitude. You've put yourself on a downward sloping trajectory, but it's difficult to tell exactly how steep your descent will be. Who's watching the altimeter? What's your air speed and rate of descent? Other factors come into play, such as wind speed, direction, and even the terrain. If you get into too steep of a dive, you can't even pull up! Thinking about all this makes you stop and wonder—can you really afford to begin your descent at all, or should you work for a few more years?

Even if you've been a good pilot for many years, consider this: *You will land your plane only once.* Autopilot income advice could be an investment representative telling you that the "rule of thumb" for a withdrawal rate is 4 percent per year. But after all of your years of working and saving, are you satisfied with using a rule of thumb?

Instead, an autopilot income service could be as simple as an online calculator provided by your investment company. You enter your portfolio and withdrawal information. It applies historical rates of return and volatility to the asset classes in your portfolio, and tells you your probability of success. Or it could be a review by an investment advisor, who uses a similar computer program combined with real-life experience. The two of you decide which holdings to liquidate in what order, and then set up a system for periodic withdrawals. Or it could even be comprehensive financial planning services, where an ongoing dialogue between you and your financial planner results in changes not only to your investment holdings but also to your lifestyle and spending habits.

Rather than flying the plane all by yourself, shouldn't you explore what types of intelligent, external, automatic systems are available to you?

The Fourth Element of Retirement Autopilot: Fiduciary Advice

Even when you have an autopilot, sometimes it's smart to have a copilot, too! Many decisions related to retirement are complex and only come along once in a lifetime. You don't get to learn by trial and error; you need to make a good decision the first time around. Many of these have high stakes attached to them. For example:

- How much do I need to save to be on track for when I want to retire?

- Are my investments allocated correctly or in the right autopilot fund?

- Should I save more in a pretax account, or an after-tax one, such as a Roth IRA?

- Can I take retirement distributions before age $59^{1}/_{2}$ without a penalty?

- Should I take distributions in order to delay my Social Security for a larger benefit?

If you want real advice instead of a sales pitch, you need to look for a *fiduciary advisor*. Fiduciary means that they are legally and ethically bound to put your interests first. These professionals are attempting to create a true *financial planning profession* from out of the larger *financial services industry*. It's not an easy task. How can you find a fiduciary advisor? There are three main places you should look. Although you can find a bad apple in any barrel, these are the best barrels!

The first is at www.fpanet.org, the website of the Financial Planning Association, where you can find a member who holds the CFP(r) Certified Financial Planner designation. Some of these advisors earn commissions, but the best approach—for fiduciary advice—is to choose a fee-only planner. Whether they work on commission or fee only, as long as they hold the CFP designation, they've had the proper training and experience. The second place to look is www.napfa.org, the website of the National Association of Personal Financial Advisors. This is a much smaller association and is for financial planners who have sworn off commissions completely and pledged to work on a purely fee-for-service basis. The third place is www.aicpa.org, the website of the American Institute of Certified Public Accountants. Look for "Personal Financial Planning" and "Personal Financial Specialist." Although most CPAs work in business accounting and taxation, a few have taken additional training to become a PFS.

Are there reputable financial advisors who don't belong to any of these three associations? Yes. Are there knowledgeable financial advisors who don't hold the CFP or PFS designations? Definitely. Are there even trustworthy financial advisors who work on a commission-only basis? Absolutely. But your chances of finding a reputable, knowledgeable, and trustworthy financial advisor are much, much greater if you use one of these three websites.

THE RETIREMENT NONCALCULATOR

When you evaluate your sources of retirement income, the most important question is about *quantities*. The question is, "How much?" As a result, retirement calculators have been multiplying like crazy! They're all over the Internet, offering both saving and income calculations.

The second most important question isn't about quantities but *qualities*. The question is, "What kind?" That is, what are the unique qualities and characteristics of your sources of income? How is each source like the others, and how is it different? That's a very different evaluation.

A *quantitative* evaluation helps you see how much your sources decreased in the recession of 2009. But a *qualitative* evaluation helps you see why, and what you might expect in the future. First, use a retirement calculator. Then, use this *Retirement Noncalculator*. It's the qualitative enhancement for your calculator!

Make enough copies of the Retirement Noncalculator worksheet (on page 123) for each one of your *specific* retirement income sources. You may wonder if your specific sources are the same as your pillars, or PERKS. The answer is maybe. Some pillars may be made up of just one source—Social Security, for example. But some pillars are made up of multiple sources. Your Employer Plans pillar might include a traditional pension, a 401(k), and an employee stock plan. If your 401(k) were split between a stock fund and a bond fund, that might be two sources. However, don't bother to complete a worksheet for small sources—just the major ones that will provide the larger parts of your income. For most people, that will be less than ten.

Read through the explanations of the qualities listed on page 121. You'll discover that each of your sources displays some of the qualities to greater or lesser degrees, which you'll be able to note on each worksheet. Retirement calculators obscure these qualities, while the Retirement Noncalculator emphasizes them. If the explanations don't make sense to you, work with a friend or a trusted advisor. Your retirement income may depend upon it.

After you've completed a worksheet for each major source, you'll be able to see the relative quantities and qualities of each one. Which three are most essential for your retirement well-being? Write the names of those three sources on your Life Circle at the end of this chapter.

Explanations of the Qualities

Liquidity. To what degree do you control the timing and amount of income from this source? Can you start, stop, and change at will? Do legal, contractual, tax, or market sale conditions restrict you? What needs to happen to receive your income, or what might prevent you from accessing it?

Examples: Social Security is subject to legal restrictions, annuities to contractual restrictions, IRAs to tax restrictions, and home equity to market sale restrictions.

Volatility. To what degree does this source fluctuate over time? Does the short term go up and down independent of trends in longer-term value? Could there be a "bad time" for you to make a withdrawal?

Examples: Stocks, bonds, and commodities (like gold) and funds that hold them all fluctuate in the short term. Real estate can fluctuate, too.

Market. To what degree is this source tied to some broad market? Is it related to long-term trends? Can the market go down and stay down for years? Could a downturn last longer than your ability to wait?

Examples: Individual stocks can decrease to zero. Stock mutual funds effectively couldn't but are tied to trends by sector, industry, style, and a broader market. Real estate is tied to trends within regions, communities, and neighborhoods.

Issuer. To what degree is this source dependent on a single entity? Could solvency problems prevent them from paying you? How many years into the future are you relying on them? Would anyone take over their obligations?

Examples: Individual bonds can default. Insurance companies can become insolvent, although state guaranty associations cover a portion of the obligations. Traditional pensions are trusts, subject to the Pension Benefit Guaranty Corporation.

Inflation. Will this source lose purchasing power if prices rise over time? Or will it increase with inflation to keep the same standard of living? Is that increase contractual, or dependent on market value?

Examples: Interest from CDs and fixed annuities can lose purchasing power to inflation. Monthly pensions may increase, or not. Inflation-protected bonds increase payments with inflation, contractually. Stocks and home values historically matched inflation, but the future is uncertain.

Interest. To what degree is this source affected by changing interest rates? If rates increase over time, is that good or bad for you? What if rates decrease?

Examples: Rising interest rates decrease bond values, while falling interest rates increase bond values. Interest from CDs rises or falls with rates in general, although not immediately. Fixed annuity interest rates are typically slow to adjust. Reverse mortgage income is based on interest rates initially but typically doesn't change over time. Home equity loans can be very sensitive to changing interest rates.

Political. To what degree is this source dependent on a political process? Would a change in tax laws greatly affect the value? Is the attractiveness dependent on complex regulations? Is continuing government support important?

Examples: Social Security and state programs for older citizens will soon become political tugs-of-war, with unknown outcomes. IRAs, employer plans, insurance products, and long-term capital gains all enjoy tax incentives that could change in the future, due to political pressure.

Foreign. To what degree is this source dependent on a foreign country? What effect might currency exchange rates have?

Examples: Foreign stocks and bonds are subject to even more market forces than domestic securities. Foreign real estate can be subject to complex legal structures.

Management. To what degree does this source require ongoing competent management? Is it a firm that can be evaluated? If you're the manager, how long will you be competent to perform the task?

Examples: Mutual funds are relentlessly analyzed and compared, but other types of funds may not be. Human managers (whether you or a professional) succumb to poor judgment now and then—and ultimately to old age.

THE RETIREMENT NONCALCULATOR WORKSHEET

(Make a copy of this page for each specific source of income.)

Name for this specific source: _____

Which of my PERKS is this source from?

____ P   ____ E   ____ R   ____ K   ____ S

The *quantities* of this source, according to my retirement calculator:

Current lump sum $_____ Retirement lump sum $ _____

Most importantly, the monthly lifetime income from this source $_____

How large a share of my retirement income is this source likely to provide?

___ Small   ___ Medium   ___ Large   ___ Extra-Large   ___ Super Size!

The *qualities* of this source, according to my understanding of these characteristics:

Liquidity _____

Volatility _____

Market _____

Issuer _____

Inflation _____

Interest _____

Political _____

Foreign _____

Management _____

Other _____

- Can I really afford to retire now, or when will I be able to?

- Should I take the pension plan monthly benefit or the lump sum option?

- How much part-time income, for how many years, will it take to make a difference?

- Is it more cost-effective to keep the money in my 401(k) or roll over to an IRA?

- Should I take a reverse mortgage or downsize to a less expensive residence?

- Does long-term care insurance make more sense for me or for my spouse?

If you're unsure, good advice is priceless. But even if you're a financial specialist and pretty sure of your decisions, getting feedback can be valuable. Think of it as peer review.

Retirement Autopilot Is Only the Beginning!

Most retirement books are completely dominated by the question of how to manage your retirement finances. But in order to cover all the dimensions of your retirement well-being, it's time for us to move along. That's why you'll find recommendations for additional books that are completely focused on finance and economics in the Resources section on page 257.

LIFE CIRCLES EXERCISE

Now review the information about your financial sources, and consider which three are most important to your well-being. Enter these in the Life Circle to use for your One Piece of Paper in chapter eleven.

My Ideal Retirement
includes managing these
financial pillars:

1. _____

2. _____

3. _____

"We shall not cease from exploration
And the end of all our exploring
Will be to arrive where we started
And know the place for the first time."

—T. S. ELIOT, twentieth-century English poet

Chapter SIX

The Nature of Space and Time

When physicists like Einstein and Hawking reference the *nature of space and time,* they're asking questions about the nature of reality itself. But we're only asking questions about where to live in retirement. In comparison, that might seem a bit trivial. But isn't it all relative?

Have you known people who stayed in the same place as they aged, long after they should have moved? They clung to a particular home, neighborhood, or part of the country. They were somehow immobilized, for one reason or another, even when it became more and more difficult to stay there. Living in the *wrong place* came to dominate their life. Then, when they finally relocated (if they ever did), they announced, "I should have moved long ago!"

Or just the opposite—you've known people who couldn't wait to relocate for retirement. They fell in love with a particular home, condo, or apartment. Perhaps they discovered a real estate development, or just a neighborhood, that offered exactly the amenities and activities they had dreamed about. Off they went, with great anticipation and excitement, to inhabit this new place. Then, for one reason or another, it didn't live up to their expectations. They were disappointed. But they stayed in the new place because it was too difficult or too expensive to relocate. Or perhaps they did set off once more, in search of yet another new place. Or, as sometimes happens, they retraced their steps and simply moved back to where they had come from, more or less. They were disillusioned, if not defeated.

Of course, there are stories of success, too. Many people stay in the same place, and it works out perfectly. Or they move somewhere new, and it fulfills their expectations. The question is this: How can you predict, in advance, how well a certain place might work for you?

This chapter answers that question. It offers you a new perspective and a practical approach for understanding the places where you might live in retirement. Equipped with this new perspective and approach, you'll see the pros and cons of moving or staying where you are now.

Most of us at least *daydream* about moving somewhere new. It could be just across town or across the country. Either way, letting go of the place where we live and making a new home somewhere else is one of the most adventurous things we could do. Even the old-fashioned, leisure-oriented approach to retirement was exciting when it included a move to a new location. (Sun City, here we come!) Any move is an adventure, after all.

It's easy to imagine moving, but it's not easy to know whether that move would really support your retirement well-being. Or if you imagine staying where you are, it's not easy to imagine how well your existing place will serve you in the future, as you get older. Geography is an important decision, because it affects almost every aspect of your life—financial, social, psychological, biological, and medical. Let's peek at those connections.

Your geography and finances are linked not only by the cost of your residence itself but also by the general cost of living that goes along with any particular location. If necessary, we can almost always find a place to live that's *cheaper* than where we live now. Or coming from the other direction, if you plan to work in retirement, geography will help or hinder your ability to do that. It's easier to make money in some places than in others. Where you live can affect both sides of your cash flow statement: expenses and income.

Location has an enormous effect on your social relationships, too. As much as you want your social ties to transcend distance, you've probably spent more time with friends and family when it was geographically easier to get together with them. The place where you live affects you psychologically, too. Hopefully it provides you with outlets for exploring your interests and using your skills. In retirement, you'll either be engaged and stimulated by your environment or lulled into boredom.

Finally, geography will affect your health in two key ways. Where you live impacts your healthy living habits, such as being physically active. Retirement offers more free time, and your geography will shape what you do with that time. Will your environment help get you moving and build your biological vitality, or will it shut you down, prematurely aging you? Even if you do take better care of your body, sooner or later you'll seek out more medical services from practitioners and institutions. Will your retirement geography be a help or a barrier to getting the treatment you want?

Will Your Dream Home Become a Nightmare?

Even if you decide to stay right where you are when you retire, that decision raises all the same questions that a new place would. You should still look at your location with fresh eyes and evaluate it from a new perspective. Will it support the kind of life you really want to live? Would a few changes make your current place into your dream place? How do you know what your dream place is, anyway? Your life changes so much from the Second Age to the Third Age to the Fourth Age that your dreams change, too. The place that was perfect for raising your kids and commuting to work may not be perfect anymore. Your dream home from the Second Age could even become a nightmare in the Fourth Age.

Not only is your choice of where to live a profound decision, it's also a high-stakes one. Making a move is such a major undertaking that you are unlikely to undo it, even if you get it wrong. If you discover you made the wrong choice, you may settle for just settling in because it's too difficult (and too expensive) to move again. Another move would likely be to another new place. You surely know the expression "You can't go home again." (That's because someone else is probably living there now.)

On the other hand, if you make plans for retirement based on not moving and then design a life around your existing place, it can be difficult to reconsider later. There are, in life, certain *windows of opportunity*.

Leaving your long-term career (and daily commute) is a major life transition that opens the window to living in a new place. If you don't make your move during that transition, the window may close. The window may be stuck—and you may be stuck, too.

The Geography of Freedom

The Four Ages depict the life stages, and life transitions, that are emerging in society. As you move from the First to the Third Age, your degree of freedom tends to increase, and that means more geographic freedom as well.

In the First Age, you lived wherever your family lived through high school, and perhaps college, too. You typically didn't have any choice about where you lived. It was just a given. Unless your family moved, you probably didn't think about moving. (There are those of us, though, who dreamt of faraway places from a very early age.) If you had a chance to go away to college that may well have been your first glimmer of geographic freedom. And for most of us, even that was quite limited freedom.

The Second Age opened up new horizons. You had the power to choose where to live. But the need to support yourself meant getting a job, which put limitations on your geographic freedom. You may have also been limited by a desire to be close to friends and family. Over the years, your work may have been a deciding factor, keeping you in place or moving you around. Having children may have kept you close to family for support. Getting your children into the schools you wanted for them may have shaped your geographic choices, too.

Yes, the Second Age is filled with responsibilities, and many of those have geographic requirements. But the Third Age offers the greatest freedom of place that you'll ever experience! Here are five reasons:

1. Your income may not be tied to living in a particular location. Unless you've been a telecommuter or a freelancer or you've done some other your-presence-is-optional type of work, your income and your geography have always been joined at the hip. But that loosens up

in retirement. Once you're receiving benefits, the Social Security Administration (and your pension plan, IRA account, bank, and so on) will send your monthly check wherever you tell them to.

2. If you want to work in retirement, you may be more geographically flexible in your search for work than you could be in the job that you retire from. Whether you work for the income, to use your strengths, or to be socially connected with other people, you can probably find work in a variety of places. There are even more options when you're open to—or even prefer—temporary or part-time work.

3. Your residence may appreciate in value by the time you retire, allowing you to sell it at a hefty profit. Or even if your residence doesn't appreciate, it may be much more expensive than a similar place in another location. In particular, if you live in a region or a metropolitan area with a thriving economy that has plenty of jobs and moneymaking opportunities, people still in the workforce will be eager to buy your residence. They need to live somewhere convenient for their work. But once you're retired, you may not need that same proximity. Many great places to live have poor job opportunities, which may not matter to you one bit!

4. Family responsibilities typically lessen in the Third Age, so geographical constraints loosen. As your brood left the nest (or flew the coop), they may have stayed nearby or moved across the country. But either way, you're not responsible for them. Staying connected with your family and being an important part of their life are affected by your geography, to be sure. But connection requires less proximity than responsibility did. In retirement, you may use your increased free time to visit them or stay in touch in other ways. If you live somewhere really cool, they may even be the ones who want to come visit you!

5. People you already know are blazing new trails for you. You have family, friends, and acquaintances who have moved to other places already, and they can provide you with opportunities to try out a different geography. It's an opportunity for you to sample places where

you may want to live. You may have had less communication with them since they moved, but planning your retirement is the perfect opportunity to reconnect with them, and possibly connect with the place that they've moved to. Getting inside information from the people who actually live somewhere is infinitely more informative than staying there on vacation.

It's great to have more geographic freedom, isn't it? Now what you need is a simple way to consider all the places you could live and compare them to where you live now. So on to this new perspective and new approach to analyzing your retirement geography.

The Four Layers of Retirement Geography

It's useful to think about any place in terms of *four layers*, the names of which form the acronym SALE. See the image that makes the acronym easy to remember.

S is for *sense of place*. The innermost layer, it's the meaning that you derive from a geographic location.

A is for *aging in place*. The micro layer, it's what most people hope to do in their retirement residence.

L is for *livable community*. The middle layer, it's a supportive environment for retirement and aging.

E is for *essential region*. The macro layer, it's the part of the country that you absolutely must live in.

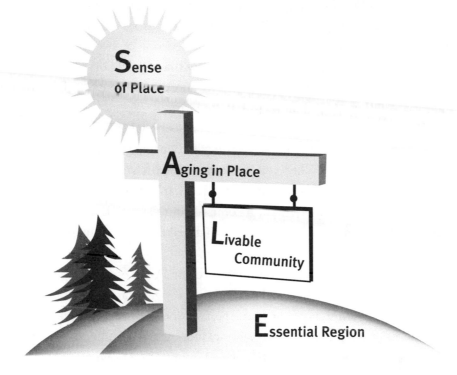

Does this acronym mean you should sell your place and move? Not at all. But you should at least evaluate your current place according to these four layers. That way, if you decide to stay there, it will be the result of a conscious decision. Consider the four layers in any order that makes sense for you. We'll explore them one at a time, starting with the big picture.

Your Essential Region:
The Macro Layer of Geography

Assuming that you really could pick up and move to another part of the country (or another country altogether), where might that be? You may have visited other regions for business, while on vacation, or to visit friends or family. Certainly there are regions that you're curious about, or even attracted to deep down, but have never been to. Retirement may be just the opportunity you've needed to visit those places or hang out in them for a while—for weeks, months, or even years. But although retirement can have a vacation quality, it's important to make a distinction between the places you plan to sample and the one or two places that you may really want to call home. You know that expression "It's a nice place to visit, but I wouldn't want to live there"? It's not just a cliché; it holds a deeper wisdom than we give it credit for.

Whether a region is just nice to visit or is one where you'd happily live out your days depends, of course, on whether that region holds what you need to truly live. When you think about the life you want in retirement, there are probably certain things you can't imagine living without; you view those as essential. If some of your essentials are tied to a geographic region of the country, then that makes it an essential region for you.

Now, you may not have an essential region. Your essential requirements may be the kind that can be found in many geographic locations— say, a first-rate symphony, year-round golf, a professional sports team, or a huge outlet mall. But a good way to explore the possibility is to consider what you absolutely couldn't live without, then see whether those things are connected to a particular area.

To identify your essential region, ask yourself these questions:

1. Is there a region that supports you socially—that is, your most important relationships? Where are the people who are essential in your life (possibly children, grandchildren, lifelong friends, elderly parents)? You may not need to be right next door, but within easy traveling distance, perhaps? Consider, too, that these loved ones may relocate someday.

2. Is there a region that offers compelling opportunities to use your skills or strengths in a way that's psychologically engaging for you? This could be a particular retirement job, an unusual volunteer opportunity, a chance to go back to school, or a once-in-a-lifetime special project, such as working to help protect the flora or fauna of a threatened ecosystem.

3. Is there a region that would allow you to pursue your interests or passions in a way that you could nowhere else? This could be physical geography like mountains or water, or cultural offerings such as the arts or entertainment.

4. Is there a region that could be particularly supportive to your health, especially if that might become more of a challenge, as you get older? You may need a climate that's beneficial to a physical condition, or proximity to uncommon medical specialists or alternative practitioners. Even basic access to medical care, such as a Veteran's Administration hospital, HMO, or PPO, could be a factor.

5. Is there a region that would make it easier to make ends meet financially, if that's an issue for you? This could mean a lower cost of living or the chance to pool resources with family or others as a way to cut costs.

6. Is there a region that's somehow connected to your deepest values? It could be the center of your religious tradition, cultural heritage, or family roots.

7. Is there a region that would uniquely support your chosen ways to live? This means the area somehow pulls together the social, psychological, biological, medical, and financial elements to support the life you want to live.

As you answer these questions, keep in mind that retirement changes over time. What's important in early retirement is different than what will be important in later retirement. At the beginning, in the Third Age, you're young and healthy enough to be very active in the world, so amenities and opportunities are at the top of your checklist for evaluating regions. Toward the end, in the Fourth Age, you'll likely want and need more help and support from others, and you may need significant medical care. This evolution may necessitate two migrations during your retirement. A first migration could be made so you can do the things you want to do. Demographers call this an *amenity migration*. A later move to get some help from your supportive relationships is called an *assistance migration*. That could be to a new place altogether, wherever your family happens to live. Or it could be back to the region where you lived before—a *reverse migration*. It's not that you made a mistake and moved to the wrong place. You may have moved to the right place for the Third Age but know in advance that it won't be the right place for the Fourth Age.

Keep these migration types in mind as you think about what's important to you and where that's located. Your essential region for retirement may be a place that's very different from your essential region for your working years. And if your essential region has anything to do with people (and I hope it does!), your essential region could change if those people migrate. After all, you may be looking at thirty years of retirement.

Of all the changes in geography that you may consider, migrating to another region is the most expensive, labor-intensive, and logistically complex, and it has the greatest effect on your relationships. It's also the least common. You may already be living in your essential region and just haven't thought of it that way! All this adds up to the obvious conclusion that migrating to another part of the country is a level of geographic change that you need to research and consider most carefully. With a fresh perspective and a bit of ingenuity, you may be able to create your Ideal Retirement in the region where you already live. Perhaps you could instead make changes at another level, such as your community or residence. (In which case you might decide that another region that had beckoned you is a nice place to visit, but you wouldn't want to live there!)

Your Livable Community: The Middle Layer of Geography

What exactly is a community? For purposes of your retirement geography, think of a community in the broad and varied sense of the term. It's simply an area that you live in during your retirement, and it usually has little in common with that specialized planned development that's marketed as a "retirement community." Livable community, as the middle layer of your retirement geography, is the area around your home that you typically travel within to fulfill your daily needs and desires.

Think about your current community. How far do you need to travel to the coffee shop, the grocery store, your faith community, the pharmacy, the post office, the doctor, the library, or dinner and a movie? How much farther, if at all, do you travel to see friends and family? How much farther for something a bit out of the ordinary, such as an airport, a major sporting event, or a top-notch regional hospital? (Although in the later years of retirement, having a hospital close to home could well become more essential.) Whatever area you travel within to fulfill those daily needs is probably what you think of as your community. At some distance from home, you know the feeling that you have left your community behind.

If you think you might even consider looking around for a new community for retirement, it's worthwhile to think about all the different kinds that exist. In looking at types of communities, you might even redefine what you think of as the boundaries of your own community. **A community can be described in a number of ways:**

- It could be a political entity with easily identifiable borders, such as a city or county (for example, Santa Fe, New Mexico, or Door County, Wisconsin).

- It could be a political entity that is contiguous with others but still retains its own character (such as Sarasota, Florida).

- It could be an area bounded by certain landforms or by water (such as Cape Cod, Massachusetts, or Bainbridge Island, Washington).

- It could be a well-known urban area in a large city (such as Buckhead in Atlanta or Wrigleyville in Chicago).

- It could be an area shaped by the presence of a university or other institution (as Clayton, Missouri, is by Washington University).

- It could be a real estate development organized by a corporation (such as Sun City, Arizona).

It could even be what was once called a neighborhood, even if it doesn't have a specific name (but these are getting harder to find). Many large cities have these enclaves, but knowledge of what makes each neighborhood special may be jealously guarded by locals.

Communities are wonderful things; more wonderful still is a livable community. This concept is a fairly recent one, but it is developing rapidly. Livable communities are good for everyone, whether they're in the first, second, or third box of life. In fact, one of the features that can make a community particularly livable is that it integrates people from all three boxes. Rather than separating age groups—young singles, families with children, retirees—from each other, all are included. People have lived in these kinds of age-integrated communities for most of human history, and there is a deep wisdom in it. You may even have spent your childhood in an environment like this, and you probably benefited greatly from your interaction with retired folks. They probably benefited from their interaction with you, too!

At the same time, there certainly are livable communities composed mostly of retirement-age people. Where these arise organically through the maturing of a neighborhood, they're called naturally occurring retirement communities, or NORCs. On the other hand, where these are created synthetically through land development, we might call them developer-organized retirement communities, or DORCs. Not all DORCs are created equal, and a few are even shining examples of livable communities. But please recognize that although DORCs always look very nice, looks can be deceiving. They may be more "lookable" than livable.

You can start thinking now about your current community and how livable it may be through your retirement years. After you retire, your awareness of the community may be heightened. For example, you could become more aware of how rich and varied the available activities are. In looking for activities, memberships, and environments to invest yourself in, you'll be able to explore your community at a deeper level. One part of that exploration will be getting to know other people in your community to build fun, engaging, and meaningful relationships with (because you'll be seeing less of your old friends from work). The more interesting and vibrant the activities are in your community, the more rewarding your explorations can be. The good news is that those activities attract interesting and vibrant people (like you!).

Is your community up to the task of being a livable community for your retirement? Or is it a dud? And you may want to gaze into your crystal ball. Not only will your own life change over the coming years, but the life of your community will, too. Is it the kind of town that relies too heavily on just one or two industries, with a Main Street that's been abandoned as strip malls sprout just outside the municipal limits? Or is your town too appealing for its own good, attracting newcomers from pricier areas, so longtime residents' children can no longer afford a starter home (if they can find one)? As your community develops, do you see yourself wanting to live there more than you do now, or less? Is there another community, or are there several (right in your own backyard), that would be a better fit? Only by making a comparison will you know. You may discover that yours stacks up very well and you didn't even realize it. Lucky you!

The Self-Contained Community

Another facet of your community is more mundane: How self-contained is it? For many, retiring from work also means retiring from commuting. Commuting is an activity that automatically routes you near many services that you need. In fact, you've probably become a loyal customer of some retailers just because they're on your commute route. Or you may have gotten into the habit of shopping or running errands near your workplace. At lunch and along the way from home to work and back again, you may often fit in the side trips needed to keep the household functioning. They're just stops along the way. But once you don't need to commute, if those services aren't available in your community you'll need to make specific trips to obtain them.

You might think that's a good thing in retirement—it will get you out of the house and into the world. That may be true for some folks. But because you're reading this book, I suspect you're not looking for meaningless time fillers just to keep yourself busy in retirement. You'd prefer to take care of as many of your needs as easily and close to home as possible. Sure, you want to get out of the house, but for meaningful, engaging activities. If your retirement has the potential to be the high point of your life's journey, it would be a shame to spend it running errands, don't you think?

Some communities are called by a single name and thought of as a single entity, but they are actually composed of several self-contained neighborhoods. Their lucky residents can fulfill their daily needs within just a few blocks from where they live. If they walk those blocks (in decent weather) instead of driving a car or taking public transit, they tend to stay more physically fit. The more activities they can participate in within walking distance, the more likely they are to know their neighbors, shopkeepers, librarians, pharmacists, and other nice folks. As people make their way further and further into the third box of life, these relationships become more valuable.

These self-contained neighborhoods exist in every region, in most cities, and in both low-rent and high-rent districts. Many smaller towns still operate on this principle. If you've never lived this way before, you owe it to yourself to experience it. Go stay a while with a friend who's fortunate enough to live in one. For a vacation, sublet an apartment or a house in an area that appears to operate this way (even though you may not get to know many residents in that short a time). There are no advertisements or marketing brochures (let alone salespeople) for these neighborhoods. They aren't trying to entice anyone, so you need to seek them out. You need to be a sleuth!

Calling It a Community Doesn't Make It One

On the other hand, there are also places that are called "communities" but are communities in name only. You've seen the signs at the gates of developments: "A Community for Those 55 and Better," "A Community of 38 Distinctive Homes," "A Community for Active Living!" These places, whatever you call them, often put their residents at a disadvantage, because they don't offer what people actually need to live day to day. (Unless all you need to do is play golf or tennis or swim.) These "communities" are isolated enclaves that force residents to rely on a car or public transportation, which can be an inconvenience or a hardship, depending on the situation. (Strangely, both gated communities and ghettos can share this limitation.) Because residents don't walk to the services they need, exercise isn't as naturally integrated into their daily lives. Because they don't walk outside as much, they are less likely to know their neighbors and others outside the gates.

As you move from the Third Age into the Fourth Age, living in this kind of "community" can easily make you more socially isolated. Although the architecture and landscaping may be pleasing to the eye, the residents may or may not interact very much. This isn't something you can normally spot from photographs or even on a tour. But a little feet-on-the-ground research should reveal how residents get around and how well they know each other.

The social life of a community is often revealed in its physical configuration. There is a saying in the field of geography: "The spatial is social, and the social is spatial." The idea is that the configuration of a neighborhood affects the social relationships of the residents. The flip side is that the social relationships of the residents will in turn affect how they create and modify the spatial configuration of the neighborhood. **Every community offers social clues:**

- Are there sidewalks? Are there people walking on them?

- Are there courtyards or parks with benches? Are residents gathering and visiting there?

- Are there commercial establishments where people linger and socialize? Or do they just hurry in and out?

Such distinctions may not be a big deal for you in the early part of retirement, when you're healthy, active, out and about in the world, and reveling in your new free time. But much later, when you may not be as active and may prefer to spend more time closer to home, this distinction could mean the difference between inconvenience and hardship, between a community that is livable and one that is not.

Your Aging-in-Place Residence:
The Micro Layer of Geography

When the time comes, as it may, that you need assistance with the activities of daily living, would you prefer to continue living in your own home or move to a nursing home? (Surveys, over and over, overwhelmingly report that people want to "age in place.")

Although this question deals with the Fourth Age, you should consider it as early as possible—right now, when you're thinking about the Third Age. The decisions you make at this point will determine, far down the road, how long you can live in your own home. Will the home in which you choose to spend your retirement be one that allows you to live out your days there? (Hand in hand with choosing that home, of course, goes making every effort to preserve your health and physical self-sufficiency, the focus of another chapter in this book.)

At the middle layer of retirement geography—your community—the key concept is livability. At the micro layer—your residence—livability is the key concept, too. Just as you'll spend more time in your community in retirement, you'll also spend a lot more time in your residence than you ever have before. The question is not simply "How livable is it?" but also "How long will it be livable?" Based on what happens to you as you age, how easy or difficult will it be to live there? As you're planning your retirement, you need to take the long view. The very long view.

Of course, even though many people claim that they want to age in place, not everyone wants to. Perhaps you imagine living in one residence for the Third Age when you're vigorous and active, then moving to another residence for the Fourth Age when you can't get around as well. That's a perfectly good plan, if you really do that kind of two-stage planning. Just don't ignore the Fourth Age because you find it unpleasant to think about. A little long-range planning now can save you (and your loved ones) a lot of frustration, work, money, and heartache down the road.

You may have been thinking of moving to a new home for your retirement, or not. Perhaps you're definitely moving, because you want to downsize and get equity out of your home for retirement income. Perhaps you're definitely not, because you have so many memories and friends (and so much stuff) associated with your home that you can't imagine moving. In that case, if you need to draw equity out of your home for retirement income, you'll look into a reverse mortgage or a home equity line of credit.

Perhaps you've hedged your bets by buying a vacation home that you plan to make into your retirement home. This will eventually lead to a sort of hybrid move, as you bring the remainder of your belongings to join those you've been keeping in the second home and adjust to living there as opposed to limited vacation visits. Perhaps you're open to moving but aren't sure yet what exactly you would be looking for, or whether a new home would be worth all the trouble. Whatever possibilities you're considering, remember this: think both near term and long term. When you evaluate a residence—existing or contemplated—ask yourself two questions:

1. How well would that residence support your active early retirement life?

2. How well would that residence support your aging in place, later in retirement?

Six Possible Ways to Use Your Home in Retirement

Let's look at some examples of the active early part of retirement, in the Third Age. Think of people you know who have recently retired; you've probably noticed that they use their homes in variations on the following six basic approaches. As you read each description, consider it in light of your own chosen Ways to Live. How have you been using your home during your working life? Is that how you'd really like to use it in retirement?

1. **Home as a Job.** These folks retire from their regular job and, in effect, take on a new job as the caretaker, handyperson, and housekeeper of their own residence. They take personal responsibility for just about every aspect of maintenance. These hardworking folks throw themselves into duties for which they might previously

have hired a professional (or a local teenager). Some retirees may find this truly rewarding; others may just be trying to keep busy, because they really don't know what else to do with their time. Either way, handling physical and technical responsibilities helps keep us sharp as we age, so some of it may be a good thing for everyone. How about you?

2. **Home as a Project.** These folks use their newfound freedom (and sometimes their retirement money) to finally get to the major home improvements they've contemplated for years. Whether they use the do-it-yourself or have-it-done approach, it's the focus of their interest and attention. If they're not careful, the remodeling ideas can be leftovers, fitting their old life more than their new one. But ideally the ideas are fresh and relevant to the way they want to live in retirement. The improvements really increase quality of life. At some point, though, the home improvement phase must come to an end. That's when these folks discover whether just living in their home is enough for their Retirement Well-Being. How about you?

3. **Home as a Museum.** These folks have accumulated a lot of physical possessions during their time in the second box, and their home is the place they display and store everything. Retirement is an opportunity to seek out and find even more of just the right stuff. Some people are true connoisseurs; others are true pack rats. For both, though, the thrill of acquiring more things or the sense of security in keeping them may be more important than the residence itself. Some may get involved as buyers or sellers at flea markets or in online auctions. The home may be just a warehouse or the ultimate display case, showing the entire collection. They may hope that their prized possessions will one day become family heirlooms. (If you're such a collector, one of the best ways to test that hope against reality is to talk with your family about it. Really, really talk with them. You may find that they treasure the time spent with you more than they would treasure having your treasure.) How about you?

4. **Home as a Community Center.** These folks turn their residence into a setting for finally spending more time with other people. In Western society, life in the second box is typically time deprived, and social relationships often suffer. Some people use their additional free time in retirement to entertain—seriously entertain. They get friends and family into their home for large and small gatherings, and they encourage overnight guests whenever possible. Unlike the first two uses of a residence, this approach is focused less on the physical structure itself and more on its usefulness as a venue. Of course, if these folks have let their relationships slip away during the second box, they may be beyond reviving in the third box, regardless of the venue. How about you?

5. **Home as a Base of Operations.** These folks may not really be interested in their residence at all. They yearn to be somewhere else, traveling hither and yon. Whatever form their travels take, their home becomes more or less the base camp. These folks feel that they've been tied down long enough in the Second Age, and as long as they've got health and money, they'll seek their happiness on the road. But consider this: Sooner or later we all must stop to rest, and rest becomes a bigger issue the further we progress toward the Fourth Age. At some point these folks will need to decide whether the residence they have is the one that they want to spend time in as their travels wind down. How about you?

6. **Home as a Retreat.** These folks may or may not be interested in their home per se, but they are interested in the privacy and serenity that it can provide. They may have found the requirements of the Second Age tiring, forcing them into more contact with the world than they really liked. Now they want to be left alone in peace and quiet and interact with the world on their own terms. Although home is a refuge even during the working years, it's usually only for a few hours each day. The long, unbroken time structure of retirement certainly allows home owners to retreat if that's what they want to do. However, as they move from the Third Age to the Fourth, a social support network will be an essential resource.

The danger of residence as retreat is that unless the residents also emerge to keep relationships alive, those may not be there when they need them. How about you?

It all comes back to the essential message of this book: making plans for the life you want to live in retirement, then considering how your residence can support that life. Life planning comes first; residence planning comes second. This is really the foundation of your micro layer geographical decision. Only after you're clear about your own Retirement Well-Being can you think clearly about whether you should stay put or go looking for your retirement dream home.

Thinking about what you'll need in your residence in the later, aging-in-place phase of retirement is more straightforward than planning for the active early retirement years, because your options are narrower. The natural process of aging, even healthy aging, means that sooner or later it can become a challenge for you to live independently. However, you probably can't foresee what your own specific challenges will be, when and if that time comes for you. There is a broad range of infirmities that become more common as you age, and you don't get to choose them; they choose you. It may be a loss of strength or balance, physical dexterity, eyesight or hearing, cardio or respiratory capacity. If you knew in advance which infirmities might eventually force you to leave your home for some type of assisted living, you could plan better. You could make sure that the home you settle on, early in the Third Age, would be hospitable to the infirmities you expect to have later on. Your family genetics, your health history, any existing conditions, and your health habits are all factors, but these are far outweighed by the unpredictable. Seeing as you can't accurately predict, it's a good idea to consider some general ideas from the new concept of universal design (see the sidebar on page 147).

Universal design offers great guidance for planning the micro layer of your retirement geography. To look at your home with a universal design perspective means asking, "If someone with [fill in the limiting health condition] were going to live in this residence, what would allow them to be self-sufficient; what would make it a lifetime home?" *Lifetime home* is a new term to describe the residence that we hope will support us in both the early and the later parts of our retirement. It has a nice ring to it, don't you think?

So what makes a home a lifetime home? Mostly, that it can accommodate your changing needs. It can be as simple and easy as adding sturdy handrails in bathrooms, or more complex and expensive, such as installing lower counters and cabinets or a chair lift on a stairway. But some livability fixes can be almost impossible to implement in the layout of many homes. For example, if rooms are on multiple levels — even if they're separated by just one or two stairs — there may not be space for a wheelchair-accessible ramp.

Thinking about your physical needs as you age may be something you'd prefer to put off. And even when you do address the issue, you don't have a crystal ball. But evaluating your residence now with these ideas in mind could eventually make the difference between continuing to live there and being forced to leave.

A Sense of Place: The Inner Layer of Your Geography

Your inner experience of your retirement geography is as important as the outer layers that we've already explored. Sense of place is that connection you feel to a particular place, your emotional reaction to it, the symbolic meaning that it has for you. Sense of place is not easy to pin down, because it is something different for each of us. It has to do with how unique or generic a place is, how personal or impersonal.

This idea has arisen in the context of sweeping changes in the way we live in Western society. Many people are uncomfortably aware of the sameness, the lack of authenticity, the *placelessness* that has proliferated across the country. Subdivisions filled with look-alike houses, business parks filled with work-alike offices, interspersed with standard-issue strip malls. National chains driving out local retailers and franchises replacing family-owned restaurants. Places that once had a distinctive local character are being made over to fit into the same mold. There are parts of many cities that look just like parts of any other city. And they don't just look the same—they feel the same. It's difficult, if not impossible, to have a sense of place in such environments. Of course, many jobs are geographically connected to them, and in your working years you may need to live there. However, retirement offers your greatest geographic freedom. Are you curious where you might discover your own personal sense of place?

Universal or Personal?

Sense of place ranges from the universal to the personal. Certain landscapes evoke a strong sense of place for just about everyone. You have surely visited some unfamiliar places that you felt an immediate connection with—the mountains, the seashore, a deep forest, green rolling hills, the desert in bloom. You could say that those locations have a universal sense of place, and most humans would probably agree.

You have surely visited other places to which you felt a culturally based connection—for example, a classic Main Street in a small town, a setting that resonates with your childhood and the image presented in your schoolbooks and in magazines. Many people who share your upbringing would experience the same sense of place.

Finally, there are places that you connect with because of your own personal life experience; you would not expect others necessarily to experience the same sense of place that you do. You may have lived there in the past or dreamed about living there in the future. You may have gone to school there or vacationed or visited relatives there. Or you may have never set eyes on the place before, but once you do, you say, "This is the place." For your retirement geography, your own personal sense of place is the one that matters most.

You can't predict what will create that sense of place for you. You can't tell from pictures or descriptions alone. You can't tell from what other people say about it. You certainly can't tell from the statistics about it. No, sense of place comes from direct experience. It could be the evident features of a place: its climate, topography, vegetation, or architecture. It could be the people you interact with there. It could be what you know about its history or its importance in the larger scheme of things. It could be your own personal memories, distinct from your current experience of the place. You may even get the sense that a particular place will support your chosen Ways to Live.

The only way to really know whether a location has a sense of place for you is to become an explorer; you need to be there and experience it. You may need to move to a new place, or you may instead need to see the place you live now as if for the first time. Only you can explore the geography of your Ideal Retirement. But it's worth exploring, because your retirement will last a very long time, if all goes as you hope.

Two factors that are critical to just how long it will last are the biology and medicine elements that make up the health dimension of your Retirement Well-Being, which is the focus of another chapter. In this chapter, as we've explored where you might spend your retirement, we have frequently touched on the need to plan for both the natural aging process and the unpredictable infirmities that may arise. It's wise to choose a livable community and a home that incorporates universal design to support your aging in place. Having done that, you'll want to do all you can to preserve your physical vigor and independence for as long as possible.

But first, you get to brainstorm the geography of your Retirement Well-Being.

LIVING IN MY GEOGRAPHICAL PLACE

You've used the Four Layers of Retirement Geography to imagine the kinds of places that could best support all the other elements of your Retirement Well-Being. You should now have plenty of raw material for your final geography exercise: identifying the geographical element of your Ideal Retirement. That place could be the one you're living in now or someplace new.

You can approach the four layers in any order that makes sense for you. The acronym SALE doesn't mean you need to sell your home; it's just a way to help remember the layers.

If it's earlier in your career, you can note just the broad or general features of each layer. If it's later in your career, you should be more specific. If you're approaching retirement, you may have all the particulars completely worked out.

My Sense of Place: The Inner Layer

What places could create a particular feeling or a sense of connection for you in retirement? These might have a sense of place on a universal, cultural, or personal level, or be especially symbolic or meaningful for you. Think of places you've already experienced and ones you would like to explore. Write the names of several types of places, or specific places, for this layer, for example, "Ocean shore; Colorado Rockies; Taos, New Mexico."

_____

_____

_____

My Aging-in-Place Residence: The Micro Layer

What role will your residence play in your retirement? Is it likely to become a job, a project, a museum, a community center, a base of operations, a retreat, or something else? To fill that role, what physical features would your home need? Financially, would your home be a significant expense, a low-cost place to live, or a source of income? Would your residence accommodate aging in place, or do you plan to move as you get older? If it's early in your career, identify a general type of residence (such as a city apartment, resort-style condo, or country house). If it's later in your career, try to identify a specific type of residence, or even a specific house (say, in your town, seen on vacation, or found on the Internet).

_____

_____

_____

My Livable Community: The Middle Layer

Considering how far into retirement you plan to live there, how supportive does your community need to be at different stages? Which livability issues are most crucial to you? A walkable neighborhood? Access to medical care and other services? Transportation? Social interaction? Activities? A retirement-age population or one that's age-integrated? What other features or amenities are most important for you? Financially, will your community provide opportunities to upscale or to economize?

_____

_____

_____

My Essential Region: The Macro Layer

Which part of the country offers what's most important to you? Could it involve the people you have relationships with? The opportunity to connect with your interests, strengths, or values? A supportive environment for your health or health care? A lower cost of living? Where are the things that you absolutely wouldn't want to live without? Is it likely your essential region will change during your retirement years?

_____

_____

_____

LIFE CIRCLES EXERCISE

Now go back to your responses for all four layers and choose the most appealing or significant responses for each layer. (These aren't set in stone; you can revisit and revise your choices later as your planning evolves.) Enter these on the appropriate lines of your Life Circle to use for your One Piece of Paper in chapter eleven.

My Ideal Retirement

includes inhabiting this

geographical place:

S _____

A _____

L _____

E _____

"It's not a health care system at all;
it's a disease management system."

—Dr. Andrew Weil,
integrative medicine pioneer

Chapter SEVEN

Medicine—Who's in Charge?

How much retirement medicine are you planning to buy? A lot or a little? What kind?

During the Second Age, those questions might not have made sense. But for the Third Age, they make complete sense. That's because, when we were younger, most of us didn't have much interaction with the medical system. If we needed care, it was often the *urgent* kind. An infection that required antibiotics. An accident that caused cuts or broken bones. An acute condition like appendicitis that demanded surgery. We didn't expect to need treatment, but then we needed it in a hurry. For treatment, we *entered* the medical system, it *fixed* us, and we *exited*. We went back to our Second Age world, where medicine didn't play much of a role. The questions "How much care?" and "What kind?" wouldn't have been relevant then.

But, for the Third Age, those are very relevant questions. That's because we begin needing treatment not just for urgent conditions but also for *chronic* ones. The ones associated with aging. You know the list: high blood pressure, high cholesterol, high blood sugar, arthritis, depression, digestive problems, and so on. These chronic conditions are very different than the *enter-fix-exit* ones of the Second Age. When these develop, it's not usually urgent. Instead, it's usually *permanent*. Whatever it is, it's going to be with us, more or less, forever. So the question changes. Instead of "How quickly can I get this fixed?" it becomes "How will I manage this over the next couple of decades?" How you answer that question affects how you design the next stage of your life!

That's why this chapter is about *retirement medicine*, which addresses how to get the treatment you want for illness (if you need to). The next chapter is about *retirement biology*, which addresses the physical aging process and how to choose practices for building and maintaining your vitality. Here's one way to think about the distinction: We each have our own personal biology, the body we walk around in. We're responsible for taking care of it, and it's the aspect of our health that we have the most control over. In contrast, medicine isn't part of us. It's a system that's outside of us, out there in the world. We use a medical system, or systems, for treatment. The system doesn't act *upon* us—we choose to interact with the system, *consciously*. That's one difference between medicine and *veterinary* medicine—conscious choice on the part of the patient!

The Medical System Is in Turmoil

Making plans for how we want to access medicine in retirement would be a complicated subject under any circumstances. But with the Patient Protection and Affordable Care Act of 2010, our society has started down a long path of change. Economic constraints and an aging population mean there will be *short-term and long-term changes* to the system. How will we pay for it? Under what conditions can we access it? What's covered, and what's not? Those questions just scratch the surface of issues that our society will need to address over the next few decades.

You can't answer those questions now. You'll need to learn about new options as they emerge and make the best decisions you can as you go along. However, you can develop a long-term perspective for how you want to access medical care in your next stage of life. You can identify what your goals are and create a foundation for your future decision making that's unique to you and your life.

There Are Really Two Medical Systems

One of the core issues you need to address is what you consider the medical system to be. On the one hand, there's the *conventional* Western medical system composed of medical schools, MDs, hospitals, and drug companies, which is completely connected to and supported by state licensing laws, insurance plans, and federal tax laws. And there is also the enormous, expanding, unconventional *alternative* medical system that has not been connected or supported in the same way until fairly recently.

When you walk into a pharmacy to fill your prescription from the conventional medical system, you walk by an entire *aisle* of alternative treatments. It includes everything from herbs to vitamin and mineral supplements to homeopathic remedies. Huge quantities of these are sold at the pharmacy (and in natural foods stores), but because they don't require a prescription, few pharmacists have any in-depth knowledge of them.

Similarly, an entire section of the bookstore is devoted to alternative treatments, but because the topic is generally avoided in medical training, you won't find many medical doctors browsing there. And even though offices of alternative practitioners such as acupuncturists and chiropractors are often right next door to offices of MDs, there is generally little acknowledgment or interaction between these different practitioners. It's as though they're from different *planets*. More accurately, they're from different *paradigms*. Yet, research has shown that up to half of Americans have used alternative approaches not recognized by conventional medicine. And when they do use alternative approaches, they tend not to tell their medical doctor.

This topic of alternative medicine becomes particularly relevant for the Third Age. Urgent conditions of the Second Age are a perfect fit for conventional treatment. But for the *chronic* conditions of the Third Age, many people view complementary and alternative medicine (CAM) as an option. Rather than take a prescription drug for the *rest of their lives*, some wonder about "natural" alternatives. You probably don't know which chronic conditions you're likely to develop, or what CAM treatments for those might possibly be. So let's start with a baseline: your medical history. Or rather, your complementary medical history. See the exercise on page 158.

Have you used complementary or alternative medicine (CAM) at one time or another? A good way to anticipate whether you might use CAM therapies in the future is to consider which ones, if any, you've used in the past. You may have had direct experience with some of the approaches listed below, heard about others, and some may be new to you.

CAM Approaches	Have you ever used this?	Would you consider using it?
Ayurveda	No / Yes / Not Sure	No / Yes / Not Sure
Biofeedback	No / Yes / Not Sure	No / Yes / Not Sure
Botanical medicines or herbs	No / Yes / Not Sure	No / Yes / Not Sure
Chiropractic	No / Yes / Not Sure	No / Yes / Not Sure
Energy therapies such as Reiki or Healing Touch	No / Yes / Not Sure	No / Yes / Not Sure
Homeopathy	No / Yes / Not Sure	No / Yes / Not Sure
Mind-body approaches such as hypnosis or visualization	No / Yes / Not Sure	No / Yes / Not Sure
Movement practices such as yoga or tai chi	No / Yes / Not Sure	No / Yes / Not Sure
Prayer or meditation for healing	No / Yes / Not Sure	No / Yes / Not Sure
Nutritional supplements or vitamin therapy	No / Yes / Not Sure	No / Yes / Not Sure
Therapeutic massage	No / Yes / Not Sure	No / Yes / Not Sure
Traditional Chinese medicine or acupuncture/acupressure	No / Yes / Not Sure	No / Yes / Not Sure
Unconventional or unproven science	No / Yes / Not Sure	No / Yes / Not Sure
Other	No / Yes / Not Sure	No / Yes / Not Sure

Now read down the answer columns. Do you notice a pattern or theme in your use—or nonuse—of CAM? Even if you haven't discovered anything new, it is worthwhile to document your past and consider your future. How does this fit into your planning for the next stage of life?

For When You're Not Feeling Up to PAR: Your Retirement Medicine Cycle

What's your medical philosophy? Do you have a medical philosophy? You've probably never been asked! Instead of asking what your philosophy is, most books and practitioners tell you what it *should* be. If they're based in conventional medicine, they offer the truths from that paradigm as though they were the only truths. If they're from one of the alternative systems (such as the approaches in the history exercise), they offer the truths from that particular paradigm as though *they* were the only truths. All these sources of information seem to pretend that they exist in a vacuum, without considering the philosophies or principles of other systems. (Unless it's to attack them.)

There is one essential truth, though. The essential truth is that you're stuck in the middle and you need to make up your *own* mind. That's why you need to have your own philosophy of medicine. If you wait until you're sick to try to identify it, you won't be at your best. You'll be more likely to just accept a philosophy that's thrust on you by a medical practitioner or a well-meaning relative or friend. You may be so overwhelmed that you may not realize you have a choice. It's better to figure this out now, while you're of sound body and sound mind. Your medical philosophy is a little bit like having an advance directive or living will. Except instead of addressing end-of-life care, it addresses *all* of your medical care. Instead of being a guide for others, it's a guide for *yourself.*

The Retirement Medicine Cycle is a way to think about, and plan for, the kind of medicine you want. It has three components: your medical philosophy, your access to medicine, and your medical relationships. You can think of it as philosophy, access, and relationships, which creates an easy-to-remember acronym: PAR.

Regardless of the changes that happen to the medical system, you'll be able to make sense of your options by understanding how the Retirement Medicine Cycle operates.

- *Philosophy* includes your preference for conventional or alternative approaches, as well as your preference for greater or lesser medical intervention in general. Your philosophy determines what type of medical services you want access to. (Conventional or alternative? High-tech or low-tech?)

- *Access* includes your methods for getting treatment. (Insurance? Out-of-pocket cash? Government plans?) Your methods of access determine which practitioners you can use and thus limit the medical relationships you can create and develop.

- *Relationships* with practitioners are your sources of both treatment and information. The information you get from those practitioners will be limited by the paradigm they operate within—their own truths—which in turn influences your medical philosophy. That's what makes it a cycle rather than a linear process.

You can see that, if you're not careful, the Retirement Medicine Cycle can become a *closed loop* system. If your philosophy leads you to

THE RETIREMENT MEDICINE CYCLE

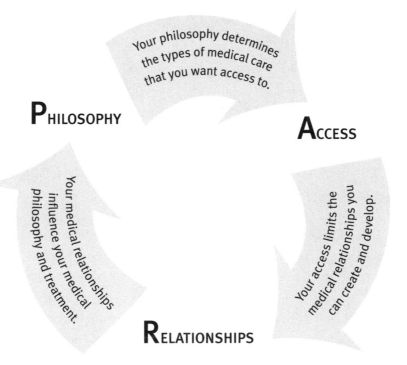

Your philosophy determines the types of medical care that you want access to.

PHILOSOPHY

ACCESS

Your medical relationships influence your medical philosophy and treatment.

Your access limits the medical relationships you can create and develop.

RELATIONSHIPS

seek out access to one particular system and you develop relationships with only those practitioners, they will tend to give you only information from inside *their* system or paradigm. That's where they live and practice. However, that will only serve to further reinforce your original philosophy. You're not being presented with *other* perspectives or options, therefore you may have blind spots about your medical treatment, and you may not even realize it.

Let's take something common that most people simply *love* about aging—back pain—as a simple example. If you have a purely conventional philosophy, you may seek access only to medical doctors, who then offer treatment options only within conventional medicine (drugs, surgery, or maybe physical therapy). If you have a particular alternative philosophy—say, Chinese medicine or nutritional approaches—you may seek access only to *those* practitioners, who then offer treatment options only within *that* system. In both scenarios, you probably wouldn't be referred to a chiropractor, even if that might be a beneficial treatment in your particular case. (Although alternative practitioners may be more aware of and supportive of other alternative practices than conventional practitioners are.)

That's why it's so important to enter into your Retirement Medicine Cycle consciously, rather than getting swept along unconsciously. You need to be the one who's in charge! The following section will help you clarify your philosophy, identify your likely methods of access, and determine which medical relationships you'll need to support your health and well-being in the Third and Fourth Ages.

PAR: Philosophy of Medicine

Your medical philosophy combines two ingredients: your perspective on conventional versus alternative medicine and your tendency toward medical intervention in general.

First, where do you stand along the conventional versus alternative *continuum?* Do you see medicine from the narrower, more orthodox perspective or from the broader, more unorthodox perspective? Those are the two ends of the continuum, and your outlook may be somewhere in

YOUR MEDICAL PHILOSOPHY

To identify your personal philosophy of medicine, consider the sets of paired statements below. For each pair, decide where your perspective is on the continuum from conventional to alternative and mark one of the boxes accordingly. Marking the far right or left box means you strongly agree with that philosophy; marking the next box in means you agree somewhat more with that philosophy than with the other; marking the center box means you're neutral or unsure. This topic is enormous and very complex, so it can't be reduced to just this set of paired statements. But this exercise can be an important step toward clarifying your philosophy.

Conventional Philosophy			Alternative Philosophy	
Medicine should be based on modern and rigorous research methods.			Medicine can be based on forms of knowledge other than modern science.	
❏ Strongly Agree	❏	❏ Neutral	❏	❏ Strongly Agree
Treatments outside of conventional medicine should be avoided.			Conventional medicine treatments should be avoided.	
❏ Strongly Agree	❏	❏ Neutral	❏	❏ Strongly Agree
All treatments must meet the same standards for safety and effectiveness.			Treatments that pose little risk and could be beneficial are worth trying.	
❏ Strongly Agree	❏	❏ Neutral	❏	❏ Strongly Agree
High-tech is almost always more effective than low-tech.			High-tech or low-tech has little bearing on effectiveness.	
❏ Strongly Agree	❏	❏ Neutral	❏	❏ Strongly Agree
Medicine is the weapon of choice in the fight against disease.			The body seeks to heal itself; medicine plays a supporting role.	
❏ Strongly Agree	❏	❏ Neutral	❏	❏ Strongly Agree
As the expert, the doctor's role is to diagnose and prescribe; the patient's role is to comply with treatment.			The practitioner and patient both have knowledge and must actively share the role of promoting the patient's health.	
❏ Strongly Agree	❏	❏ Neutral	❏	❏ Strongly Agree

Now consider your tendency to seek medical intervention *distinct* from how sick or healthy you are. This isn't about how sick you've been or how sick you're likely to be. This is about how likely you are to seek treatment for any given level of health. Your propensity to seek out medical care during your healthier Second Age may be an indicator of your propensity to seek it out in the Third Age. You can't know for sure whether your history of getting a little or a lot of help for small aches and pains is a predictor of how you'll react to the chronic issues of old age. (Unless you've already had major health issues.) To the extent you think about this consciously, though, you may become aware of a certain *consistency* in your tendency to seek intervention.

For each of the following pairs of statements decide where your perspective is on the continuum from high intervention to low intervention, and mark one of the boxes accordingly. Marking the far right or left box means you strongly agree with that philosophy; marking the next box in means you agree somewhat more with that philosophy than with the other; marking the center box means you're neutral or unsure.

High-Intervention Philosophy		*Low-Intervention Philosophy*		
Too much treatment is usually better than too little.			Too little treatment is usually better than too much.	
❑ Strongly Agree	❑	❑ Neutral	❑	❑ Strongly Agree
It's better to seek care sooner rather than later.			It's better to wait; conditions often resolve themselves.	
❑ Strongly Agree	❑	❑ Neutral	❑	❑ Strongly Agree
Relying on a range of specialists provides better care.			Relying on a single trusted practitioner provides better care.	
❑ Strongly Agree	❑	❑ Neutral	❑	❑ Strongly Agree
Using multiple treatments for multiple conditions all at the same time makes sense.			Receiving multiple treatments at the same time can cause problems in and of itself.	
❑ Strongly Agree	❑	❑ Neutral	❑	❑ Strongly Agree
Medical treatment is the most important thing, even when it may be inconvenient.			Medical treatment that is difficult or disruptive must be considered within the context of day-to-day life.	
❑ Strongly Agree	❑	❑ Neutral	❑	❑ Strongly Agree

between. You already have one good indicator in your history of using—or not using—CAM approaches. However, that's a measure of your past actions, not your current perspective. Second, where do you stand on the *level of intervention* continuum? The high extreme of that continuum is hypochondria, where people seek treatment for symptoms that aren't real. The low extreme is denial, where people ignore symptoms or don't take prescribed medicines. But well within those two unhealthy extremes, there is still a significant variation in the level of intervention that reasonable individuals consciously choose. To discover your preferred ways of using the medical system, complete the medical philosophy exercise in this chapter.

Now we'll put these two aspects together to illustrate an overall way of thinking about your medical philosophy. In the following figure, you'll see that *conventional* is on the left side and *alternative* on the right, *high intervention* on the top and *low intervention* on the bottom. For each of these two aspects, mark the point that indicates where your philosophy lies on the continuum (the line with two arrows).

To identify your philosophy, mark the point where a line drawn across from your spot on the High Intervention–Low Intervention (ver-

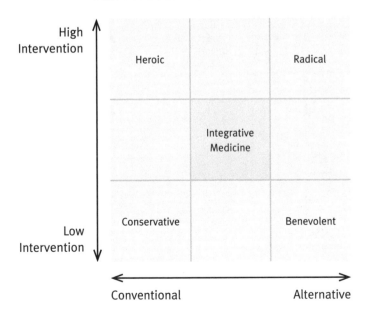

THE FIVE MEDICAL PHILOSOPHIES

tical) continuum would intersect with a line drawn up from your spot on the Conventional–Alternative (horizontal) continuum.

The figure combines these two different aspects of your medical philosophy and provides a simplified way to think about them in the practical world. The four corners each crystallize a particular perspective. If you tend toward a high level of intervention using conventional treatments (upper left), that's a *heroic* philosophy. A low level of conventional intervention (lower left) is a *conservative* philosophy. That same tendency for low intervention, but using alternative treatments (lower right), is a *benevolent* philosophy. And if you use alternative treatments and also tend toward a high level of intervention (upper right), that's *radical*, dude.

An Integrative Approach

What if you're somewhere in the middle? You should be delighted to learn that there is actually a fifth perspective, and you can see it right in the middle of the shaded area. *Integrative* medicine is a fast-growing movement that integrates these different perspectives.

Integrative medicine is midway between conventional and alternative, and high and low intervention. Of course, even without integrative medicine, it's possible to use both conventional and alternative treatments in an eclectic way. You know, some of this and some of that. However, that's definitely not what integrative medicine does. At its core, it's based on adherence to the same *scientific method* that is the foundation of conventional medicine. However, for treatment options, it accesses both conventional *and* alternative approaches. It uses a rigorous approach to explore alternative treatments that are less dangerous and disruptive to the body than many conventional treatments but are often just as effective. It looks for the best of both worlds.

The scientific approach that integrative medicine takes is somewhat different from that of conventional medicine, however. Conventional medical science is sometimes *skeptical* toward phenomena that it should be *curious* about. Or dogmatic about assumptions that it should be questioning. In terms of the Retirement Medicine Cycle, conventional medicine can act like a closed loop system that isn't open to some types of new information.

In contrast, integrative medicine is open to information from *more sources.* Specifically, it studies treatments from alternative medicine that may be beneficial, yet because it does adhere to the scientific method, it's rigorous about which alternative medicine treatments to use. However, there may be different standards for evaluating the safety of traditionally used natural substances that are less likely to cause harm versus newly developed powerful pharmaceuticals that may have strong side effects.

As for a low or high level of intervention, integrative medicine assumes that the lowest level that supports the body's own healing is the place to start. (Often the best intervention is a healthier lifestyle!) If a condition doesn't respond to the lower-level intervention, then it's time to move up the ladder. For example, instead of prescribing the standard dose of a drug, integrative medicine may start with the *minimum* dose, to see whether that's effective. If so, there are few side effects. But if a higher level really is necessary, so be it.

Specific to the Third and Fourth Ages, integrative medicine suggests that biological aging is a natural part of life. Technically speaking, there is no such thing as an "antiaging" treatment. No one has figured out yet how to reverse the natural aging process that inevitably ends in death. But it's possible to optimize your health at any age. And it's definitely possible to optimize how healthy you feel and act in your daily life. Often, ironically, when you focus on the symptoms and diseases that you *don't want,* they expand to assume a bigger role in your life. When you instead focus on how to support your body's own *self-healing* process, that's what expands. Which would you prefer?

Integrative medicine helps you (1) build habits that support your biology and (2) use any natural treatments that are effective for your condition (with fewer adverse side effects). This helps you focus on (and expand) your awareness of health and healing, rather than focus on diseases or treatments. This issue becomes more and more important as you age. In the First and Second Ages of life, because health conditions are the *enter-fix-exit* type, they go away and may be quickly forgotten. But in the Third Age, many conditions related to aging can't be cured. Even if you need to gracefully accept those conditions, do you want *disease* to be the focus of your life? Or would you prefer to focus on the *health and healing* that are operating in your life?

The goal of integrative medicine is healthy aging, even though you may also have chronic health conditions.

COMPLEMENTARY AND ALTERNATIVE MEDICINE USE BY AGE

Barnes, P.M., B. Bloom, and R. Nahin. *CDC National Health Statistics Report #12.* Complementary and Alternative Medicine Use Among Adults and Children: United States, 2007. December 2008.

Now that you've had a chance to identify the fundamentals of these five medical perspectives, you'll have an easy way to identify them in the real world. If you read a book or magazine, talk to a practitioner, or get a recommendation for treatment, you'll have an idea which perspective it's coming from. Before you consider the specific information, you can consider your *compatibility* with the source. How does that perspective relate to your medical philosophy?

You need to ask, "How valid is that perspective, approach, or paradigm in general?" And if it's valid, you can ask, "How knowledgeable is that practitioner within the scope of that perspective or approach?" Even after you determine that your perspective and the practitioner's perspective are compatible, there's always the question of whether the individual practitioner is experienced or inexperienced, competent or incompetent.

So, for the first stage of the Retirement Medicine Cycle, would you describe your medical philosophy as heroic, conservative, benevolent, radical, or integrative? Is there yet another term that better describes you? The answer is an important part of planning your Ideal Retirement.

PAR: Access to the Care You Want

Now that you know your medical philosophy, you can plan how to gain *access* to the types of medical care that you want.

First, will conventional treatments be enough for you? If not, which alternative approaches do you plan to use? How will you gain access financially? One of the first observations we made about these two systems is that conventional medicine is supported by insurance companies, the Medicare system, and the tax laws. Much alternative medicine is not supported (although that's been changing), which leads to higher out-of-pocket costs. However, who knows what will be covered, and not covered, under future health care system reforms? If you didn't have access to an expensive conventional treatment, would you then consider an inexpensive alternative treatment? Another part of your access can be geographical—if the provider for that type of treatment is far away, it may not be feasible. If you live in a remote area, most treatments may be out of reach. If you want a particular specialist, or a particular CAM practitioner, can you travel to see them? What will it cost to live near the treatments you want or to travel to gain access to them? Geographical access becomes a bigger issue in the Third Age and especially in the Fourth Age.

Second, what level of intervention do you expect? Do you tend toward more intervention rather than less? Are you more likely to pay a visit to your practitioner? More likely to pursue advanced treatments? This isn't about how sick or healthy you'll be (although that is another important question). Rather, the question is, for a given level of sickness or health, do you tend to *seek out* a lot of care or just a little? Do you tend to be lured by those prescription-drug commercials that coax you to "Ask your doctor if this New Miracle Drug is right for you"? Even when you have insurance, if you tend toward high intervention, you'll have higher out-of-pocket costs.

Let's review our medical philosophy table from the perspective of cost. In the figure, total cost means the actual true cost, *ignoring* subsidies such as insurance plans or tax breaks. Out-of-pocket cost means what you might typically pay, taking into account subsidies such as insurance plans or tax breaks. Again, who knows how the health care reforms will affect what treatment is covered under your plan at that time? However, the general principles underlying this table should operate for the foreseeable future. If you favor an "expensive" approach, you need to think about how to pay for it!

RELATIVE COSTS OF EACH MEDICAL PHILOSOPHY

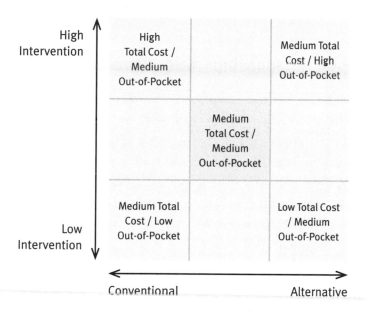

Now consider common methods for accessing medicine in retirement, recognizing that all of these may well be *changing* over the course of your retirement:

- Social programs, such as Medicare A and B, the Prescription Drug Plan (Medicare D), or your state's "Senior Care" type plan

- Insurance plans, such as a working spouse's group insurance, your own retiree medical coverage, a former employer plan through COBRA, or an individual medical policy

- Membership rights, such as access to the Veteran's Administration for those who served in the armed forces, or facilities that serve members of religious or fraternal organizations

- Out-of-pocket expenditure, such as earmarked funds like health savings accounts, or general funds—any of your PERKS (see chapter five) that you would draw on to pay for out-of-pocket medical costs

Based on your philosophy, which one of these is likely to provide your primary method of access? Which one will take some advance planning to make it available? Where should your focus be?

PAR: Relationships with Practitioners

Now that you know your medical philosophy, you can identify the practitioners to help you implement it. Although you'll probably be looking for good practitioners as long as you live and breathe, this is about identifying *types* of practitioners. Is your family practice MD's expertise enough? Do you already have a condition that will make a medical specialist important? If you want to use alternative medicine, which approaches will you use the most? Which types of practitioners will provide the most treatment and be your sources of information and advice? To stay healthy, this is an important part of your Ideal Retirement.

It's time for a reality check. Look back over your Retirement Medicine Cycle. Does it fit together as a whole? Does your philosophy fit your method of access? Will your access pay for the types of treatments and relationships that you want? Will your relationships provide treatment and advice that fit your philosophy?

In addition to your relationships with medical practitioners, there's an even more important relationship for you to develop. That's your relationship with your *own body*. If you're like most people, the relatively good health of the Second Age allowed you to pay less attention to your biology than you probably should have. The next chapter will give you a chance to start making amends. As you think about your next stage of life, remember to think about how you'll take care of your body. It's the only one you've got!

LIFE CIRCLES EXERCISE

Looking back over the Retirement Medicine Cycle sections, consider the three components: philosophy, access, and relationships. In your Life Circle, write the name of your medical philosophy next to the "P." Next to the "A," write your primary method of access, or the method that you most need to focus on in your planning. Next to the "R," write the medical relationships that will be most important for you to develop. All together, these help you create a vision of how medicine will support your Ideal Retirement, and you will use this when you fill in your One Piece of Paper in chapter eleven.

My Ideal Retirement
includes accessing this medicine:

P _____

A _____

R _____

"For an individual, the pattern of growth, plateau, and decline is mandated by personal biology."

—JAMES FRIES, MD,
renowned longevity researcher

Chapter EIGHT

Health from the Inside Out

For retirement, are you more concerned about staying alive—or staying healthy?

As average human longevity has increased and more people are living into their eighties and nineties, the issue is becoming less and less whether we'll live long enough. We may know people who've lived longer than they expected to, or even wanted to. No, for most of us it's about staying healthy as we spend decades in old age. What we really want is a health span that matches our life span. However long our journey lasts, we want to be healthy along the way. But how do we make that happen?

The Equation Is Biology + Medicine = Health

In the Retirement Well-Being Model, health is called the Bio-Medical dimension. No one ever forgets about the medical part, but the biological part is easily overlooked. The term *biology* reminds us that, before we even consider medical care, we're first and foremost biological organisms. We're in charge of our own bodies, and the way we live affects our health—our *physical vitality*. Everything we do either supports or depletes that vitality. Once we become conscious of our vitality, we may decide to build it up the way we build our personal savings or build our social networks. We can even think of all of these things as unique forms of *capital* that we draw on in different ways, for different purposes, during retirement.

Even though our personal biology is unique, it's also governed by universal principles. The biological trajectory is the same for everyone: growth, plateau, and decline. We need to factor that trajectory into every other aspect of planning our life. But we can influence our trajectory in two ways. One way is through accessing the medical system out there in the world. The other is to act in ways that support our own biology directly. So, how's that been going for you?

We each have our own measures of how it's been going for us, of course. The most basic one is purely subjective: It's simply how good we feel. (Which is actually a good measuring instrument, when we take the time to calibrate and use it.) We may have other, more objective measures, too: our clothing size or weight measured on a scale; how many days of work we've missed; whether we're meeting the goals of our exercise program. These are probably all good measures, but on occasion we realize we need something more objective, more official. We go for a physical.

Measuring Your Biological Health

In the early days of the old retirement, a checkup with a medical doctor involved a lot more poking and prodding than it usually does now. For example, to assess a patient's health, physicians would listen as they palpated and gently thumped on different points of the patient's abdomen, sort of like testing a watermelon or cantaloupe for ripeness. A healthy organ has a certain *sound*. If it doesn't sound right, that's a reason to investigate.

These days, doctors don't spend as much time *listening* to their patients. They gather data using much more high-tech methods. They take biological samples from us and run laboratory tests. Our body chemistry supplies the raw data, which is then analyzed using sophisticated statistical methods. How do we measure up compared to thousands of other people? For most tests, the goal is simply to be in the normal range. But for others (such as cholesterol) the goal is actually to be better than normal. Gathering raw data and doing a statistical analysis is much less personalized than thumping on our organs, it's true. But it does provide a different, and extremely helpful, kind of analysis. Biotechnologies made the new kind of checkup possible.

Now, there's another technology that's making another kind of new checkup possible. It's called a *health risk assessment* (often available through your medical insurance plan or hospital). But instead of collecting your bodily fluids, it collects your biological data. Then it does what you'd expect: It statistically analyzes your data against that of thousands of other people. But a health risk assessment is completely different from a lab report. Instead of telling you that you may have a particular health condition in the *present*, it tells you whether you're likely to have a particular health condition in the *future*. A health risk assessment is like a crystal ball, but it's powered by statistics.

You may wonder why people would want to know what diseases they're more likely to get. You may even feel that you wouldn't *want* to know. Wouldn't it just be better to live a healthy lifestyle and forget the crystal ball? After all, many of your health risks are inherited from your parents, and it's too late to choose different ones now.

Some people find health risk assessments useful, because they put the information to good use. Let's take an example: Say that a person—based on her heredity, her health history, her current data, and her general lifestyle—discovers that the area she should be most concerned about is heart disease. One possibility is that she *wasn't* aware of her elevated risk for heart disease. But now that she has this new information, she'll adjust her behavior accordingly, make lifestyle changes, and reduce her risk.

However, another possibility is that she already *suspected* she had an elevated risk of heart disease. She knows her family history. She knows she's overweight and that her cholesterol is too high. She just hasn't been motivated to exercise more control over her biology. But seeing the health risk assessment changes how she *feels*. It's right there in black and white. It motivates her to finally make the changes that she already knew she should make.

In our society, the problem isn't a lack of information about healthy lifestyles. We live in a sea of information. Haven't you already been told a million times to exercise and eat healthier? How many more times do you want to be given the same suggestions? No, information isn't the problem—*motivation* is the problem. And not just motivation to make healthy lifestyle changes. Motivation to really stick with them over the long term and make them a part of our lives.

How Old Are You Really?

So, back to our biological question: How are you doing? Well, there's a new way for you to answer that question. It's an entirely *new form* of measurement. This form of measurement is beyond your subjective feelings, beyond being thumped like a melon, beyond giving up bodily fluids, and even beyond a health risk assessment. From a technical standpoint, in relation to a health risk assessment, it's just a small step forward. But from a conceptual standpoint, it's a giant leap. It's a form of measurement that uses statistics to tell you how old you are. Not your chronological age, but your *biological age*.

Let's review this whole *concept* of age. For most of human history, people didn't have a record of when they were born. The concept of how old they were didn't require mathematical computation; it was *functional*, not chronological. Age was how a person looked, sounded, moved, and thought. Age was a function of appearance, strength, flexibility, and mental sharpness. But then we started to keep written birth records, and by the industrial era, chronological age had become the standard. Industrialists standardized everything, including people. So of course retirement was based on chronological age rather than functional age. That kind of thinking still drives the timing of retirement all these years later. Don't people plan when to retire based on their date of birth rather than their appearance, strength, flexibility, and mental sharpness?

Now imagine for a moment that you're fifty-seven years old. That's what it says on your driver's license. However, your "age" of fifty-seven is only a tally of how many times the earth has orbited the sun since you've been in residence. That's an astronomical description, not a biological one! But that tally of orbits determined when your school allowed you to attend first grade and also when the state allowed you to take a driver's test. It will determine when the Social Security Administration allows you to apply for retirement benefits. Other than satisfying legal red tape, your chronological age has never done that much for you. (Although the birthday parties were nice.) But what if you also could measure your *biological age*? How would that affect your life stage planning?

Biological Age

Imagine again that you're looking at your driver's license and it says you're fifty-seven years old. You plan to retire in five years, when you turn sixty-two and first become eligible for Social Security. By then, you'll have enough PERKS (see pages 103–106) to afford the retirement that you want. Now, imagine that you take this assessment that measures your biological age. Much to your horror, you discover that your body's age is *already* sixty-two. According to the government you're only fifty-seven, but according to your body, you're five years older than that.

You do the math in your head and realize that in five years, when your driver's license says you're sixty-two, your biological age by *then* could possibly be . . . (gulp) . . . sixty-seven! You need to stop and reconsider the retirement life you had imagined. You realize that it may not be as physically *active* as you had hoped. You realize that it may not last as *long* as you had hoped. According to your financial plan, you thought you were retiring on the early side (going by your driver's license). But for your biology, you may actually be retiring a bit on the late side. Multiple-choice question: What should you do?

A. Focus on your driver's license age, ignore your biological age, and retire in five years as planned. If your retirement is short and sedentary, so be it. At least you probably won't run out of money. And maybe you'll beat the statistics and have a long and healthy retirement anyway.

B. Focus on your biological age and retire as soon as you can possibly afford to. If you need to reduce your cost of living to make ends meet, so be it. You want to make sure you have as healthy and active a retirement as possible. If it turns out you beat the statistics, then that will be a bonus.

C. First, find out what health changes you can make to reduce your biological age. Make those changes and monitor your biological age. Second, reduce your cost of living and save money like crazy. Third, create a new plan for when to retire.

There is, of course, no right answer. But look at how powerful the concept of biological age is. Now, change the scenario so that your biological age is five years *younger* than your driver's license, and the entire story changes dramatically.

We don't know what the correct answer to the problem is. But there's no question that biological age should be factored into retirement planning *somehow*! And although the stakes are much higher in the years close to retirement, knowing your biological age at every stage of your career is useful information. Like any health risk assessment, it can provide you with information on the changes you should make to become healthier. And probably *more* than any other type of health risk assessment, it can motivate you to make those changes. Any way you look at it, knowing your biological age is a good thing.

Other than a health risk assessment through your medical plan, how can you gain access to this new form of electronic data *checkup*? The original method for calculating your biological age is www.RealAge.com. A different approach to this concept can be found at www.BlueZones.com. Or, if you're looking for a good life expectancy calculator, use www.LivingTo100.com. Although you'll need to register to take these, the assessments are free. You'll find related books in the Resources section.

Why has staying healthy and "young" become the hot topic for retirement biology? Because longevity has already been steadily increasing, for generations. However, understanding how long you're likely to live isn't easy. Even when people calculate their life expectancy, it doesn't show them how it changes over time. To see another perspective on how life expectancy works, take a look at the Longevity Class Reunion in this chapter.

To see how long you're likely to live, consult one of the online calculators in the Resources section. But to really understand your life expectancy, you need to see how it changes over time. So let's pretend you're part of an imaginary group, during the heyday of the old retirement. Even though your group is imaginary, the mortality and life expectancy data is real, compiled by the Center for Disease Control over the last hundred years.

You're one of a thousand babies born in Longevity, USA, in the year 1900. The infant mortality rate is high, so the life expectancy for your group is only forty-nine years. That doesn't mean you'll all die at age forty-nine, of course. Half of you are expected to die before age forty-nine and half of you after.

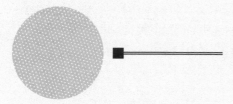

Due to sickness and accident, some of you don't live to graduate from Longevity High. Of the original thousand babies, 781 are still alive. The unhealthy and unlucky have died off. But the healthier and luckier teenagers who remain have a longer life expectancy. You now have a remaining life expectancy of forty-five years—which means the ripe old age of sixty-three! Isn't that better?

You all begin your careers and families. In the year you turn thirty-five, the Social Security Act is passed. Your class is so excited that you hold a reunion at the Longevity Hotel. Everyone attends, except that "everyone" means 691 of you. However, because you're the healthy and lucky ones, your life expectancy has now increased to age sixty-seven. So on average, each of you can expect to enjoy a Social Security retirement that will last for two years. Yahoo!

You all return to managing careers, raising children, and saving money. Thirty years pass, and now you're sixty-five. You hold a class retirement party. The room at the Longevity Hotel isn't as full as last time—there are 409 of you left. However, you had all anticipated living for just two years in retirement. But now you have a remaining life expectancy of twelve years! That will take you to age seventy-seven. You all agree to return in ten years for a Diamond Gala.

You all go off into lives of leisure. At first it's wonderful to simply not work. But boredom sets in, and you wonder if you could have done something more engaging and meaningful in your retirement. Finally, you turn seventy-five, and attend the Diamond Gala. You're surprised to see only 230 are left. But you have good reason to party, because your life expectancy is now age eighty-two. Everyone has so much fun that you promise to meet in ten years.

You all go off to lives of friends and family. Ten years later invitations go out, but the post office returns most of them—unopened. When you arrive at the Longevity Hotel, you're one of only sixty-one classmates. At the age of eighty-five, some still enjoy dancing, while others are in wheelchairs. The hardy group that remains has only a four year life expectancy—to age eighty-nine. Instead of ten years, it seems wiser to meet again in five years.

You all go off to quiet lives of deep reflection. As you open the next invitation at the age of 90, you feel a sense of accomplishment. This time the reunion is held at the Longevity Nursing Home. The 19 who are left, amazingly, still have a three year life expectancy.

As the reunion is winding down, a classmate raises her glass to toast the paradox of life expectancy:

"When I was born, I was only supposed to live to forty-nine.

But I graduated from high school, and so was supposed to live to sixty-three.

Then when the Social Security Act passed, I was going to make it to sixty-seven.

But attending our retirement party meant I'd live to seventy-seven.

At our Diamond Gala, I was expected to live until eighty-two.

But then I made it to the next reunion, so I was supposed to live to eighty-nine.

Here I am at 90, and now my life expectancy is ninety-three.

It's strange that the longer I live, the older I'm supposed to get. It feels like I might live forever!"

But she didn't.

However, if you were born in 1950, you'll get significantly closer. At birth, your life expectancy wasn't forty-nine—it was over sixty-eight. Instead of nineteen classmates at your age ninety reunion, you'll have more than sixty. Of course, that doesn't mean you'll be in attendence!

REM: Your Dream Body for Retirement

When you decide to exercise more control over your biology, perhaps you'll go to your doctor for a checkup, take a health risk assessment, or calculate your biological age. Or perhaps you won't. Maybe you feel that you don't need additional information from experts suggesting changes you should make in your lifestyle. You may feel that you already know what you should do to become healthier. If you've had an epiphany and are now *motivated* to get started, that's wonderful—get going. Then go see your doctor too, for heaven's sake!

You support your biology by making healthy lifestyle decisions. You've certainly tried out various healthy changes in the past; some were likely short-lived, while others became a part of your life. Obviously, the ones that become a part of your life are the ones that help the most.

This section will help you identify three biological *practices* that you'd like to include in the picture of your Ideal Retirement to support your health in the next stage. These are three practices to do on an ongoing basis to increase your vitality from the inside out. There are three categories of practices that you'll want to include: relaxation, eating, and movement. By making sure you address all three, you're taking a comprehensive approach to supporting your vitality. You can remember them by the acronym REM (for your *dream* body).

THE THREE TYPES OF BIOLOGICAL PRACTICES

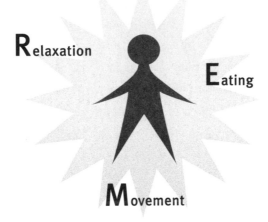

How Do You Get to Carnegie Hall? (Practice.)

The word *practice* in this case has a fairly specific meaning. To qualify as a practice, it has to pass a few tests. First, it's something that is *challenging* enough that you can't just learn it quickly. Or if you can learn it quickly, you may never fully master it. Or if you were to become a master, it's so engaging that it would draw you again and again. (You get the idea.) Second, it's something that offers a *body of knowledge* that will help you learn and grow in the practice. Others have explored it before you and have left accounts of their own practice that can inspire you. Third, it's something that has *other practitioners* for you to connect with, other people who are also learning and practicing it, so that you can either exchange information with them or do the practice together with them. When you complete the exercise below, you'll see why choosing something that meets these high standards is more likely to create *long-term* results for you.

Here's an example from the third category, movement. Martial arts could easily fit the definition of a practice; jumping jacks could not. A martial art (there are many types) is challenging enough that you might never master it. You could access a large body of knowledge about it. And you could exchange information with other devotees or practice it with them. A martial art might keep someone involved for many years, or even a lifetime. But how long could anyone keep up a practice of jumping jacks? For each of these three categories, you want to choose something that you can get really excited about, too!

These practices may be things that you currently do and want to make absolutely sure that you keep doing. Or they may be things that you tried in the past and they worked for you, but for one reason or another you stopped; now you'd like to incorporate them into your life again. Or they may even be things that you've never done but for some mysterious reason, you really want to give them a try.

Relaxation Does Not Involve TV or the Internet

Relaxation is the first category. Some people may think of it as stress reduction. We're not talking about sitting in front of the television or having a few cocktails. Far from it. A relaxation practice is a specific activity that elicits what Herbert Benson identified as the *relaxation response* in the famous book of the same name.

The relaxation response is the biological opposite of the much more famous fight-or-flight response. The fight-or-flight response triggers the release of chemicals that put us on edge to better deal with danger. In our society, that response is triggered many times every day, from obvious stressors like driving in traffic or dealing with work deadlines to seemingly passive and innocuous activities like watching TV or listening to the radio. We can expect to keep experiencing this response even in retirement. Being subjected to the fight-or-flight response so frequently has a strong negative effect on our biology. The best antidote is to *intentionally* evoke its opposite: the relaxation response.

A relaxation practice is a specific activity that you engage in to elicit the relaxation response. Benson originally focused on meditation but later identified many additional ways to do it. Prayer, especially repetitive prayer—such as with a rosary—is another way. So is visualization or self-hypnosis. There are also physical ways to elicit the relaxation response, including tai chi, yoga, and some types of walking. You can even make up your own relaxation practice, or perhaps you already have. You will find that your relaxation practice probably has a very small positive effect on you initially. Don't look for thunder and lighting. However, the nature of a practice is that it deepens over time—that's what makes it a practice! So be patient, and try a different practice if you need to, but keep going on this path. It will pay off. What relaxation practice are you going to start with as part of your Ideal Retirement?

You Are What You Eat and Eat and Eat

Eating is the second category. Of course, we all have to eat. And to a greater or lesser degree, at different times, we all try to eat "healthier," whatever that means for us. There is no shortage of official recommendations for healthy eating, no shortage of diet books, and no shortage of miracle diet supplements. (No shortage of fast-food commercials, either!) But the idea of an eating practice has nothing to do with following a diet or trying to eat more healthfully for a particular time period. An eating practice, like the other practices, is an approach that could be permanent, for you.

To follow an eating practice means adopting a way of thinking about the foods that you imagine *wanting* to eat. About what foods you imagine shopping for and buying. About how you would prepare the foods, and how you would actually consume them. How all that would affect your choices when you dine out. An eating practice is an approach that you've seen real people adopt in their lives, consciously or unconsciously, and then stick with for years. Some easy-to-identify examples of eating practices are low-fat, Mediterranean, vegetarian, and organic. But you could also create your own healthy eating practice. What about "home cooking" the way your grandmother thought of it? You resolve to simply never buy, prepare, or eat anything that comes in a box.

Think about people you've known who seem to have some internal guidance system for healthy eating habits. Can you identify what their internal standards might be? For example, you may know someone who simply doesn't eat any kind of fast food, ever. Or you may know someone who has an internal standard for eating at least one salad every day. Others may have a standard for what size portions they eat, regardless of what they're eating.

The casual observer wouldn't even be aware that each of these people has particular standards, and you probably couldn't fit their standards into any official approach. These people, intentionally or intuitively, came up with healthy practices for eating. You yourself may already be doing exactly that—if so, congratulations. If not, consider what your most *natural* inclinations would be for establishing your own internal standards. Rather than trying to adopt some system created by others, is there some healthy homegrown system already inside you, just waiting for you to give it a try? If so, how would you describe this eating practice?

Poetry in Motion

Movement is the third category. This means some type of *full-body* movement, although it doesn't have to be what you normally think of as exercising. What's more important than meeting specific guidelines for aerobic activities, or for strength and flexibility activities, is meeting your own internal standards for sustainability. It's about finding something that can become nearly automatic and a lifelong practice. For most people, this will be a specific activity, such as swimming, bicycling, or golfing (without a golf cart, please).

The lifelong part is what can make finding a movement practice trickier than finding a relaxation or eating practice. Most of those other practices are not affected by aging. But your ability to continue a particular form of movement is. There are some practices that you might not be able to keep up, such as running. What do you do then? Try to find a different practice, just when it becomes even more important to keep moving? So explore and experiment with practices that can be done at a higher intensity while you're younger and a lower intensity when you're older. Part of the equation is the expectation that you bring to the movement practice. If you anticipate that your running will someday scale back to jogging, and then someday scale back to walking, you'll find it easier to keep it up. On the other hand, if your movement practice is the pole vault, it's not so easy to scale back.

One opportunity you may want to consider is combining or pairing your relaxation and movement practices in some way. Again, the point is not to identify the "best" type, according to the experts. It's to identify—based on your own body and your own experience—what's likely to work for you over the long term. What would you call this practice that you want to put in your Life Circle?

LIFE CIRCLES EXERCISE

Looking back at the section on biological practices, consider the three categories: relaxation, eating, and movement. In the Life Circle, next to the "R," write
the name of the relaxation practice that you can imagine engaging in. Next to
the "E," write the name of the eating practice that you can most easily imagine
following. Next to the "M," write the name of the form of movement that you
could practice at a higher intensity first and then at a lower intensity as you get
older. Together, your REM practices support your biological vitality and help you
create your Ideal Retirement. Use these responses in your One Piece of Paper in
chapter eleven.

My Ideal Retirement

includes deepening these

biological practices:

R _____

E _____

M _____

"Your vision will become clear only when you can look into your own heart. Who looks outside, dreams; who looks inside, awakens."

—CARL JUNG, pioneering Swiss psychiatrist

Chapter NINE

A New Chapter in Psychology

Without the well-being model, many people are a bit lost in their thinking about happiness. Some think that if they have prosperity, then *that* will bring them happiness. Others think that if they have health, then *that* will bring them happiness. But you, dear reader, know how well-being works. You know that being poor or sick can prevent a person from being happy, but no amount of prosperity or health can *make* them happy.

But who can blame them? They know they can focus their attention and energy on building prosperity or health in life, and they're likely to get results. They can use knowledge and specific approaches to improve their finances, their environment, their biological health, and how they access medicine. They can create results in those areas, directly.

This chapter reveals a similar way of thinking about creating our happiness. That's because recent breakthroughs within the research field of psychology offer knowledge and specific approaches for *learning how to become happy*. These are ways of focusing our attention and energy on building happiness directly, similar to the ways we can build prosperity or health, directly.

There's a special challenge, though, for the topic of retirement happiness. When people dream about creating a happy retirement, it's usually based on a version from the old retirement. Society still puts some pressure on us to simply go after carefree fun and enjoyment. But that's an outdated idea for worn-out old people. This new chapter in psychology tells us that lasting happiness is linked to a critical factor that the fun-and-enjoyment approach overlooks: *engagement*. The old retirement was sometimes even described as a process of *disengagement*. That's definitely not what we want for the new retirement!

Engagement is the missing ingredient in lasting retirement happiness. And the key to engagement is identifying our *strengths*—those talents and abilities that we receive great satisfaction in using.

We can certainly get lucky and be happy without knowing how we did it. (If you win the lottery you can be prosperous without knowing anything about money.) But because the new retirement offers the greatest opportunity for our fulfillment in life, we shouldn't count on luck. Science is a better bet.

Moving Beyond a Problem-Focused Approach

As it turns out, psychology is finally learning as much about happiness as unhappiness. Instead of studying happiness, most psychological research studies over the past five decades looked at its opposite: depression, addiction, neurosis, and so on. Some very smart and well-intentioned people have spent billions of dollars to create a mountain of detailed knowledge about the *thousand and one* ways that people can be unhappy. This is important information, to be sure. It's also why, when we think of psychology, it's usually in the context of fixing people's problems, to help them lead normal lives. If you're *already* normal (or at least somewhat normal), then psychology hasn't had much to offer you. Psychology couldn't help you learn how to create happiness in your life. Trying to prevent or avoid unhappiness isn't *at all* the same as creating happiness.

To balance out all this knowledge about unhappiness, a new discipline called positive psychology emerged around the turn of the new millennium. This is *not* just a variation on "positive thinking." The inquiry into positive psychology was championed by the renowned research psychologist Martin Seligman and others. They take a clear-thinking, hard-nosed, let's-measure-it-and-see-if-it-stands-up approach to the study of human strengths, positive emotions, and other aspects of optimal human experience. Positive psychology has really caught on, and these days there are many more researchers who are studying how humans thrive.

Thanks to systematic research in other fields, we know about approaches for increasing our "economic well-being" as well as our "health and well-being." Finally, there is systematic research into our "psychological well-being," too.

Seligman suggests that there are, essentially, three approaches to happiness; that is, three basic *ways* to be happy. Although there are, thank goodness, an unlimited number of specific ways in which you can be happy, each comes under one of these three basic approaches.

Three Ways That You Can Be Happy in Retirement

What, you ask, are these three approaches to happiness?

- Pleasure

- Engagement

- Meaning

Let's explore them one by one.

Pleasure or Enjoyment

This one sounds obvious, doesn't it? When you first think of happiness, it's usually pleasure and enjoyment that come to mind, right off the bat. An afternoon at the ball game. Eating a delicious meal. Watching an entertaining movie. Buying something that you want. These involve being comfortable and *having fun* in an easy or relaxed way. Pleasure like this brings a burst of positive emotions that come and go quickly, though, usually not lasting much longer than the event itself. When you use this approach (and I sincerely hope that you do), you need to keep going back and doing enjoyable activities, over and over again, to get more of that happiness.

Engagement or Involvement

This one isn't very obvious. Another word for engagement is involvement. Positive psychology researcher Mihaly Csikszentmihalyi uses still another word for this experience that you can almost feel: He calls it *flow*. (His name, by the way, is actually easier to say than it looks; it sounds like "Me high. Chicks sent me high.") Flow happens when your abilities are well matched to some challenging task. You get so deep into the activity, whatever it is, that you lose all track of time. You may feel like it's been only a few minutes, but it's been much longer. Or a few seconds may feel like an eternity. Either way, when you're that engaged, you lose yourself in what you're doing. You may not even be aware that it makes you happy *while* you're doing it, but *afterward* you say, "That was great!"

Engagement involves challenge, and it demands something from you, so it's not as simple as pleasure. It can't be purchased or consumed in the way that pleasure can be. When you use this approach (and you may be using it more than you realize), it can stick with you *longer* than pleasure does. Over time, it can build up into a lasting satisfaction with life.

Meaning or Purpose

This approach to happiness is somewhat more obvious than engagement, but it's not so easy to pin down. Of course having meaning in your life would make you happy! But how do you get it? The way you get it, my friend, is to use your abilities in the service of something larger than yourself. This approach requires something from you, too. Note that meaning doesn't come from just *believing* in something larger than yourself; it comes from being in service to that something. This is part of living your life in alignment with your core values.

What's *larger* than yourself? Take your pick, depending on your belief system: God, your family, the environment, your political party, your ethnic culture, the free enterprise system, your community. It may not be service to something larger than yourself but to something *beyond*